EUROPE'S LAST
RED TERRORISTS

GEORGE KASSIMERIS

Europe's Last Red Terrorists

The Revolutionary Organization
17 November

NEW YORK UNIVERSITY PRESS
Washington Square, New York

First published in the U.S.A. in 2001 by
NEW YORK UNIVERSITY PRESS
Washington Square
New York, NY 10003

Typeset in Bembo by Bookcraft Ltd, Stroud, Gloucestershire
Printed in England

CIP data available from the Library of Congress
ISBN 0-8147-4756-6

For Carol, Dora,
and for you, Kyra-Evgenia

ACKNOWLEDGEMENTS

This book has taken over four years to write and it owes a great debt to many people. I offer my sincere thanks to Paul Wilkinson, US Ambassador Thomas Miller, Ken Robertson, Tim Dixon, Dennis Pluchinsky, Nikos Papadakis of the Greek Embassy in London, A. G. Stephens, Bruce Hoffman of RAND Corporation, Robert Hall, Anthea Harris, Michael Dartnell, Mark Kavanagh, Bob McKeever and A.J. Coates. In Athens, I am grateful for the help of Vassilis Kapetanyiannis, Mary Bossis, Leon Karapanayiotis of *Ta Nea* newspaper, Anna Papadakis, Dimitri Livieratos, Angelos Stangos, Christos Papoutsakis of *Anti* magazine, Manolis Stavrakakis, Angelos Elephantis, the editorial team at *Pontiki* and the staff and archivists at the Library of the Greek Parliament. Yiota Oikonomidou helped me understand the labyrinthine world of the Greek extra-parliamentary left and Olympios Dafermos, Dionyssis Mavrogenis and Marios Sarakiniotis provided pre-1974 documents which would have otherwise eluded me. I should like to record a debt of gratitude to Seraphim Fyntanidis, editor of *Eleftherotypia*, who in 1995 invited me to move into the offices of his newspaper where for several months I had access to archive material.

Lastly, I want to record my gratitude to three amazing women. One is Carol Millwood, who is my best friend, mentor, editor and most forthright critic. Any confidence I have in my work is due solely to her. The other is Tricia Hicks for her truly extraordinary goodness, generosity and friendship. I owe her a debt I can never repay. My greatest debt though is to my mother, Dora, who has never failed me. Without her support and confidence in me over the years, I would have never reached the point where a book such as this would have been contemplated, much less written.

George Kassimeris
Athens, 2000

CONTENTS

ABBREVIATIONS

AD	*Action Directe* (Action Direct)
BR	*Brigatte Rosse* (Red Brigades)
CCC	*Cellules Communistes Combattantes* (Fighting Communist Cells)
Clodo	*Comité liquidant ou détournant les ordinateurs*
CPM	*Colletivo Politico Metropolitano* (Metropolitan Political Collective)
DEA	Drug Enforcement Agency
DEI	*Dimossia Epichirissi Ilektrismou* (Public Power Corporation)
DNL	*Dimokratiki Neolaia Lambraki* (Lambrakis Youth Movement)
EAM	*Ethniko Apeleftherotiko Metopo* (National Liberation Front)
EDA	*Eniaia Dimokratiki Aristera* (United Democratic Left)
EDIK	*Enossi Dimokratikou Kentrou* (Democratic Centre Union Party)
EEC	European Economic Community
EK	*Enossi Kentrou* (Centre Union Party)
EKAM	Greek police special unit
EKKE	*Epanastatiko Kommounistiko Kinima Elladas* (Revolutionary Communist Movement of Greece)
ELA	*Epanastatikos Laikos Agonas* (Revolutionary Popular Struggle)
ELAS	*Ethnikos Laikos Apeleftherotikos Stratos* (Greek People's Liberation Army)
ESA	*Elliniki Stratiotiki Astynomia* (Greek Military Police)
ESY	*Ethniko Systima Ygeias* (National Health Service)
ETA	*Euskadi ta Askatasuna* (Freedom for the Basque Homeland)
EU	European Union

EYP	*Ethniki Ypiressia Pliroforion* (National Intelligence Service)
GRAPO	*Grupos de Resistencia Antifascista, Primero de Octubre* (1st October Anti-Fascists Group)
IMF	International Monetary Fund
IRA	Irish Republican Army
JUSMAGG	Joint US Military Advisory Group in Greece
KEM	*Kommounistiko Epanastatiko Metopo* (Communist Revolutionary Front)
KKE	*Kommounistiko Komma Elladas* (Communist Party of Greece)
KKE-es	*Kommounistiko Komma Elladas-esoterikou* (Communist Party of Greece-Interior)
LMAT	*Lumpen megaloastiki taxi* (lumpen big bourgeois class)
MAT	Greek Riot Police
NATO	North Atlantic Treaty Organization
ND	*Nea Dimokratia* (New Democracy)
OKDE	*Organossi Kommouniston Diethniston Elladas* (Communist Organization of Greek Internationalists)
OMLE	*Organossi Marxiston Leniniston Elladas* (Marxist-Leninist Organization of Greece)
OPEC	Organization of Petroleum-Exporting Countries
OSE	*Organossi Sosialistiki Epanastasi* (Organization Socialist Revolution)
PASOK	*Panellinio Sosialistiko Kinima* (Panhellenic Socialist Movement)
PKK	Kurdistan Workers' Party
RAF	*Rote Armee Faktion* (Red Army Faction)
RO-17N	*Epanastatiki Organossi 17 Noemvri* (Revolutionary Organization 17 November)
TREVI	Terrorism, Radicalism, Extremism, International Violence
UN	United Nations
YAAEV	Sub-Directorate for Special Crime and Violence

1

INTRODUCTION

> Killing a man is murder unless you do it to the sound of trumpets.
>
> *Voltaire*

On 23 December 1975, three gunmen stalked Richard Welch, the CIA station chief in Athens, shooting him at point-blank range in front of his wife and driver. A previously unknown group called Revolutionary Organization 17 November (RO-17N or 17N) claimed responsibility for the assassination. It was the first serious terrorist attack against the country's dramatic attempt to wipe away the legacy of its seven-year dictatorship and establish the foundations for an effectively functioning democracy. Since then, Greece has endured one of the most protracted and intransigent of all ideological terrorist campaigns in Western Europe; a vendetta pursued mainly by the 17N and ELA revolutionary communist groups, which has resulted in several deaths and serious injuries, hundreds of bombings and billions of drachmas of damage to property. During this period, the Greek state has failed to make a correct diagnosis of the problem and its security and intelligence agencies have failed to capture or even identify a single terrorist.

The focus of this study is the more violent and dangerous of the two groups: the Revolutionary Organization 17 November. For the past 15 years, the US State Department's counter-terrorism division has ranked it among the world's most active and lethal urban guerrilla groups. The group, often referred to as *organossi phantasma* (phantom organization), took its name from the date back in 1973 when students occupied Athens Polytechnic demanding an end to military rule. On the night of 16/17

November, riot police backed up with tanks were sent in to put an end to the occupation, causing the death of at least 34 students and the injury of another 800. Although the students were bloodily repressed, their unprecedented action intensified public dissatisfaction with the regime and accelerated the collapse of the Colonels.

Fanatically nationalistic, 17N is anti-Greek establishment, bitterly anti-American, anti-Turkey and anti-NATO and is committed to removing US bases from Greece, the Turkish military presence from Cyprus, and to severing Greece's ties to NATO and the European Union. During the past two-and-a-half decades, the group has carried out over 100 attacks, openly defying both the Greek and US security services by striking at will against carefully selected and mostly heavily protected targets. Twenty-three people have been assassinated, ranging from US diplomatic and military personnel to eminent Greek politicians, publishers, policemen, magistrates, leading industrialists and Turkish diplomats. Yet, astonishingly, in all this time, successive Greek governments have been unable to capture any member of the group. Further, not one 17N terrorist has been killed or injured in an operation or as a result of action by the Greek security forces. Nor has any undercover agent ever succeeded in penetrating the group, and the astronomical rewards offered by the Greek and US authorities for information that would lead to an arrest have come to nothing.

Tracing the history of 17N from 1975 to 2000, the aim of this work is to examine the nature and effects of terrorism by focusing on the ideology and activities of the last armed communist organization still active in Europe and explain how the phenomenon was allowed to grow so uncontrollably that it finally became a permanent fixture of contemporary Greek political life. Like the Red Army Faction (RAF) in Germany, Red Brigades (BR) in Italy and Action Direct (AD) in France, 17N proposed revolution as the solution to Greece's predicament. This study attempts to examine 17N's purposes, notion of political power and understanding of the international political system and to explain why the group could never pose a realistic threat to Greek institutions and society. It also shows that 17N's 'terrorist discourse' involved the elaboration and refinement of ideological themes and interpretations which derived from a problematic reading of the given socio-economic context. The organization based its rationale for violence on a distinct range of political images and symbols but 'confused the capacity for protest with the potential for revolution, overestimated the extent of social disequilibrium and underestimated the resilience of liberal democracy'.[1]

A central concern for studying political terrorism is defining what terrorist groups seek to achieve, what motivates their actions and how their goals and strategies are conceived. This study characterizes 17N as an armed communist organization with a revolutionary vocation within a non-revolutionary context. As shown in the following chapters, 17N is a distinctively Greek, 'closed' and apparently impenetrable urban guerrilla group which explains the organization's operational continuity and remarkable resistance to infiltration.

This is also a study of political history. It seeks to describe and analyze the emergence and evolution of the major violent groups and actors involved in extremism and document the political violence perpetrated in Greece since 1974. It particularly locates 17N in the context of post-junta Greece and explains what prompted the group to conclude that violent direct action rather than public discussion was the most effective form of political intervention. Although 17N never posed a lethal threat to Greece's sociopolitical order, the group gradually came to be accepted as a political form in its own right. To this end, a single-case study of a politically violent organization such as 17N requires an approach which

- examines the organization's character
- integrates the actions of the organization into the political events which conditioned its violent behaviour
- determines the social and political context in which such behaviour took place.

By looking systematically at 17N, the present study provides a focused investigation of why, amid numerous options, dissident groups choose particular strategies and violent tactics to achieve their goals. Such a single-case study approach isolates specific themes and influences which facilitate interpretation of the meaning 17N gave to its violence and throws light on the conflictual

---

[1] Martha Crenshaw (ed.), *Terrorism in Context* (Pennsylvania: Penn State Press, 1995), pp. x-xi.

nature of Greek politics. Ultimately, this method is selected because it points attention to the manner in which 17N's violence was conceived to affect its host political system and clarifies the centrality of ideological motives for political extremism and violence in Greece.

However, a single-case approach does suffer from limitations, especially in relation to conspiratorial political organizations. Groups like 17N are difficult for students of terrorism and policy analysts to examine since 'they operate without the mass relays that characterize contemporary Western political behaviour'.[2] Given the difficulties in observing a conspiratorial political organization like 17N on a first-hand basis, the method selected for this study focuses on ideologies and symbols that produce a distinctive frame of action. Like other West European political organizations, 17N used violence to intervene in Greek public life and symbolically communicate messages to its host political system. The use of symbols by terrorists can be a prevalent and effective strategy since it facilitates the interpretation of 'complex and undifferentiated feelings and ideas, making them comprehensible to oneself and communicable to others'.[3] By deploying symbolically dense metaphors such as 'forces of American imperialism', 'bourgeois democracy' and 'violent catharsis', 17N sought to unsettle established authority and exercise ideological influence over Greek political culture.

Like all other political cultures, Greek political culture is 'the product of both the collective history of a political system and the life histories of the members of that system'.[4] Understanding the complex traditions rooted in modern Greek political history is crucial for understanding the ideological sources of 17N's worldview. In Greek political culture, ideologies 'operate as facilitating factors, resources or constraints, in the formation of actors and in the definitions of their strategies'.[5] Depending on the context of action, an ideology may legitimate the established socio-political

---

[2] Michael Y. Dartnell, *Action Directe: Ultra-Left Terrorism in France, 1979–1987* (London: Frank Cass, 1995), p. 4.

[3] Sherry B. Ortner, 'On Key Symbols', in *American Anthropologist*, Vol.75, No.5 (October 1973), p. 1340.

[4] Lucian Pye, 'Political Culture', in *International Encyclopedia of the Social Sciences*, Vol. 12, p. 218.

[5] Donatella della Porta, 'Left-wing Terrorism in Italy', in *Terrorism in Context*, p. 122.

order or become a weapon of contestation and opposition. Using ideology, 17N attempted to 'alter the attitudes and behaviour of multiple audiences' and acquire a pre-eminent position in the Greek political system.[6] This approach towards the functionality of violence also clarifies the basis for 17N's conception of the political environment as one of protest, resistance and violence. In the following chapters, an attempt is made to locate 17N's ideology and values in the specific context of Greek political radicalism. Extreme-left traditions and a distinct idea of national legitimacy shaped a revolutionary ideology whereby violent disagreement against political rules became the basic mental frame around which 17N sought to construct a viable strategy. The historical endurance and significance of these traditions affected how 17N interpreted methods of resistance and provided both justification and the forces to which the group saw itself responding.

17N aspired to carry out a protest 'role' linked to changes that were under way in Greek political culture during the late 1970s and early 1980s. From the beginning, 17N rationale, vision and methods focused on working towards the fulfilment of the group's revolutionary aims. The group saw the 1974 democratic transition or *metapolitefsi* as a defining historical moment and sought to create 'a new frame for action, initially organized as a projection of an existing political conflict'.[7] However, 17N's attempts to repoliticize conflict and nurture revolution came to nothing because such objectives had no relevance to the post-1974 public debate. As a result, 17N failed to undermine the stability of the emergent political system and remained a fringe phenomenon operating in extreme isolation.

17N's goals and methods were motivated by a distinct political tradition based on a number of historical antecedents regarded by the group as critical determinants of contemporary political identities. 17N's consistent attachment to universalism, idealism, salvation and militarism can explain why the group resorted to terrorism as a primary method. 17N violence was intended to

---

[6] Martha Crenshaw, 'Thoughts on Relating Terrorism to Historical Contexts', in *Terrorism in Context*, p. 12.

[7] David Moss, 'Politics, Violence, Writing: The Rituals of "Armed Struggle" in Italy', in David E. Apter, *The Legitimization of Violence*, (London: Macmillan, 1997), p. 120.

counter the coercive character of American imperialism and offer a coherent ideological alternative to the domestic neo-liberal hegemonic order. Militant opposition to the establishment and the creation of a communist society were thus central to 17N's interpretation of the Greek political scene. At the same time, the group's violent reaction against existing political rules entailed a 'messianic' dimension and was presented as a response to 'a crisis of national legitimacy'. More specifically, 17N undertook a series of ritual acts of purification to 'liberate' Greece from a parliamentary system that it believed to be unable to remedy social and economic deterioration and which deployed a battery of coercive methods to maintain political conformism among the population.

17N emerged in a period in which the political climate was changing and ideological polarization was declining. Given the impact of the political and constitutional changes introduced under the Third Republic, *metapolitefsi* was a major national event in twentieth-century Greek history. The installation of the Third Republic in a country repeatedly traumatized by social strife and institutional discontinuities, epitomized the possibility of a pluralist and politically moderate society and decisively altered the terms of political argument. *Metapolitefsi* was embodied by national referenda, de-juntification, the Karamanlis premiership, a focus on the EC, the installation of a socialist government and demagogic populism, and was expressed by implicit slogans such as '*Karamanlis or the tanks*',[8] '*Greece belongs to the Greeks*',[9] and '*Allaghi*'.[10] Like Greece's other prominent revolutionary group,

---

[8] Campaign slogan used in November 1974 general election. Conscious that large sections of the electorate remained fearful of the prospect of a new *coup d'état*, Karamanlis called elections a mere four months after the collapse of the junta and using alternately the slogans '*Karamanlis or the tanks*' and '*Karamanlis or Chaos*' won a virtually unprecedented 54 per cent share of the poll which translated into a massive majority of 219 out of 300 seats in parliament.

[9] Political slogan used by PASOK's leader Andreas Papandreou during the 1977 election to portray Greece as a 'client state' of the West, demand the evacuation of US military bases in the country and denounce Karamanlis's foreign policy efforts for Greek entry into the EEC.

[10] '*Allaghi*' or 'Change' was PASOK's catch-all slogan in the 1981 general election. Promising 'socialization' and a 'restructuring' of the key industries, stronger trade unions, decentralization, immediate improvements in pensions, welfare and education, sweeping changes in the banking system, withdrawal from NATO, closure of the US bases and much else besides, Papandreou's socialist party swept to power

Epanastatikos Laikos Agonas (ELA),[11] 17N viewed *metapolitefsi* as nothing more than a democratic façade: a massive confidence trick on the nation by a political class which sought to legitimate its authority through the deliberate cultivation of fantasies of stability, transparency and pluralism. Both groups feared for the depoliticization of Greek society, distrusted parliamentary democracy and institutional discourse, were dogmatically anti-American, anti-NATO and anti-EC and made tireless efforts to expose the 'political doublespeak' of the Greek establishment.

Overall, 17N has been an extreme response to a process of substantial political and cultural change. Drawing upon the languages of class, nationalism and revolution, 17N moved to the centre of domestic ultra-left terrorist violence to challenge the political and economic *status quo*. The group rationalized its campaign of revolutionary terrorism with an ideology which reflected an amalgam of intransigent nationalism, Marxism-Leninism and Greek communist traditions. Believing itself to be a unique agent of political change, 17N engaged through its violence in a life-and-death confrontation with the state authorities and the 'American imperialist order'. It drew inspiration from the November 1973 events, the wartime resistance movement, the civil war legacy and West European extreme-left protest patterns, but failed to attract active support within Greek society. Despite this, the group has never abandoned the conviction that revolution is a real and practicable possibility in the Greek situation and that 'the road to reform through the parliamentary system leads nowhere but to the perpetuation of capitalist dependency'.[12] Dogmatically antagonistic and operating in a geographical and ideological microcosm, 17N attempted to undermine the legitimacy and institutions of *metapolitefsi* but ultimately its actions have had no perceptible effect on the post-1974 Greek political process.

with 48 per cent of the vote.

[11] In English, Revolutionary Popular Struggle. For a brief ideological and organizational profile on ELA, see Ch. 3.

[12] 17N communiqué on the assassination of the publisher of the *Apogevmatini* newspaper, Nikos Momferatos, in Athens in February 1985.

2

GREEK TRADITIONS OF POWER, VIOLENCE AND PROTEST

Revolutionary behaviour cannot be studied apart from its socio-political and ideological environment. Ultra-left terrorism in Greece resulted from a complex series of political conditions and long-standing cultural influences that drew politically active individuals towards the utopian world of revolution. These conditions and influences provided the foundations upon which extreme-left terrorism took firm root in the mid-1970s and therefore must be analysed in greater depth and be placed within the wider context of the evolution of the Greek political culture. Within this primarily political context, the focus is more specifically on the origins and characteristics of violence and the 'extent' and 'intensity' of protest to the political establishment, and less on a wide-ranging historical narrative of events and developments through Greece's original and complex history.

The birth of a state

History, geography and memory determined modern Greece's civic ethos and political traditions. The period of Turkish occupation had a direct and, in many ways, detrimental influence in shaping Greek political institutions and culture. At the most fundamental level, it produced 'an extremely weak civil society, with none of its constituent groups capable of effectively checking the authoritarian or despotic tendencies of the huge state bureaucracy and the self-serving, particularistic orientations of the major parties'.[1] Four hundred years of Ottoman rule served to insulate

---

[1] Nicos P. Mouzelis, 'Greece in the Twenty-first Century: Institutions and Political Culture', in Dimitri Constas and Theofanis G. Stavrou (eds), *Greece Prepares for the Twenty-first Century* (Baltimore: Johns Hopkins University Press, 1995), p. 19.

Greece from the Renaissance, the Reformation, the Counter-Reformation, the Enlightenment and the French and Industrial Revolutions which have had such profound effect on the historical evolution of west European culture.[2]

The revolutionary break of the war of independence (1821–30) marked the beginning of an era of profound identity crisis for the newly born nation. Until 1833, Greek politics was characterized by inordinate factionalism which seriously threatened, for a time, the ultimate success of the uprising. In fact, the crucial importance of state power had never been as obvious before and therefore came to be seen 'as "the apple of discord", the capture of which would bestow upon the victor the ability to protect his followers from harm and retaliation'.[3] The inter-Greek struggles, which quickly degenerated into civil conflict, were exclusively between different factions of the political élite since the interests of the labouring poor, peasants and artisans 'were put aside and suppressed quite early on in the game'.[4] More precisely, local feudal and warrior chiefs on the mainland, whose perception of politics and conflict had been structured primarily through their involvement and socio-economic relations with the Turkish state authorities, competed for 'privilege and power with fiercely individualistic seafaring traders and mercantile adventurers from the islands, and returning expatriate Greek diplomats, financiers and entrepreneurs who had been educated in the capitals of Europe'.[5] The political conflict between the Greek bourgeoisie of the diaspora and the local élites in the post-independence period assumed critical importance because

it tended to subsume pre-existing cleavages, social, political or cultural, and to recast them in new terms which emphasised this basic conflict between society and a new state ... The imposition of political institutions which were ultimately the products of capitalist social

[2] Richard Clogg, *A Concise History of Greece* (Cambridge: Cambridge University Press, 1992), p. 3.

[3] P. Nikiforos Diamandouros, 'Greek Political Culture in Transition: Historical Origins, Evolution, Current Trends' in Richard Clogg (ed.), *Greece in the 1980s* (London: Macmillan, 1983), p. 46.

[4] Nicos P. Mouzelis, *Modern Greece: Facets of Underdevelopment* (London: Macmillan, 1978), p. 13.

[5] 'Thucydides', 'Greek Politics: Myth and Reality', in *Political Quarterly*, Vol. 41, No. 2 (1970), p. 455.

formations with powerful middle classes upon a pre-capitalist social order which lacked the structures to receive them created in Greece a tense and sterile symbiotic relationship between state and society that was to have lasting consequences on the modern Greek political system, and which profoundly reinforced inherited attitudes of distrust and manipulation towards the state, and helped produce a deeply alienative political culture.[6]

Post-1821 Greek political culture was also influenced by the direct and lasting involvement of foreign powers in the nation-building process which essentially undermined national autonomy and rendered the meaning of independent nationhood highly problematic. England, France and Russia

manipulated their rights of 'protection' in the course of their mutual hostilities and combinations with little sincere concern for the country they had guaranteed. Greece, endowed with frontiers which condemned her to military and economic weakness ... was compelled to become the client of the power, or the powers, which favoured her claims.[7]

Greek parties even labelled themselves as French, English and Russian, operating within a political system in which 'nonmembers of a national society participate directly and authoritatively, through actions taken jointly with the society's members' either to allocate values or to mobilize support.[8] It is not surprising, therefore, that public institutions were fragile from early on since a political consensus was missing and the social one was not enough.

Independence was achieved but the vision of liberty remained unrealised. Othon's regency continued the politics of enforcing institutional modernisation from above. During the period of absolute monarchy, liberties continued to be suppressed through the practices of the government, especially with the appearance of authoritarian ideologies which collided with the cultural heritage of the Enlightenment.[9]

---

6 P. Nikiforos Diamandouros, *Greece in the 1980s*, p. 47.

7 John Campbell and Philip Sherrard, *Modern Greece* (London: Ernest Benn, 1968), p. 91.

8 John Anthony Petropulos, *Politics and Statecraft in the Kingdom of Greece, 1833–43* (Princeton, NJ: Princeton University Press, 1968), p. 44.

9 Paschalis Kitromilides, 'The Vision of Freedom in Greek Society', in *Journal of the Hellenic Diaspora*, Vol. 19, No. 1 (1993), p. 21.

As a result, there was no genuine agreement either on the objectives for which political power is to be used, or on the procedures through which disputes over such objectives were to be resolved. Parliamentary debate, for instance, did not 'centre around issues emerging out of class differences, but out of personalistic struggles over the distribution of spoils'.[10]

The overall picture that emerges from this early period of political independence up until the end of the nineteenth century is of a politically and economically beleaguered state in which:

- national leadership and authority suffered between periods of governmental deadlock and immobility
- political parties were merely loose coalitions of political barons each one of whom based his power on regional clienteles
- controversies over political institutions and values repeatedly led to violence
- the absence of popular participation excluded all possibility of class politics.[11]

Greece in the inter-war period

Greece entered the twentieth century in a state of social and political flux.[12] The dynamic emergence of new social forces of a predominantly middle-class character resulted in the creation of 'a more urbanised, occupationally more differentiated society'.[13] These new forces were eventually to challenge the continuing economic and political supremacy of the *tzakia* (established oligarchic families) and force them to accept the deepening of the political system and the inclusion of the new strata in the political arena.[14] The disintegration of oligarchic parliamentarism was also accelerated by conjunctural events, such as Greece's defeat in the Greco-Turkish war of 1897, the severe economic

[10] Mouzelis, *Modern Greece*, p. 16.
[11] Keith R. Legg, *Politics in Modern Greece* (Stanford: Stanford University Press, 1969), pp. 41–61.
[12] See Michael Llewellyn Smith, *Ionian Vision: Greece in Asia Minor* (London: Hurst & Company, 1998), pp. xxi–xx; see also George Dertilis, *Koinonikos Metaschimatismos kai Stratiotiki Epemvasi, 1880–1909* [Social Change and Military Intervention, 1880–1909] (Athens: Exandas, 1977).
[13] Nicos Mouzelis, *Politics in the Semi-Periphery* (London: Macmillan, 1986), p. 42.
[14] Konstantinos Tsoucalas, *Taxidi sto Logo kai tin Istoria, Tomos B'* [Journeys to Logos and History, Vol.2] (Athens: Plethro, 1996), pp. 205–13.

12 *Europe's Last Red Terrorists*

crisis that followed the war, and the chronic failure of successive administrations to militarily strengthen and modernize the armed forces which led to the military coup of 1909.[15]

However, the transition to post-oligarchic politics and the broadening of the political system did not automatically translate into the inclusion of lower middle class, artisans, shopkeepers and peasantry. Not only would they continue to be kept outside the sphere of active and autonomous politics but they would also be drawn into numerous intra-bourgeois conflicts which had very little relevance to their own class interests. The *ethnikos dichasmos* (national division) of 1915–16 which began merely as a passionate constitutional disagreement between King Constantine I and his Prime Minister Eleftherios Venizelos over the issue of Greece's participation in the First World War, but evolved into a fanatical political conflict of republicanism versus monarchy which 'soon spilled over into the entire society, consumed all its attention and energies' and poisoned the body politic for the entire inter-war period.[16] Hatred, persecution and open terrorism between the two opposing camps degenerated into a virtual civil war, with the monarchy versus republic issue blurring most others and superseding the grave social problems which had originally been its cause.[17]

The atmosphere of chaos reached its climax in 1922. Greece by then was a country in irreversible crisis. The aftermath of the First World War, culminating in the most devastating defeat of the Greek armed forces by the Turks in Asia Minor in 1922, shook the political and civic order of Greece to its very foundation. The collapse of the 'Greece of the Two Continents and the Five Seas' was an important turning point in more than one respect.[18] Asia Minor

[15] Mouzelis, *Politics in the Semi-Periphery*, p. 43; On the 1909 military intervention or 'revolution' as it often referred to in Greek historiography see S. Victor Papacosma, *The Military in Greek Politics: The 1909 Coup d'Etat* (Kent, OH: Kent State University Press, 1977).

[16] P. Nikiforos Diamandouros, 'Regime Change and the Prospects for Democracy in Greece: 1974–1983', in Guillermo O'Donnell, Philippe C. Schmitter, and Laurence Whitehead (eds), *Transitions from Authoritarian Rule: Prospects for Democracy* (Baltimore: Johns Hopkins University Press, 1986), pp. 140–2.

[17] Constantine Tsoucalas, *The Greek Tragedy* (Harmondsworth: Penguin, 1969), p. 34; see also Christos Theodoulou, *Greece and the Entente: August 1, 1914 – September 25, 1916* (Thessaloniki: Institute of Balkan Studies, 1973).

[18] See Mark Mazower, *Greece and the Inter-War Economic Crisis* (Oxford: Clarendon Press, 1991), pp. 18–21.

became the burial ground of panhellenic irredentism and expansionism, producing an enormous zone of ideological uncertainty, even deeper political divisions and chaos which probably changed Greek society more profoundly than any other period of comparable brevity.[19] The vision of 'Greece of Two Continents and Five Seas' had acted as

a powerful ideological instrument of social demobilisation and social control, managing to contain social conflict, and to impart some semblance of unity to a deeply fragmented society. Its death left Greece with a huge ideological vacuum precisely at the time when it was badly shaken by defeat and ... tensions produced by the rapid transformation of Greek society [which] rendered all the greater the need for an ideological principle of legitimation.[20]

At the same time, the sudden and massive influx of over 1.5 million refugees into a country of barely 5 million had fundamental consequences for Greece's inter-war social structure. A 20 per cent population increase, during a period in which Greek society was already experiencing rapid political change, combined with a quickly deteriorating economic situation exacerbated by huge war indebtedness abroad, had a catalytic impact on the country's inter-war socio-economic and demographic morphology.[21] In short, it was this new and volatile element inside Greek society which gradually began to 'change the style of the political debate and the ideological orientation of the traditional dominant classes'.[22] Constituting 'the only compact voting bloc of nationwide importance', the refugees crucially affected the internal balance of power by strengthening the socio-political dynamic of a hitherto

---

[19] The young novelist George Theotokas wrote: 'The wars had ended, the "Disaster" had abruptly and rudely closed the first century of modern Greek independence. The second century was beginning in anarchy and discontinuity. Greece had suddenly found herself without a form of government, without a constitution, without institutions or state organizations, without ideologies, because all had been bankrupted in the conscience of the nation.' Cited in Thomas Doulis, *Disaster and Fiction: Modern Greek Fiction and the Asia Minor Disaster of 1922* (Berkeley: University of California Press, 1977), p. 93.

[20] Diamandouros, 'Regime Change', in *Transitions from Authoritarian Rule*, p. 141.

[21] Alkis Rigos, *I B' Elliniki Dimokratia 1924–1935: Koinonikes Diastasseis tis Politikis Skinis* [The Second Greek Republic, 1924–1935: Social Dimensions on the Political Scene] (Athens: Themelio, 1992), p. 17.

[22] Mouzelis, *Modern Greece,* p. 26.

amorphous, underdeveloped and quiescent Greek working class.[23]

The post-1922 decade was therefore marked by two developments: 'the rising demands of the working classes for a greater share of social goods and services and the determination of the fragile and divided middle class to safeguard the Greek liberal state from what it perceived to be a mortal threat'.[24] Against rising industrial unrest[25] and political agitation exacerbated by the Great Depression and the Bolshevik victory in Russia, the *astikos kosmos* (the bourgeois parties), anxious to preserve the pre-war social equilibrium, responded with a series of repressive measures designed to block change and punish 'whoever sought the implementation of ideas whose manifest purpose is the overthrow of the established order by violent means'.[26] Meanwhile, the Greek communist party (KKE), which claimed to be the exclusive political expression of both the working class and labour movement, remained mysteriously indecisive and ineffectual. Despite the fact that a mass basis for political mobilization came into existence, the KKE, 'espousing an ideology of ouvrierisme, chose to ignore the radical potential of the two most frustrated socio-economic groups, the peasants and the refugees, and followed a course of political and social isolation'.[27] Overall, emergent problems from 'the new social and economic conditions were left unattended, while anachronistic political attitudes prevailed alongside rather advanced formal political structures of constitutionalism and parliamentary democracy'.[28] After 1922 and for more than a decade, a chaotic succession of elections, plebiscites, pronunciamentos, coups and counter-coups paralyzed public life and discredited the political establishment.[29]

---

[23] George Th. Mavrogordatos, *Stillborn Republic: Social Coalitions and Party Strategies in Greece, 1922–1936* (Berkeley: University of California Press, 1983), p. 184.

[24] Diamandouros, 'Regime Change', p. 141.

[25] There were 247 strikes in the first seven months of 1936. Cited in David H. Close, *The Origins of the Greek Civil War* (London: Longman, 1995), p. 36.

[26] Dimitris Livieratos, *Koinonikoi Agones stin Ellada, 1927–31* [Social Struggle in Greece, 1927–1931] (Athens: Enallaktikes Ekdoseis, 1987), pp. 120–2.

[27] Haris Vlavianos, 'The Greek Communist Party: In Search of a Revolution' in Tony Judt (ed.), *Resistance and Revolution in Mediterranean Europe, 1939–1948* (London: Routledge, 1989), p. 193.

[28] 'Thucydides', 'Greek Politics', p. 457.

[29] Tsoucalas, *Taxidi sto Logo, Vol. 2*, p. 205.

The 1936 Metaxas crown-sponsored dictatorship offered the clearest, albeit short-term, solution to 'an increasingly destabilizing organic crisis':[30] the failure of the Greek governing class to look away from its antagonisms and concentrate on how to contain the growing threat from below.[31] The regime, with its emphasis on nationalism and anti-communism, was profoundly anti-democratic and authoritarian.[32] Imitating the domestic practices of other South European dictatorships prevalent at the time, the Metaxas regime made no secret of its contempt for the 'decadent political world', and idealized notions of family, religion, morality and patriotism.[33] Meanwhile, the police force became the regime's state-control agency and its main instrument of reforming political values and public morality.[34] Police officers were ordered to attack their 'traditional enemies' (primarily left-wing dissidents and strikers) and suppress any sign of political opposition and industrial unrest with no restraint. It was during Metaxas' dictatorial rule that

the dreaded police file, with the necessary corollary, systematic spying on the population and classification of citizens in discriminatory categories, became an established administrative practice. It was then that signed declarations of loyalty to the regime became compulsory. It was then that criminal prosecution of radical ideas, as distinct from communist activities, was introduced and the practice of exhorting denunciations of communism from unwilling citizens by intimidation, even torture, became prevalent. It was then, too, that job victimization for political opposition became systematic. Finally, arbitrary arrest and banishment to distant islands or imprisonment in concentration camps was generalized.[35]

---

[30] Mavrogordatos, *Stillborn Republic,* p. 349.

[31] See P.J. Vatikiotis, *Popular Autocracy in Greece, 1936–1941: A Political Biography of General Ioannis Metaxas* (London: Frank Cass, 1998), pp. 185–95, 202–17.

[32] David H. Close, 'The Power-base of the Metaxas Dictatorship', in Robin Higham and Thanos Veremis (eds), *The Metaxas Dictatorship: Aspects of Greece 1936–40* (Athens: ELIAMEP-Vryonis Centre, 1993), pp. 22–8.

[33] Haris Vlavianos writes that 'Communism, parliamentarism, and the political world in general provided the villains which justified the dictatorship and were accordingly vilified as the "double yoke" or the "infection" under which the people suffered. Parliamentarism in particular, with the concomitant economic system of a capitalist economy, had allegedly reduced the people to a corrupt selfishness and materialism', H. Vlavianos, 'The Greek Communist Party under Siege' in *The Metaxas Dictatorship,* p. 149.

[34] See D.H. Close, 'The Police in the 4th August Regime' in *Journal of the Hellenic Diaspora,* Vol. 13 pp. 91–105.

[35] Andreas Papandreou, *Democracy at Gunpoint: The Greek Front* (London: Andre Deutsch, 1971), p. 46.

Official paranoia about any form of public dissent and the full-scale repression that came with it diffused mass protest but formed, at the same time, a violent and claustrophobic society. Far from healing the rifts that had gravely threatened the country's national well-being during the 1920s, the monarcho-fascist experience of 1936–41 served to fragment the nation more than ever. The Axis invasion and occupation that followed the Metaxas dictatorship temporarily silenced but did not weaken the growing popular dissatisfaction with the pre-war socio-political *status quo*. Sooner or later a dramatic reaction was to be expected.

Revolution averted: the legacy of the civil war

The end of the Second World War was met with popular enthusiasm and a strong desire for a new institutional order was felt. Calls for a new type of state and the replacement of the disintegrating bourgeois state, which had first become audible before the occupation, now re-emerged more loudly, echoing the frustration and alienation of the population from its traditional political leaders. Established systems of rule, thought and legitimacy came under attack from a variety of forces demanding radical change.[36] This time, the Communist KKE, the driving force behind the resistance organizations during the Nazi occupation, appeared determined to seize this unique opportunity and play a decisive role in shaping the country's political future. For a while, it appeared that political change had found its way forward. However, fundamental reform and a no-return to the pre-war institutions and practices could only be achieved through the overthrow of the established political order. Predictably, such moves provoked in turn reactionary efforts from home and abroad to stop the clock and reimpose the traditional balance of social and economic power.[37] Indeed, in post-war Greece there were only two solutions: revolutionary violence or reactionary violence. Full-scale confrontation was imminent and cou ld no longer be staved off.

[36] See J. O. Iatrides, 'Greece at the Crossroads', in John O. Iatrides and Linda Wringley (eds), *Greece at the Crossroads: The Civil War and its Legacy* (University Park, Penn: Pennsylvania University Press, 1995), pp. 1–30.

[37] Mark Mazower, *Inside Hitler's Greece: The Experience of Occupation 1941–44* (New Haven: Yale University Press, 1993), pp. 265–97.

The civil war of 1946–9 was the culmination of a series of uneven struggles between the forces of reform and reaction that had dominated Greek society ever since the mid-1920s.[38] It represented the ultimate expression of the attempts by the old political élite and their foreign patrons to hold back social progress and crush any economic reforms that might upset the *status quo*.[39] In the end, the existing order survived, partly because of the indecisiveness of the left in seizing the initiative[40] but more crucially because of direct US intervention in the conflict through the Truman doctrine.[41] From March 1947, the United States, which had hitherto remained aloof from national affairs, assumed full politico-military control of the Greek state, seeking the eradication of 'the communist armed rebellion without delay, vacillation or compromise'.[42] As Greece became the first battleground of the Cold War,[43] the main objective of the US policy and military planners was

not a peaceful settlement of the Greek civil war, which would have given legal status to the Greek communists. Peaceful reconciliation and negotiations with the communists would have hindered American Cold War policy. The true US purpose was, first, to win the civil war as a victory against the Soviet Union and its allies, thus curbing their 'conspiratorial efforts to subvert and incorporate Greece into the communist bloc'; and, second, to establish an obedient Greek anti-communist state, thus ensuring US strategic interests.[44]

Two things became clear from this terrifying episode in which over 80,000 Greeks were killed and 700,000 lost their homes:[45] first, as

---

[38] J.O. Iatrides, 'Greece at the Crossroads', p. 10.

[39] Nitsa Loule-Theodoraki, *Harilaos Florakis* (Athens: Ellinika Grammata, 1995), pp. 82–5; see also David H. Close, 'The Changing Structure of the Right, 1945–1950' in *Greece at the Crossroads*, pp. 122–56.

[40] Ole L. Smith, 'Communist Perceptions, Strategy, and Tactics, 1945–1949' in *Greece at the Crossroads*, pp. 90–121; see also Ilios Yannakakis, 'The Greek Communist Party', in *New Left Review* (March–April 1969), pp. 46–54.

[41] Amikam Nachmani, 'Civil War and Foreign Intervention in Greece: 1946–9, in *Journal of Contemporary History*, Vol. 25 (1990), pp. 489–552.

[42] Vassilis Kapetanyiannis, *Socio-Political Conflicts and Military Intervention: The case of Greece, 1950–1967*, (unpublished PhD dissertation, University of London, 1986), p. 6.

[43] See Alonzo L. Hamby, *Man of the People: A Life of Harry S. Truman* (Oxford: Oxford University Press, 1996), pp. 390–94.

[44] Minas Samatas, 'Greek McCarthyism: A Comparative Assessment of Greek Post-Civil War Repressive Anticommunism and the US Truman-McCarthy Era' in *Journal of the Hellenic Diaspora*, Vol. 13, Nos. 3–4 (Fall–Winter 1986), p. 15.

other European countries were rebuilding themselves from the Second World War, a physically ravaged and war-devastated Greece continued to destroy itself and, second, that a state-organized campaign of mass political repression extrapolated the civil war schism to the entire Greek population, perpetuating, at the same time, 'the bondage of a system that was already exhausted, frustrated and incapable of any dynamic development'.[46] The pattern of Greek politics for the next 30 years was set: 'an impenetrable ideological and political ghetto'[47] was developed with the victors (the right) launching an Orwellian anti-communist campaign against the vanquished (the communist left) in the name of republicanism, religion, patriotism and 'national security'. The communist KKE was outlawed and a draconian set of emergency laws (modelled on US anti-communist legislation) and political control techniques (used extensively during the Truman-McCarthy era) were introduced for the politico-economic exclusion of the Greek left and the consolidation of the anti-communist state.[48] Politico-ideological criticism and dissent were banned: until the early 1960s, there was 'no grouping, newspaper or periodical advocating a non-Communist alternative to reaction in the political, social and cultural sphere'.[49]

Anti-communism bolstered authoritarianism everywhere: in the civil service, the army, the police, and the university. Discrimination and politico-economic exclusion was enforced by

a large police bureaucracy which kept files on all Greek citizens. With red pen police underlined critical information about citizens (or their relatives) who had been stigmatized as communist, leftist, sympathizer or 'crypto'. The police file (*Fakelos*) and the police-issued civic-mindedness certificates implemented that brand of totalitarianism which entailed collective family responsibility and mass political surveillance by using hundred of police informers.[50]

---

[45] Figures in Richard Clogg, *A Short History of Modern Greece* (Cambridge: Cambridge University Press, 1979), p. 164.

[46] Tsoucalas, *The Greek Tragedy*, p. 118.

[47] Ibid. p. 115.

[48] Samatas writes in his 'Greek McCarthyism' that 'Greek emergency laws 512 and 516 (1948), plus a similar law 1540 (1950), restated almost verbatim the basic civil service loyalty-security provisions of the US "Hatch Act" of August 2, 1939, which was passed to prevent "pernicious political activities", but prescribed harsher penalties'. pp. 17–18.

[49] Tsoucalas, *The Greek Tragedy*, p. 115.

Special paraconstitutional legislation (laws 509/1947 and 516/1948), which operated alongside, and in flagrant violation of the Greek constitution, enabled the security police to terrorize, persecute and ostracize citizens of 'doubtful' political morality.[51] By the end of 1950s, anti-communism had been transformed from a political instrument of state legitimation to the governing principle of an aggressive strategy of social demobilization and of social control designed to safeguard the closed nature of the Greek political system, to reinforce it and, above all, to ensure its perpetuation.[52]

Until *metapolitefsi*, all Greek citizens were categorized into *ethnikofrones* ('healthy', nationally-minded citizens) and the non-*ethnikofrones* (the communists, fellow-travellers and sympathizers). Such deep ideological divisions had serious side-effects on the evolution of Greek political culture in which extreme-left terrorism later developed.

Meanwhile, the Greek state urgently needed new institutions, systematic reconstruction policies and a coherent national plan.[53] The prospect of another communist bid for power in combination with the absence of a foreign policy consensus made Greece totally dependent on US military and financial patronage.[54] The activation of the Cyprus problem and fear of Turkey provoked deep uneasiness and led to alliances as a way to ensure territorial integrity and national prestige.[55] The strongly anti-communist atmosphere in the West and in the NATO alliance (which Greece joined in 1952) allowed the Greek right to consolidate its power and to institutionalize a politically exclusivist parliamentary system. NATO, at

---

[50] Samatas, 'Greek McCarthyism', p. 35; By 1962, the number of paid police informers is estimated to have reached over 60,000. See Nicos C. Alivizatos, *Les Institutions politiques de la Grèce à travers les crises, 1922–74* (Paris: R. Pichon & R. Durand-Auzias, 1979), pp. 147, 197–8, 201–2; and Jean Meynaud, *Les Forces Politiques en Grèce* (Paris: Etudes de Science Politique, 1965), pp. 251, 263 and 352.

[51] See David H. Close, 'The Legacy' in David H. Close (ed.), *The Greek Civil War, 1943–1950: Studies of Polarization*, (London: Routledge, 1993), pp. 214; 218–20.

[52] Diamandouros, 'Regime Change', p. 142.

[53] Stavros B. Thomadakis, 'Stabilization, Development, and Government Economic Authority in the 1940s', in *Greece at the Crossroads*, pp. 173–80.

[54] See Alexis Papachelas, *O Viasmos tis Ellinikis Dimokratias: O Amerikanikos Paragon, 1947–1967* [The Rape of Greek Democracy: The American Factor, 1947–1967] (Athens: Estia, 1997), pp. 17–54.

[55] Evanthis Hatzivassiliou, 'Security and the European Option: Greek Foreign Policy, 1952–62', in *Journal of Contemporary History*, Vol.30 (1995), pp. 191–3, 195–6.

the same time, was seen as 'a panacea for the most crucial problems, so the terms and implications of admission were not even discussed'.[56]

The right's 11 years of uninterrupted rule (1952–63), first under the leadership of Marshall Alexander Papagos, and, after his death in 1955, under Konstantinos Karamanlis, perpetuated norms of non-participation and polarized political stances and forces. However, socio-political tension began to rise over inadequate housing, transport, poor access to higher education, urban unemployment, income inequalities, weak unions, uneven modernization, and a manipulative electoral system that disenfranchized a large minority.[57] Popular discontent grew throughout the 1950s and took a much more crystallized form in the early 1960s when Greece's post-civil war mechanisms of political control came, for the first time, under strain.[58] The election victory of George Papandreou's Centre Union progressive party in November 1963, and again in February 1964, was the result of growing vocal demands for the democratization of the post-civil war exclusionist system.[59] Under Papandreou

political participation and mobilisation were encouraged under freer conditions of expression and conduct. Politics became a respectable pursuit once more and a less risky personal and collective enterprise. A new sense of civic morality was emerging and a new feeling of participating citizenship. The newly acquired civil and political rights, though not legally sanctioned, were sufficiently established in people's minds not to be surrendered too easily. Thus the political map was redrawn. The Right lost its exclusive claim to govern and the old political divide between Right and Left could not be sustained any longer.[60]

Many other transformations started in this period:

- expansion of the educational system
- wage increases to large sections of the workforce and strengthening the independence of trade unions
- greater freedom to the press

---

[56] Tsoucalas, *Greek Tragedy*, pp.153–4.
[57] George Th. Mavrogordatos, 'The 1940s between Past and Future', in *Greece at the Crossroads*, pp. 45–7.
[58] Constantine Tsoucalas, 'Class Struggle and Dictatorship in Greece', in *New Left Review*, No. 56 (July-August 1969), pp. 4–7.
[59] Mario S. Modiano, 'Greek Political Troubles', in *The World Today*, Vol. 21, No. 1 (January 1965), pp. 35–40.
[60] Vassilis Kapetanyiannis, *Socio-Political Conflicts and Military Intervention*, p. 259.

- better social security and subsidies for the peasants
- new military-civil relations
- development of consensually based institutions.[61]

Given the dynamic of political democratization, it soon became evident that the politically repressive and exclusivist parliamentarism could no longer survive without radical changes. At the same time, however, such radical rearrangements were bound to affect deeply the main institutional pillars of the political system (the throne-army-parliament alliance in which the military was dominant) and to alter fundamentally the distribution of power among them.

Either parliament, through its opening up to the masses, had to become the dominant force in this triarchy, in which case the army would lose its leading position with inevitable internal consequences for holding posts within it; or else the army had to prevent this by the overall abolition of parliamentary rule.[62]

The 1967 coup was therefore an assault from within the political system, signifying an anxious attempt by an apprehensive military to preserve its supremacy. Committed to their own survival and to the perpetuation of the divisive ideology of the civil war, the armed forces abandoned their post-war role in the Greek state as mere arbitrators to intra-bourgeois squabbles and forcibly acquired a dominant role in the power structure in order to re-organize the country's political life by 'clearing up the mess'[63] and putting an end to the conditions of 'anarchy and chaos' to which the political class (the right and the King) had reduced Greece.[64]

---

[61] George Karambelias, *Kratos kai Koinonia stin Metapolitefsi: 1974–1988* [State and Society in Metapolitefsi, 1974–1988] (Athens: Exandas, 1989), pp. 76–81.

[62] Mouzelis, *Modern Greece*, p. 133.

[63] Kollias, the new premier, said in his statement on the day of the coup that: 'We have long been witnessing a crime committed against our people and our nation. Unscrupulous and base party compromises, shameful recklessness of a great part of the press, methodical attack on and undermining of all institutions, complete debasement of Parliament, all-round slander, paralysis of the state machinery, complete lack of understanding of the burning problems of our youth, moral decline, secret and open collaboration with subversion, and finally, constant inflammatory slogans of unscrupulous demagogues, have destroyed the country's peace, created an atmosphere of anarchy, chaos, hatred and discord, and led us to the brink of national catastrophe' cited from Keith R. Legg, *Politics in Modern Greece,* p. 227.

Although the military had intervened at different times during the century and a half (1909, 1916 and 1922) since Greece's independence from Ottoman Turkey, it never questioned parliamentary rule nor sought to permanently replace civilian and parliamentary institutions. Until 1967, military interventions were 'essentially restricted to a moderator pattern' as they advanced the interests of specific political groups or sought to punish the political class for its failings.[65]

The Colonels shared most of Metaxas' obsessions.[66] However, their image as simple patriots crusading against communism, their loud commitment to the principles of Hellenism and Orthodox Christianity and their populist rhetoric of spurious egalitarianism did not succeed in concealing the fragility of the regime and its essential political weaknesses.[67] Despite this, although anachronistic and with 'no clear policies and consistent views on the shape of the regime or the nature of its future options',[68] the regime of 21 April maintained power for seven years through its use of open political repression and with the help of an unprecedented international boom. At the same time, sporadic and uncoordinated resistance[69] and the apathy and resignation of a large section of a populace deeply disillusioned with parliamentary politics fed a belief that the military junta, though archaic and authoritarian, was better than the available alternatives.[70] Until the 1972–3 world oil crisis, rapid growth raised living standards and minimized the potential for protest. However, the economic crisis weakened confidence in the regime which appeared to be floundering in

---

[64] See Richard Clogg, 'The Ideology of the Revolution of 21 April 1967', in Richard Clogg and George Yannopoulos (eds), *Greece Under Military Rule*, (London: Secker & Warburg, 1972), p. 36.

[65] See Thanos Veremis, *The Military in Greek Politics: From Independence to Democracy* (London: Hurst & Company, 1997), pp. ix–x.

[66] Many of the Colonels, writes Veremis in his *The Military in Greek Politics*, 'entered the Military Academy when General Metaxas was already firmly established in power.', p. ix.

[67] Nancy Bermeo, 'Classification and Consolidation: Some Lessons from the Greek Dictatorship', in *Political Science Quarterly*, Vol. 110, No. 3 (1995), pp. 438–41, 449–50.

[68] Veremis, *The Military in Greek Politics,* p. 159.

[69] Yannopoulos, 'The State of the Opposition Forces Since the Military Coup' in *Greece Under Military Rule*, p. 177.

[70] Panayote E. Dimitras, 'Changes in Public Attitudes', in Kevin Featherstone & Dimitrios K. Katsoudas (eds), *Political Change in Greece: Before and After the Colonels* (London: Croom Helm, 1987), p. 78; see also *The Economist*, Survey: Greece, 31 July 1971, p. xxxvi.

problems beyond its competence. The events of November 1973 and the brutal military suppression of the student occupation of Athens Polytechnic turned public opinion against the regime and activated popular resistance, cementing the impression that political transformation might be possible.[71] Finally, the junta collapsed in the summer of 1974 when, in an effort to gain domestic support through the manipulation of nationalist sentiment, it attempted to influence events in Cyprus and lost the northern part of the island to Turkey.[72] At a deeper level, the Colonels' regime dissolved because it failed to overcome the problem which haunts most bureaucratic-authoritarian models of government: 'the establishment of a political system with an appearance of a legitimacy that could succeed the dictatorship'.[73]

The Third Hellenic Republic

Metapolitefsi, the 1974 transition from an authoritarian rule to a democratic constitutional order, was not the result of a clear and sharp break with the Colonels' regime but the product of a whole range of compromises and negotiations between élite-level political actors and the military. Despite this, 1974 was a turning point for several reasons:

The establishment, in that year, of full political democracy, for the first time, changed the structures of political life in profound and lasting ways. Obscured by unquestionable continuities embedded in the restorative rather than the instaurative element of the transition, the

---

[71] Angelos Elephantis, *Ston Asterismo tou Laikismou* [In the Constellation of Populism] (Athens: O Politis, 1991), pp. 77–83.

[72] The end of the dictatorship, it must be emphasized, and the surrender of power to a civilian government was neither the result of a military counter-coup in Athens nor of a popular upheaval from below. Rather, it resulted from the 20 July Turkey invasion of northern Cyprus (38 per cent of the island) and the inability of the Colonels to handle the crisis and deal with a rapidly deteriorating military situation. When a general mobilization collapsed in chaos, revealing that the politicization of the armed forces over the previous seven years had compromised their capability to defend the country's territorial integrity, the chiefs of staff with the acquiescence of the military President of the Republic, General P. Gizikis, decided to call in the politicians. In less than 24 hours, Konstantinos Karamanlis returned from his French exile to rescue Greece from the brink of war with Turkey and to preside over the transition to a civilian rule.

[73] Raymond Carr, *Modern Spain 1875–1980* (Oxford: Oxford University Press, 1980), p. 106.

advent of political democracy set off novel and powerful long-term processes of social and political change.[74]

Aside from propelling Konstantinos Karamanlis back into power, the two fundamental purposes which underlay the establishment of the Greek Third Republic were: 'to remove the obscurantist "parallel state" and to end the "exclusivism" that had tainted the post-war political system'.[75] By defining national goals, Karamanlis expressed the widespread view that democracy never functioned smoothly in Greece because conditions were either missing or could not be created. These conditions were 'a moderate political climate, peaceable political mores and institutions adapted to the particular circumstances of our country'.[76] The fratricidal issue of monarchy-versus-republic which had divided the nation for 60 years was settled through a national referendum in which two-thirds of the electorate (69.18 per cent) voted against the King's return and were strongly in favour of a presidential democracy.[77] The result reflected the general mood of the country and the electorate's determination to make a fresh start. From 1974 onwards

the issue of the form of the regime benefited from a broad consensus, a diffuse support, something hitherto unprecedented and which made the new Republic by far the most legitimate modern Greece has experienced.[78]

At the same time, Karamanlis had three fundamental and most immediate problems to resolve. First and foremost was the question of Cyprus: how to work out a speedy political solution to the problem and, given the imbalance between the two countries' armed forces, defuse the risk of war with Turkey? Second was the question of the army: how to bring the armed forces firmly under

---

[74] P. Nikiforos Diamandouros, 'Politics and Culture in Greece, 1974–91: An Interpretation', in Richard Clogg (ed.), *Greece 1981–89: The Populist Decade* (London: Macmillan, 1993), p. 7.

[75] Yannis Papadopoulos, 'Parties, the State and Society in Greece: Continuity within Change', in *Western European Politics*, Vol. 12, No. 2 (April 1989), p. 57.

[76] Richard Clogg, *Parties and Elections in Greece: The Search for Legitimacy*, (London: Hurst & Company, 1987), p. 223.

[77] There had been six earlier referenda in 1920, 1924, 1935, 1946, and 1973 but the December 1974 was the only one not to have been conducted in abnormal conditions and free of allegations of manipulation.

[78] Papadopoulos, 'Parties, the State and Society', p. 56.

government control and to break up the network of officers which enabled the military to rule for more than seven years? Third was the question of a purge: how far should the fascists and fascist sympathizers be punished or removed from public posts? The problem of the purge proved especially difficult. The dilemma faced by Karamanlis was that

on the one hand he had to be seen to respond to the demands – which were particularly insistent on the part of the students whose resistance to the dictatorship had been instrumental in its destabilisation – for the severe punishment of the tyrants, and the *apohountopoiisi* or 'dejuntification' of the entire state apparatus of the appointees of, and collaborators with, the military regime. On the other hand, indiscriminate revenge could easily have provoked a backlash on the part of junta sympathizers still firmly entrenched in the armed forces.[79]

Military officers and the extreme right repeatedly tried to paralyze public life. During the first six months of democratic change, four attempted *coups d'état* were uncovered. With this threat in mind, Karamanlis adopted a strategy of a swift but contained retribution.[80] A strategy centrally designed

to enhance the legitimacy of the new regime, further to delegitimate its discredited predecessor, and, at the same time, to appear equitable, to avoid the potentially negative repercussions from too protracted a public focus on past traumas, and to prevent excesses that might undermine the climate of national solidarity so crucial to the regime's long-term consolidation chances.[81]

The first years of *metapolitefsi* were thus marked by a curious amalgam of continuity and change. The symbols, the rhetoric, and even the constitution changed; but without any systematic purge of the bureaucracy and the police apparatus, key sections of

---

[79] Clogg, *A Concise History of Greece*, p. 173.

[80] Karamanlis's strategy of contained retribution was mostly evident in the deliberately slow pace at which the government proceeded in dealing with the most sensitive and explosive popular demands: purges of the military, the state bureaucracy, the universities, the security forces, and, above all, the prosecution of the protagonists in the 1967 coup, in the bloody suppression of the Polytechnic uprising, and in the torturing of political prisoners during the seven-year fascist regime.

[81] Diamandouros, 'Regime Change', in O'Donell, p. 161; see also Harry J. Psomiades, 'Greece: From the Colonels' Rule to Democracy' in John H. Herz (ed.), *From Dictatorship to Democracy* (Westport, Conn: Greenwood Press, 1982), p. 256.

the state continued in the hands of the old order.[82] When the Karamanlis government proved itself unable to deliver its promise of 'irreversible change', the credibility of the new republic was seriously weakened in the eyes of many ordinary Greeks, especially the students whose resistance to the Colonels had been catalytic in its destabilization.[83] Their disillusionment was expressed in the form of protest movements, anti-establishment journalism and, ultimately, political terrorism.

At the same time, the new institutions were initially identified with Karamanlis and his newly established New Democracy (ND) party and were openly used to control and channel the processes of political change.[84] ND capitalized on its founder's strong charisma and great personal prestige as the leader who stood between democracy and the return of the Colonels' junta.[85] Like de Gaulle, Karamanlis projected himself as the best guarantor of political stability and asked for and obtained solid majorities.[86] The implicit slogan '*Karamanlis or the*

---

[82] Karamanlis's strategy meant that within the remarkably short space of five months, the protagonists of the 1967 coup, the leaders of the foiled coups, together with the major figures in the brutal suppression of the Polytechnic uprising, and the torturers in the military police and secret services were brought to trial, and received sentences ranging from the death penalty to life imprisonment for the major figures to lesser if not nugatory sentences for others. Indicative of Karamanlis's firm strategy of contained retribution was the government's decision to commute the death sentences being passed on the three leaders of the junta to life imprisonment – without awaiting the results of any appeal. Not surprisingly, perhaps, the government's decision provoked a storm of criticism and resentment in opposition circles and not only there. Andreas Papandreou, the leader of the then newly established PASOK, spoke of 'a mere change of guard'. By the end of 1975 the air was thick with rumours that the commutation of the death sentences and the light sentences given to ministers who had served in the junta administrations 'smacked of a deal'. In the end, pragmatism won out, and attempts to conduct a thorough and systematic purge of the entire state apparatus were dropped. See Richard Clogg, 'Karamanlis's Cautious Success: the Background', in *Government and Opposition* (Summer 1975), pp. 338–42.

[83] See Lina Alexiou, 'Katharsi-Apochountopoiissi-Ekdimokratismos: Chamenes Elpides, Olethries Parachorisseis' [Catharsis-Dejuntification-Democratization: Lost Opportunities, Calamitous Concessions'] in *Anti* (No. 24, 1975), pp. 7–9; see also *Anti* editorials (Nos. 3, 10, 1974); (No. 12, 1974); (Nos. 21, 23, 1975); (Nos. 44, 61, 1976); (Nos. 63, 65, 73, 86, 1977).

[84] Roy C. Macridis, 'Elections and Political Modernization in Greece', in Howard Penniman (ed.), *Greece at the Polls: The National Elections of 1974 and 1977* (Washington DC: American Enterprise Institute, 1981), pp. 3, 6–8 and 11–12.

[85] C.M. Woodhouse, *Karamanlis: The Restorer of Greek Democracy* (Oxford: Clarendon Press, 1982), pp. 75–89.

tanks' struck the heart of a sentimental and insecure electorate, and persuaded a substantial number of voters across the political spectrum to support Karamanlis's visibly reshaped, neo-conservative New Democracy party.[87]

Both in rhetoric and in practice, the Karamanlis governments of 1974 and 1977 made consistent efforts to reshape the culture of governance and initiate a break from the patterns of the past. The regime sought to de-polarize political stances and forces, which explains the 'incorporation into the political system of social forces which since the end of the civil war, had remained excluded from, or marginal to, the political process'.[88] After more than three decades of political and ideological demonization of the left, the regime institutionalized right-left coexistence through a series of actions 'designed to underscore that a system open to all Greeks was in the process of being reconstructed'.[89] The essential goal of the leaders of the Third Republic, working in the midst of the Cyprus crisis and against military plots and neo-fascist terrorist conspiracies, was to produce distinctive new patterns of governmental behaviour and legislative output. Determined not to repeat mistakes of the past, Karamanlis and his government were concerned with establishing state institutions and procedures which could be both efficient and autonomous. This explains why the main constitutional changes were directly related to the legislative process. As such, the measures can be divided into two basic types: (1) structural assets which enhanced in a constant manner the government's power *vis-à-vis* the parliament and, (2) an arsenal of constitutional weapons to be wielded, if and when needed, to combat particular problems. Under the 1975 constitution:

executive power was to be exercised both by the president of the republic and by the government, with the powers of the head of state more rigorously defined than under the 1952 constitution. While the

---

[86] Christos Lyrintzis, 'Political Parties in Post-Junta Greece: A Case of "Bureaucratic Clientelism" ', in Geoffrey Pridham (ed.), *The New Mediterranean Democracies* (London: Frank Cass, 1984), pp. 106–9.

[87] 'In the event', writes R. Clogg, 'the implicit slogan "Karamanlis or the tanks" produced a massive 54.4% vote in favour of ND. Clearly a significant element in the electorate had placed the continued consolidation of the country's newly re-acquired democratic freedoms above their personal political preferences'. Source: Richard Clogg, *Parties and Elections in Greece*, p. 66.

[88] Diamandouros, 'Politics and Culture' in *Greece 1981–89: The Populist Decade*, pp. 10–12.

[89] Diamandouros, 'Political Regime', in *Transitions from Authoritarian Rule*, p. 162.

influence of the Fifth Republic is manifest and the powers of the president considerable, these were only to come into play in times of political and national crisis, and the president was precluded from intervening in the day-to-day running of the government.[90]

The president was to be 'the guardian of national interests' and the 'regulator' of the regime. Although he was not supposed to be a substitute for the cabinet, the president 'would have more powers than his Bonn counterpart but less than the president of the French Fifth Republic'.[91] In short, he would have sufficient pre-rogatives 'to perform his regulatory role, that is to harmonize relations between the people and the Chamber and between the Chamber and the Cabinet, in order to ensure the normal course of parliamentary government'.[92]

Because of the country's long-standing tradition of political authoritarianism, both PASOK and the communist parties (KKE and KKE-es) feared that the new regime would produce a system of selfish, hyper-presidential control that would lead to the creation of a Greek de Gaulle. In their view, although elected, the head of the state 'should have only nominal and formal powers, while real power should lie in the hands of the cabinet and the Chamber, to which the former should be exclusively accountable'.[93] The debate led to a major clash but since they were numerically too weak to oppose Karamanlis, their actions concentrated on protests inside parliament and partisan rhetoric in the national media.

In the early years of *metapolitefsi*, the Greeks were obsessed by restoring their national credibility and independence of action. Pre-dictably, the process of democratic consolidation was played out against a background of continuing tension with Turkey and the Atlantic Alliance.[94] The Karamanlis government's tactical move to

[90] Clogg, *Parties and Elections in Greece*, p. 68; See also Nicos C. Alivizatos, 'The Presidency, Parliament and the Courts in the 1980s, in *Greece 1981–89*, pp. 65–78; D.K. Katsoudas, 'The constitutional framework' in *Political Change before and after the Colonels*, pp. 14–33; Evangelos Venizelos, *I Logiki tou Politevmatos kai i Domi tis Ektelestikis Exoussias sto Syndagma tou 1975* [The logic of the Regime and the structure of the Executive in the 1975 Constitution] (Thessaloniki: Paratiritis, 1980).

[91] Nicos Alivizatos, 'The President', p. 66.

[92] Greek Parliament, Official Minutes of the Chamber, 7 June 1975, p. 1904.

[93] Alivizatos, 'The President', p. 66.

[94] P.J. Vatikiotis, 'Greece and the Mediterranean Crisis', in *Survival*, Vol. xviii, No. 1 (Jan/Feb. 1976), pp. 25–6.

take Greece out of the military wing of NATO's American-dominated command structure proved a case in point. The 1974 NATO withdrawal represented both a political and psychological break with the historical experience of foreign intervention.[95] Additionally, it brought about a number of structural changes in the country's external relations: (1) a departure from an exclusive and subordinate relationship with the United States and NATO; (2) the strengthening of political and economic ties with Europe and the EEC; and (3) the development of closer links with a number of states in the Balkans, Eastern Europe, Africa and the Soviet Union.[96]

Capitalizing on the vicious atmosphere of the period, Karamanlis waged a constant and occasionally obsessive campaign pushing for Greek entry into the European Community. This was seen as a political umbrella which could safeguard the country's young democratic institutions from internal enemies and its territorial integrity from external threats.[97] At a deeper level, however, Karamanlis had hoped that Greek participation in the institutional structures of the Community would act as a catalyst for the modernization of the country's political and financial systems.[98] Mainstream opposition to EC membership focused on old-fashioned and intransigent ideological grounds.[99] Typically, the pro-Moscow KKE viewed the European Community as merely 'an arm of the multinationals and NATO, designed to snuff out the last vestiges of Greek economic independence and to ensnare the country ever more firmly in the arms of the West'.[100] However,

---

[95] George Andreopoulos, *I Chrissi kai i Katchrissi tou Antiamerikanismou stin Ellada* [The Use and Abuse of anti-Americanism in Greece] (Athens: Polytypo, 1994). pp. 50–3.

[96] Theodore A. Couloumbis, 'Defining Greek Foreign Policy Objectives', in *Greece at the Polls*, pp. 170–5.

[97] 'Membership', Karamanlis argued, 'was not only essential for economic reasons but was also a safeguard for Greece's democratic regime'. EC full integration meant that 'it would be impossible for any coup to be attempted against democracy. For those who would dare such an action would know that on the morrow they would have been dismissed from the community, with grievous consequences for the country', *Herald Tribune*, Special Report, 31 October, 1979.

[98] See P.C. Ioakimidis, 'Greece in the EC: Policies, Experiences and Prospects' in Harry J. Psomiades and Stavros B. Thomadakis (eds), *Greece, The New Europe, and the Changing International Order* (New York: Pella, 1993), pp. 405–420.

[99] Loukas Tsoukalis, 'Greece in Europe: the tenth member', in *The World Today*, Vol. 37, No. 4 (April 1981), pp. 121–126.

the socialist PASOK was the loudest in denouncing the EC as an 'aggressive international capitalist club, a front for the multinationals seeking to exploit countries such as Greece that were on the capitalist periphery'.[101] Only the KKE-es welcomed membership because it quickly realized that the EC could be the only substantial counterweight to US influence and broaden Greece's foreign policy options. Ultimately, party-political debate over EC membership fulfilled a vital need, giving an important indication of the nature and prospects of the new democratic process.[102]

Overall, Karamanlis used single-minded ambition and nationalist economic self-interest to set a foreign policy consensus. He was willing to acknowledge more clearly than Venizelos (the architect of the short-lived 'Greece of the Two Continents and the Five Seas') had ever done the degree to which Greece needed Europe.[103] With a great sense of history he

avoided Venizelos' error of imposing the commitments of a major power on the infrastructure of an underdeveloped country. He first advanced its infrastructure to the level of a secondary power, and then sought commensurate responsibilities. He recognized that in association with major powers, through NATO and the EEC in particular, he could exercise greater leverage on international affairs than a secondary power could exercise on its own.[104]

Until 1979, the Greek Third Republic was closely associated with Karamanlis. His main achievement was the creation of a new political system acceptable to almost the entire population. For the first time since 1830, there was a general consensus in favour of republican institutions. Karamanlis's departure from the political centre stage left the New Democracy party in a state of complete confusion. Deprived of the charismatic personality of its

---

[100] James Pettifer, 'Greek Polity and the European Community, 1974–1993' in Philip Carabott (ed.), *Greece and Europe in the Modern Period: Aspects of a Troubled Relationship* (London: King's College, 1995), p. 101.

[101] Clogg, *A Concise History of Greece*, p. 181.

[102] Susannah Verney, 'To be or not to be within the European Community: the party debate and democratic consolidation in Greece' in Geoffrey Pridham (ed.), *Securing Democracy: Political Parties and Democratic Consolidation in Southern Europe* (London: Routledge, 1990), p. 212.

[103] On Venizelos, see Clogg, *A Concise History of Greece*, p. 226.

[104] Woodhouse, *Karamanlis*, p. 287.

leader and fractured by internal disputes over policy differences and electoral tactics, the party gradually lost its electoral appeal.

PASOK's landslide election victory in 1981 ended almost half a century of right-wing political monopoly and gave Greece its first ever socialist government.[105] Intoxicated by victory (48 per cent share of the vote and 57 per cent of parliamentary representation) the intelligentsia of the left spoke forcefully about a change of regime:

> The coming of power of the first left-of-centre political force in modern Greek history seemed to bring to a close a long historical cycle whose salient characteristic had been the repeated failed attempts at incorporation of the rural and urban masses into the Greek political system. While the 1974 transition made possible the incorporation of the heretofore excluded rural and working class masses into the new political system (a decisive step toward the normalisation of Greek politics), the 1981 change in government actually brought to power the party representing them.[106]

Although the *Allaghi*[107] of October 1981 with its promises for a dramatic break with the recent past and its radical proposals for changing Greek society was a clear anathema to the traditionalist right, post-1974 national political institutions and electoral arrangements had demonstrated both to the public and to most participants that they had become healthy, flexible and democratic. Under Papandreou's guidance, the non-communist left proved that the regime had room for perceptive, well organized and innovative political parties of all colours. PASOK symbolized a 'new political synthesis – national, consensual and participatory – that supersedes the previous one'.[108] Ready to go beyond the old dogmas of right and left, PASOK transformed the terms of political engagement by becoming itself the

---

105 For a detailed analysis of the 1981 general election, see George Th. Mavrogordatos, *The Rise of the Green Sun: The Greek Election of 1981,* Centre of Contemporary Greek Studies, King's College, Occasional Paper No. 1 (London, 1983); see also Richard Clogg, 'Greece: The Year of the Green Sun' in *The World Today*, Vol. 37, No. 11 (November 1981), pp. 401–4.

106 Richard Gunther, Hans-Jurgen Puhle and P. Nikiforos Diamandouros, 'Introduction' in Richard Gunther, P. Nikiforos Diamandouros and Hans-Jurgen Puhle (eds), *The Politics of Democratic Consolidation: Southern Europe in Comparative Perspective* (Baltimore, MA: Johns Hopkins University Press, 1995), p. 29.

107 *Allaghi* = Change was PASOK's principal campaign slogan in the 1981 general elections.

108 Roy C. Macridis, *Greek Politics at a Crossroads: What kind of Socialism?* (Stanford: Hoover Institution Press, 1984), p. 47.

vehicle of collective demands that can no longer be satisfied through the traditional patron-client networks. The ideology of the party (both nationalist and socialist) is committed to a radical restructuring of the economy and society through nationalisation and state intervention.[109]

The Socialists managed to galvanize public support over a whole range of claims which Karamanlis had failed to meet. Under the banner of root-and-branch reform and renewal, PASOK pledged to meet these claims and satisfy even more:

to redistribute wealth, punish tax evasion and tax exemptions, increase salaries and pensions, raise the floors on agricultural prices, increase subsidies to small enterprises, maintain the stability of incomes, promote social security, provide special care for women and children, and improve education.[110]

Moreover, Papandreou was able to exploit the widespread discontent caused by the deepening economic crisis and the changing pattern of social aspirations which reflected significant changes in socio-professional structures. His appeal across the class divide succeeded because he understood that inequality in the 1970s had drained New Democracy's individualistic paleoliberalism of its remaining credibility. Papandreou was also quick to evoke emotions of national pride. He told the Greek people what they believed to be true: 'that in every crucial phase of Greece's modern history, the Bavarians, the notables, the Palace, the Metaxists, the Pentagon, NATO, the multinationals, the CIA, etc. – had all, at every opportunity, turned the country against itself'.[111]

Papandreou wished Greece to be autonomous and capable of asserting her independence in matters more crucial to her. His radical political vision thus promised to strengthen Greece's standing in the world, re-assert the wounded sense of Hellenic nationhood, ensure her a minimum of independence and freedom of manoeuvre in her international relationships, shelter her drive for social and economic progress at home, and inculcate a sense of national identity and national interest in the body politic. Astonishingly, PASOK was able to

[109] Ibid, p. 46.
[110] Angelos Elephantis, 'PASOK and the Elections of 1977: The Rise of the Populist Movement', in *Greece at the Polls*, p. 116.
[111] Angelos Elephantis, *Ston Asterismo tou Laikismou*, p. 184.

lump together the authoritarian right-wing forces, foreign intervention, US imperialism and the privileged conservative forces associated with them, and to identify them simply as the enemy. At the same time, PASOK took advantage of the split within the Greek communist Left to present itself as a new Left which not only differed from the traditional Left, but also truly represented the popular forces. The Right, against which these forces were mobilized, was presented not merely as conservative, but as obsolete, morally wrong and responsible for all the evils present in Greek society.[112]

In the early years of *Allaghi*, a period of public dialogue replaced the furious polemics of the electoral campaign. Rather than constantly attacking one another in pursuit of short-term political advantage, parties increased space for political debate and even took small steps towards broad consensus. Smooth alternation of power between right and left increased public confidence over the functioning of institutions and drew political protest off the street. As the 1980s progressed, a new generation of political activism – ecology, feminism, alternative lifestyles and other independent groups – emerged, putting issues on to the agenda which were never raised before. Extreme-left terrorism subsided: 17N did not carry out an attack for two years. Respecting the popular mandate the group decided 'to postpone' its operations so that 'it would not create additional obstacles' to the implementation of PASOK's political programme.[113]

Despite launching a number of positive and long overdue social and legal reforms,[114] Papandreou's insistence on maintaining generous

---

[112] Christos Lyrintzis, 'The power of populism: the Greek case', in *European Journal of Political Research*, 15 (1987), p. 672.

[113] 17N communiqué taking credit for the attack on US Navy Capt. George Tsantes and his Greek driver Nikolaos Veloutsos, dated October 1983.

[114] The most important reforms introduced by the Greek Socialists were:
- The recognition of the national resistance and abolition of legislation remaining from the Metaxas dictatorship and civil war years, thus promoting national reconciliation.
- The establishment of the National Health System and the creation of the National Drug Organization.
- The establishment of civil marriage, the creation of the Council of Equality between men and women, and the ratification of international conventions for the protection of motherhood and abolition of discrimination against women in the job market.
- The reform of the agrarian sector run by cooperatives, thus ensuring their democratic cooperation.

wage and welfare payments at a time of stagnant growth took public sector borrowing to record levels. It soared from '12.5% of GDP in 1983 to 17.5% in 1985 without having any effect on domestic output'.[115] Furthermore, the already bloated state sector was enlarged and the state bureaucracy became 'colonized from top to bottom by the party faithful, other hangers-on and voters in the best traditions of patronage, clientelism and the distribution of the spoils of power'.[116] In the end, double-digit inflation, high public deficits, a remarkably low growth rate and an unfavourable balance of payments depressed an already vulnerable economy and eroded the country's financial stability and international credibility.[117] However, despite the government's poor economic performance, PASOK remained electorally viable.[118] Reflecting a mixture of fondness, right-wing disdain and superstition, the electorate trusted Papandreou in 1985 with a second term. Unlike other Greek political leaders, Papandreou spoke with the voice of the people. The voters wanted to hear

their own voice. And, indeed, it was *their* voice that came from Papandreou's lips unchanged – contradictory, disjointed, vague, neither more nor less refined, but enormously amplified, like the echo of a voice in a canyon or an empty room. For the myth of the Saviour always goes hand in hand with the myth that the People are always right. They only need someone to tell them they are right. And thus the frenzied applause and cheers of the crowd muffled the contradictions and dissonances of the PASOK manifesto.[119]

[115] James Petras, 'The Contradictions of Greek Socialism', in *New Left Review*, No. 163 (May-June 1987), p.13.

[116] Vassilis Kapetanyannis, 'The Left in the 1980s: Too Little, Too Late', in Clogg, *The Populist Decade*, p. 81.; see also Dimitrios A. Sotiropoulos, 'Bureaucrats and Politicians: a case study of the determinants of perceptions of conflict and patronage in the Greek bureaucracy under PASOK rule, 1981–1989', in *British Journal of Sociology*, Vol. 45, No. 3 (September 1994), pp. 349–64.

[117] See Richard Clogg, 'PASOK in power: rendezvous with history or with reality' in *The World Today*, Vol.39, No.11 (November 1983), pp.436–42.

[118] Efthalia Kalogeropoulou, 'Election promises and government performances in Greece: PASOK's fulfilment of its 1981 election pledges', in *European Journal of Political Research*, 17 (1989), pp. 289–311.

[119] Elephantis, *Ston Asterismo*, p. 120; 'By lending his voice to the demands of individuals from most social strata', writes T.S. Pappas in his *Making Political Democracy in Greece*, 'Papandreou succeeded in moulding them into an effective, *even though fictitious*, collective identity, the (non-privileged) "people". He also managed to inspire them with a hazy and unrealistic picture of what Greece should ideally be', in Takis S.

Greek Traditions of Power

By the mid-1980s, however, any semblance of consensus-politics
was replaced by political polarization. The French-style institutional balance of *metapolitefsi* between the president of the Third
Republic and premier was abruptly redressed in favour of the
latter.[120] Under the revised charter, the president was no longer
able to take vital issues directly to the people by referendum, nor
could he air any differences with the government by speaking to
the people: he now needed the prime minister's consent. As the
holder of complete executive authority, Papandreou became 'the
Julius Caesar'[121] of the post-1974 parliamentary system whereby

a ceremonial President, a powerless cabinet, a degraded Parliament, a
subservient judiciary, governmental trade unionism, and a very
weak local government were counterbalanced by an autocratic and
omnipotent party leader and Prime Minister.[122]

A year after its electoral triumph, PASOK began to display several
of the classic features of a party suffering from too long a period in
power. Running the country from *Kastri*,[123] Papandreou 'made a
habit of making himself scarce in parliament'.[124] At the same time,
parliament became more 'a platform for spectacular confronta-
tions between government and opposition than a place for debat-
ing the real issues'.[125] By the end of 1986, the rapidly worsening
economic situation shattered any illusions of recovery and effectively brought Greece's socialist experiment to an end.[126] Under
strong pressure from the EC, the Papandreou government introduced a stringent economic stabilization programme – with wage

Pappas, *Making Party Democracy in Greece* (London: Macmillan, 1999), p. 179.

[120] Stavros Lygeros, *To Pechnithi tis Exousias* [PowerGames] (Athens: Nea Synora, 1996),
p. 16; see also Theodore C. Kariotis in *The Greek Socialist Experiment*, 14–15.

[121] Elephantis, *Ston Asterismo,* p. 133.

[122] Minas Samatas, 'The Populist Phase of an Underdeveloped Surveillance Society:
Political Surveillance in Post-Dictatorial Greece', in *Journal of the Hellenic Diaspora*, Vol.
19, No. 1 (1993), p. 51; see also Michalis Spourdalakis, *PASOK: Domi, Essokommatikes
Krisseis kai Sygkentrossi tis Exoussias* [PASOK: Structure, Intraparty Crises and Power
Concentration] (Athens: Exandas, 1988), pp. 306–310.

[123] Papandreou's residence.

[124] Michalis Spourdalakis, *The Rise of the Greek Socialist Party* (London: Routledge, 1988),
p. 243.

[125] Alivizatos, 'The Presidency', in *Greece, 1981–89: The Populist Decade*, p. 68.

[126] See James Petras, 'The Contradictions of Greek Socialism' in *The Greek Socialist
Experiment*, pp.97–126; Spourdalakis, *The Rise*, pp. 286–288.

freezes as its dominant characteristic – in an effort to offset years of macroeconomic mistakes and irresponsible debt-funded public spending. Far from restoring business confidence, the austerity package alienated many of its trade union supporters who joined forces with the communists to fight the wage freeze. This resulted in a series of bitter industrial disputes. Strikes, a rarity during the first four years of PASOK rule, became an everyday phenomenon. Journalists, teachers, taxi and transport drivers, state and private employees, pharmacists and hospital doctors all took to the streets in Athens and Salonika.[127]

Attacked from all sides of the political spectrum and the media for the absence of clear policies and a sense of direction, the PASOK leadership used foreign policy 'crises' as a diversion from domestic problems.[128] In 1987, for example, Greece almost went to war with Turkey over Turkish exploration of oil in disputed Aegean waters. Having found it politically expedient to condemn US foreign policy at every opportunity, Papandreou declared his determination to defend the country's territorial integrity from external threats and held Washington responsible for the crisis, demanding, at the same time, that both NATO and the EEC took a clear stand on the issue.[129] In the end, excessive personalism in public affairs and a multitude of political and financial scandals undermined the credibility of the administration directly calling Papandreou's style of leadership into question. The Bank of Crete affair for which Papandreou and members of his cabinet were

---

[127] In 1986 1,106,330 people went on strike and 8,839,363 hours of work were lost.

[128] John Loulis, 'Papandreou's Foreign Policy', in *Foreign Affairs*, (Winter 1984/85), pp. 375–391; see also John O. Iatrides, 'Papandreou's Foreign Policy' in *The Greek Socialist Experiment*, pp. 158–159. 'During the general strike of the bank employees in the summer of 1982', writes Loulis, 'the Socialist government dramatized disagreements with NATO. Papandreou appealed to strikers "to take into consideration the crucial international crisis facing the nation". Following the municipal elections of 1982, in which PASOK suffered a débâcle, Papandreou made a series of tragedian appearances close to the Greek borders, as if war was imminent. The prime minister urged Greeks, and particularly "those residing in large cities" (i.e., those who are hardest hit by inflation and who were evidently most disillusioned with PASOK), to "understand that the main issue that the country is facing at this moment is defending national integrity", rather than the issue of the economy which was cutting into the government's popularity'. p. 382.

[129] On Papandreou's tactical exploitation of anti-Americanism see John O. Iatrides, 'Beneath the Sound and the Fury: US Relations with the PASOK Government' in *Greece 1981–89*, pp. 154–8; 164–5; and Spourdalakis, *The Rise of the Greek Socialist Party*, p. 59.

indicted for bribery and embezzlement had devastating effects on the economy and humiliating consequences for the country's reputation abroad.[130] At the most fundamental level, PASOK's political behaviour and organizational practices

enhanced the existing view of politics as a 'dirty' business and that politicians seek only the promotion of their personal or group interests. Politics became associated with embezzlement and theft ... Disenchantment and frustration led to apathy and above all to the legitimation of illegal or semi-illegal practices, profiteering and moonlighting. This general disenchantment with politics is linked to the diminishing appeal of much-discussed concepts such as socialism and the left. PASOK's use and abuse of these concepts led to disenchantment with the transformation of society and turned the few remaining romantics and visionaries into pragmatists and cynics.[131]

In 1989, according to an MRB poll, 60 per cent of Greeks said that a sweeping *catharsis* of political life was needed, though only 44 per cent believed that those really responsible would be punished.[132] Ten months of special court hearings and the testimony of hundreds of witnesses polarized Greek society and did nothing to alleviate political differences. Although Papandreou conceded that he was responsible for the scandal in a political sense, he boycotted the legal proceedings and was eventually acquitted by a majority of one.

From 1990 onwards, the use of scandal and ethical accusations as political weapons became an accepted feature of Greek political life.[133] Repeated accusations and counter-accusations of political

---

[130] See Robert McDonald, 'Greece's year of political turbulence', in *The Word Today* (November 1989), pp. 194–7.

[131] Lyrintzis, 'PASOK in Power' in *Greece 1981–89*, p. 40.

[132] See Kl. S. Koutsoukis, 'Sleaze in Contemporary Greek politics', in *Parliamentary Affairs*, Vol. 48, No. 4 (October 1995), p. 698.

[133] The New Democracy leader and former premier Konstantinos Mitsotakis was also accused of corruption, political abuse and perverting the course of justice. Mitsotakis was formally charged with two scandals: illegal wiretapping and the questionable sale of the cement company AGET-Heracles to the Italian firm Calcestruzzi, a subsidiary of Ferruzzi. Throughout the 1993 election campaign, PASOK claimed that there was 'a web of corruption and kick-backs implicating AGET, the ND government and the National Bank of Greece'. Furthermore, in April 1993, a former employee of the state telephone company OTE, Christos Mavrikis, claimed to police that he was hired by Mitsotakis' security chief, Nikos Gryllakis, to tap the telephones of Papandreou and other leading political figures from 1988 to 1991. Mitsotakis' daughter, former culture

abuse, corruption and economic mismanagement degraded public spirit. However, the political crisis and moral malaise did not lead to the disintegration of the party political system as in Italy. Instead, it revived divisive politics and reconstructed memories of civil conflict. After 1989, political discourse took the form of continuing vendettas. Political debate became confrontational without being creative. More interested in the politics of revanchism and recrimination, politicians resembled each other and became interchangeable. Parties remained populistic, clientelistic, and uncooperative.[134] More precisely, the main aim of opposition parties was not to

> influence government policy in a particular direction, but rather to discredit the governing party and drive it from power. In consequence, oppositional tactics have been based on a concept of 'structural opposition' involving a direct challenge to the government on all issues, even when this entails the adoption of a stance incompatible with party policy.[135]

Overall, parties became highly convergent around a common, superficial analysis of the country's needs, offering little opening to heterodox ideas and solutions. As it became extremely difficult to secure absolute parliamentary majorities, political competition and inter-party relationships were characterized by the preservation and perpetuation of artificial cleavages and polarization which allowed the two rival parties to claim, obtain and exchange power.[136]

Papandreou's return to office in 1993 for a third term established PASOK as the natural party of government in Greek politics but

---

minister Dora Bakoyiannis, was also accused of complicity in wire tapping. The charges followed an eight-month inquiry by magistrates, whose 30,000-page dossier was presented to Parliament and eventually the trial was cancelled in January 1995 by Papandreou just as his own charge for wiretapping had been dropped by Mitsotakis when prime minister.

[134] Calliope Spanou, 'Penelope's Suitors: Administrative Modernisation and Party Competition in Greece', in *West European Politics*, Vol. 19, No. 1 (January 1996), pp. 97–124; Kevin Featherstone, 'The Challenge of Liberalization: Parties and the State in Greece after the 1993 Elections' in *Democratization*, Vol. 1, No. 2 (Summer 1994), pp. 280–94.

[135] Geoffrey Pridham and Suzannah Verney, 'The Coalitions of 1989–90 in Greece: Inter-Party Relations and Democratic Consolidation' in *West European Politics*, Vol. 14, No. 4 (October 1991), p. 47.

[136] Spanou, 'Penelope's Suitors', p. 98.

solved very little on the domestic front.[137] Greece entered a phase of economic stabilization and convergence with the rest of the EU but little happened by way of administrative reform and political modernization. Although PASOK claimed to have learned from its past mistakes, the main structural reforms introduced in the organization of the state apparatus and the country's vast state sector were soon undermined by short-term populism and political clientelism.[138] At the same time, incessant speculation about the poor health of the PASOK leader and continuing personality clashes undermined policy-making and cemented public scepticism.[139] As the premier's health deteriorated, Papandreou's *entourage,* led by his wife Dimitra Liani, continued to camouflage the reality that the Socialist leader was little more than an observer in the running of day-to-day policy until his resignation in 1996.[140]

In foreign policy, governmental disunity and diplomatic intransigence weakened Greece's international position at a time when the country needed national purpose and strength. The collapse of the satellite communist regimes of Eastern Europe and the subsequent disintegration of the Soviet Union weakened Greece's geostrategic significance for the West, thus undermining its eligibility for special treatment and financial support enjoyed when the country was a front-line state in the Cold War. The Yugoslav crisis arrived like a *deus ex machina*: a unique opportunity for Greece to cut a figure on the post-Cold War international stage. More precisely, Greece, the most stable, democratic and ethnically homogeneous Balkan state, a

---

[137] See Michalis Spourdalakis, 'PASOK's Second Chance' in *Mediterranean Politics*, Vol. 1, No. 3 (Winter 1996), p. 321; PASOK's share of the vote, 47 per cent, was marginally less than that achieved in the party's great electoral triumph of October 1981.

[138] Spourdalakis, 'PASOK's Second Chance', p. 326; see also Konstantinos Ifantis, 'From Factionalism to Autocracy: PASOK's De-radicalization during the Regime Transition of the 1970s', in *Democratization*, Vol. 2, No. 1 (Spring 1995), pp. 77–89.

[139] Spourdalakis writes in his 'PASOK's Second Chance' that 'internal party disputes, which have taken place primarily through the media, have been so extensive that they have contributed to, or perhaps generated, dysfunctions in the government. Phenomena such as a cabinet minister boycotting the initiatives of another department simply because of his differences with another department's head have been daily events', p. 328.

[140] See Richard Clogg, 'Andreas Papandreou – A Profile', in *Mediterranean Politics*, Vol. 1, No. 3 (Winter 1996), p. 386; and Alexander Kitroeff, 'Andreas Papandreou: A Brief Political Biography' in *Journal of the Hellenic Diaspora*, Vol. 23, No. 1 (Special Issue, 1997), p. 30.

member of both the EU and NATO, was ideally placed to act as a force of stability in the region and thus become its economic and political leader. Instead, the PASOK government not only created friction with most of its Balkan neighbours, but its exaggerated fears over the alleged long-term expansionist ambitions of the small republic of Macedonia seriously threatened, for a time, the stability of south-eastern Europe as a whole.[141] Under Papandreou, the nationalism of resentment which had characterized the first years of *metapolitefsi* was replaced by the nationalism of pride. To give foreign policy the appropriate level of emotional significance to its audience, Papandreou emphasized terms like Hellenism, independence, national interest and national integrity. Declaring that '*Greece belongs to the Greeks*', Papandreou turned anti-Westernism into a national mantra, threatening several times to pull Greece out of every international organization to which the country belonged. Although none of these threats ever materialized, Papandreou's rhetorical violence and anti-American, anti-NATO, anti-Turkish polemics fulfilled the need for recognition and offered security, national identity and pride to a confused and anxious people, increasingly unsure of their place in a rapidly changing European and international environment.[142]

In the latter part of the 1990s, the characteristics of the post-Papandreou years are not yet clear.[143] However, Papandreou's populist nationalism abroad and personalism, patronage and clientelism at home meant that Greece received negative international attention and that its political culture and institutions remained anachronistic and underdeveloped.[144] In short, while Papandreou liberalized and broadened the political community whereby 'all ideologies and divergent viewpoints and principles legitimately constituted part of the political landscape, he failed to encourage or even facilitate the emergence of a civil society'.[145]

---

[141] Thanos Veremis, *Greece's Balkan Entanglement*, (Athens: ELIAMEP, 1995), pp. 67–93.

[142] Keith R. Legg and John M. Roberts, *Modern Greece: A Civilization on the Periphery* (Boulder, CO: Westview Press, 1997), p. 153.

[143] See I.K. Pretenteris, *I Thefteri Metapolitefsi: prosopikes simeiosseis apo mia megali anatropi* [The Second Metapolitefsi: personal notes from a big upset] (Athens: Polis, 1996).

[144] See Loukas Tsoukalis, 'Beyond the Greek Paradox' in Graham T. Allison and Kalypso Nicolaides (eds), *The Greek Paradox: Promise vs. Performance* (Cambridge, MA: MIT Press, 1997), pp. 163–74.

[145] Adamantia Pollis, 'Modernity, Civil Society and the Papandreou Legacy' in *Journal of the Hellenic Diaspora*, Vol. 23, No. 1 (Special Issue, 1997), p. 67; On the loss of

Elected in 1981 on the basis of radically transforming Greek political structures and institutions by decentralizing the state and rev-
olutionizing clientelistic politics, Papandreou soon switched
direction and 'retained the traditional centrality of the state, transformed it into a party state, expanded its penetration throughout
society and reinforced its patriarchal features'.[146] In post-
Papandreou Greece, the two largest parties (ND and PASOK)
continued to dominate most discussions about politics, but there
was hardly any significant policy difference between them. In fact,

so indistinguishable have the main parties become that neither of them
seems capable of proposing radical solutions, providing fresh social
visions, let alone untarnished images and, finally, satisfying the high
expectations the parties once gave rise to and thereafter nurtured in
society.[147]

Polls continually showed deep levels of cynicism and contempt
for the political process. A dramatic drop in party membership
and increasing electoral abstention indicated 'an unprecedented
crisis in the party system'.[148] Surveys confirmed that electors were
profoundly disappointed with the institutional performance of
parties and had lost faith in the capacity of governmental action.[149]
By the mid-1990s, holding the major parties together had become
PASOK's and ND's main priority task.[150] Although this indicated
that Greek political culture had the potential of becoming far
more fluid, fragmented and factionalized, the regime reduced violence by allowing the incorporation of most ideologies into institutional politics. Since 1991, 138 political parties have been
founded in Greece.[151] The fact that these groups could openly seek
sympathy and support from all sections of Greek society made anti-

autonomy by interest groups in Papandreou's Greece see George Th. Mavrogordatos,
'Civil Society Under Populism' in *Greece, 1981–89*, pp. 47–64.

[146] Pollis, 'Modernity, Civil Society and the Papandreou Legacy', p. 67.

[147] Pappas, *Making Party Democracy in Greece*, p. 207.

[148] Spourdalakis, 'PASOK's Second Chance', p. 328.

[149] See, for example, the 31 July 1995 survey organized and published by *Eleftherotypia*
newspaper in which only a mere 2.2 per cent of Greek people have faith in political
parties. According to the same survey, the Armed Forces and the Church topped the
list of the institutions most trusted, with 34.4 per cent and 29.5 per cent, respectively.

[150] See *Anti* Special issue 'I Chreokopia ton Kommaton' [The Bankruptcy of the Greek
Political Parties], 22 July 1994, pp. 17–22.

[151] See *Odyssey*, (September-October, 1996), p. 22.

system violence inappropriate. Both government and opposition continued to be attacked by different types of groups (human rights activists, ethno-Marxists, ecologists, anarchists) for 'conspiring' to prevent domestic reform to a system which exclusively benefits them, but political protest declined. In Greece in the mid-1970s, extreme-left terrorism emerged in a political system which

not only provides fewer civil and political rights to its citizens but also is unable to focus attention on, identify, and locate the real obstacles to effective political and social reform.[152]

Reacting to the ideological consensus of *metapolitefsi,* both 17N and ELA used violence 'to effect a change in the body politic'.[153] Like other European communist militant groups, 17N opposed the US, American NATO-ism, the EC and a capitalist-dominated society. Entrenched by visions of class war and a violent upheaval of the *status quo,* 17N rejected *metapolitefsi* as junta by another name. Unlike most extra-parliamentary extreme-leftist groups, 17N never moved its protest into the mainstream. With no community support to draw strength and recruits from, 17N remained on the fringe, viewing itself as the armed vanguard of the working class and the *primum mobile* of Greek national independence. Drawing on the complex traditions of Greek communism and nationalism and the civil war legacy, 17N bitterly attacked the political structures of post-1974 Greek society. The group never forgave Papandreou and his party for abandoning socialism. In 1983, it reached the conclusion that only 'popular revolutionary violence and not parliamentary elections' could lead to socialism. After the end of the Cold War and the death of Marxist socialism, 17N struggled to camouflage its outdated political agenda. By 1996, a combination of successive operational failures and bizarre verbal outbursts against TV stations and newspaper editors typified the group's ideological fatigue and organizational confusion. In Greece in the late 1990s, 17N and ELA had become an ultra-left terrorist anachronism and were no longer relevant.

---

[152] Nicos P. Mouzelis, 'Greece in the Twenty-first Century: Institutions and Political Culture', in *Greece Prepares for the Twenty-first Century,* p. 24.

[153] T. P. Thornton, 'Terror as a Weapon of Political Agitation', in Harry Eckstein (ed.), *Internal War* (London: Free Press of Glencoe, 1964), p. 71.

3

THE TERRORIST ROUTE

NOVEMBER 1973, *METAPOLITEFSI*, AND THE EXTRA-PARLIAMENTARY LEFT

Both Revolutionary Organization 17 November (17N) and *Epanastatikos Laikos Agonas* (ELA) drew their belief that socialism in Greece could only be achieved through an armed struggle under the leadership of a revolutionary vanguard from the November 1973 revolt and *metapolitefsi*. The 1973 events in particular spawned a radical social idealism that inspired 17N. The group took its name from the November events when a student-worker alliance occupied Athens Polytechnic demanding an end to the military dictatorship. Inspired from the 1973 'incomplete revolution' and deeply disillusioned with the post–1974 *metapolitefsi*, both groups went underground in an attempt to raise the banner of radical communist revolution in Greece.

During the 1960s, large-scale economic and demographic changes placed the post-civil war political system under great strain for the first time. After 1964, vocal demands for political liberalization increased dramatically. Until then a combination of parastate violence, police intimidation and harassment of activists had managed to contain dissent. In addition, trade unionism was fragmented and student activism was merely confined to bread and butter issues. The communist Left, still devastated and demoralized by its civil war defeat, lacked the confidence and programmes needed to attract supporters for political change. In fact, the Communist Party of Greece (KKE) did everything to avoid direct confrontation with the regime.[1] Forced to choose

---

[1] Christoforos Vernardakis and Yiannis Mavris, *Kommata kai Koinonikes Symmachies stin prodiktatoriki Ellada* [Parties and Social Alliances in pre-dictatorial Greece] (Athens:

between political silence and ostracism, party leaders had opted for the latter, taking refuge abroad, mainly in the Soviet Union. Despite all this, the United Democratic Left (EDA), an alliance of a number of leftist groupings which stood as a front for the outlawed KKE, gradually developed into a well-organized party and in the 1958 general election even became the main opposition in parliament with 79 seats and 24.4 per cent of the total vote.[2] Encouraged by the election result and supported by prominent communist and non-communist personalities, EDA began, under the leadership of Yiannis Passalidis, to call openly for political pluralism, the dismantling of the repressive state apparatus, full amnesty for civil war political prisoners and the legalization of KKE. Strongly anti-American, EDA repeatedly attacked both the right and the centre for their slavish dependence on the Western alliance, questioned the country's association with the European Community and campaigned for the removal of nuclear weapons from Greece. In effect, EDA was assigned by KKE's leadership in exile the task of advancing the Greek communist movement and thus preparing the ideological ground for the KKE.[3] According to the KKE analysis, once this was strategically accomplished the exiled leadership would return to take over and change the course of Greek politics in a left-ward direction through the implementation of its maximum programme of socialism.[4]

At the same time, rapid urbanization coupled with a high rate of economic growth had a significant effect on the country's socio-political geography. Restored confidence in the drachma, modernization of social patterns and a rapid rural exodus into Greece's main cities generated fresh optimism about the possibilities of meaningful progress and political reform. More precisely, the anonymity of Athens and Salonika

Exandas, 1987), pp. 109–17.

[2] For a detailed analysis on the May 1958 elections see Illias Nikolakopoulos, *Kommata kai Vouleftikes Ekloges stin Ellada, 1946–1964* [Parties and Parliamentary Elections in Greece, 1946–1964] (Athens: EKKE, 1985), pp. 230–54.

[3] The majority of EDA leaders were Communists and among them a group called the 'Interior Office' of the Central Committee was in charge of executing KKE's policies. But appointments to key posts within EDA were submitted for approval to the KKE leadership in exile.

[4] Vernardakis and Mavris, *Kommata*, pp. 98–108; see also 'KKE kai EDA: Sta Chronia tis Dimokratikis Antistassis, 1949–1967' [KKE and EDA: The Years of Democratic Resistance, 1949–1967] in *Dialogos*, No. 1, (January–February 1972).

offered more diversified opportunities for political activities, made avoidance of political surveillance and repression much easier, gave the political activists alternative chances in seeking solidarity with other social and political groups and rendered them less vulnerable to clientelistic ideologies and practices.[5]

At a deeper level, however, socio-political tension was diffusing to several sectors of the population. With popular expectations rising, social problems accumulating and new social forces entering the political arena, a spirit of militancy among workers, peasants, students and even civil servants began to grow at a threatening pace for the regime.[6] The regime, at the same time, seemed to be able to manage discontent, albeit with great difficulty. However, the assassination of the EDA MP Grigoris Lambrakis[7] in May 1963 at a peace rally in Salonika by extreme-right militants (linked with the gendarmerie) 'sparked off already inflammable material: latent discontent and dissatisfaction with a life impoverished in opportunities of self-expression, creative and constructive action'.[8]

The Lambrakis murder catalyzed the gathering pressure and became in the public mind a symbol against the repressive and authoritarian style of government. In less than a year, a broad-based political movement named after the murdered deputy grew and spread rapidly in both cities and the countryside, becoming the most active pro-democracy force in the country with 20,000 members.[9] Demanding moral and political catharsis, the *Democratic Youth Movement – G. Lambrakis*, as it was initially named, captivated the imagination of the young people and turned Lambrakis into 'the hero of a new generation which having not had

---

[5] See Vassilis Kapetanyiannis, *Socio-Political Conflicts and Military Intervention: The case of Greece, 1950–1967* (Unpublished PhD dissertation, University of London, 1986), p. 188.

[6] Vassilis Kapetanyiannis, 'The Making of Greek Eurocommunism' in *Political Quarterly*, Vol. 50, No. 4 (October–December 1979), p. 448.

[7] Grigoris Lambrakis was in fact elected in 1961 as independent MP on EDA's ticket. The Lambrakis affair became known worldwide through Costa Gavras's film 'Z'.

[8] Kapetanyiannis, *Socio-Political Conflicts*, p. 224.

[9] Katerina St Martin writes, in her Paris VIII doctoral thesis on the Lambrakis movement, that in 1965 there were approximately 100,000 Lambrakides organized in more than 150 offices and clubs around the country. Published in Greek under the title *Lambrakides: I Istoria mias Yenias* [Lambrakides: The history of a generation] (Athens: Polytypo, 1987), p. 15.

previously experienced discord and conflict sought a different message from that of hatred and bloodshed unleashed by the Civil War'.[10] The movement's autonomy and heterogeneity were also seen as a response to the communist left's revanchism, sectarianism and political ineffectiveness. Although it structured criticism of the regime, the Lambrakis movement also provided, through an expanded network of youth clubs, a mass of young people for the first time with a venue in which to meet to discuss and exchange ideas and an opportunity to develop elementary forms of cultural and political identity as a social group with separate and distinctive needs.[11]. When EDA merged its own youth section with the Lambrakides in 1964, it marked an important moment in the political culture of the period since the united movement, renamed *Lambrakis Democratic Youth* (DNL), became the country's 'leading, democratic, anti-fascist, patriotic, pacifist, anti-imperialist' political organization.[12] Moving away from the traditional forms of political activism, the *Lambrakis Democratic Youth* aspired to educate and intellectually improve the new generation and 'propose, at the same time, a different problematique against a socio-political order founded upon obscurantism, foreign power subjugation and police terrorism'.[13] Despite enormous pressure and persecution from an omnipresent secret police, DNL's influence continued to grow. Together with George Papandreou's *anendotos agonas*[14] (relentless struggle) campaign launched in 1962 against 'fraud and violence' they set a precedent for political activism and popular mobilization. Promising to clean out the country's Augean stables, Papandreou spoke of social justice, fairer distribution of income and welfare reforms. At a deeper level he sought

---

[10] Ibid., p. 45.
[11] Kapetanyiannis, *Socio-Political Conflicts*, p. 225; see also Catherine St. Martin, 'Organized and Spontaneous Youth Movements', in *Anti*, 20 June 1980.
[12] *Lambrakides*, p. 124.
[13] Ibid., p. 119.
[14] Disputing the legitimacy of the right's victory in the 1961 elections which, Papandreou argued, were the product of 'fraud and violence', he launched *anendotos agonas* to overturn the results. 'Papandreou's refusal to legitimize the new government', writes Kapetanyiannis in his *Socio-Political Conflicts and Military Interventions*, 'left him no other option for a come-back than that of *going to the people*. He had therefore, not only challenged the government, but also the King and the repressive apparatus of the state, in short to use the political methods unknown to a bourgeois party, to test the validity of the political system and its claim to be liberal and democratic', pp. 231.

to redress the balance between the various components of the established constitutional order by restricting the role of the Throne to ruling rather than governing and meddling in party politics, by asserting the authority of the civil government over the army and the security services and by curbing the influence of extra-parliamentary and non-national centres of powers over the government.[15]

Inevitably, popular mobilization became too visible to be ignored. Mass demonstrations in favour of amnesty for political prisoners, peace rallies and a barrage of large-scale industrial strikes shook the country. Between 1963–5, the number of strikes had risen to a total of 1,001 and the streets of Athens and Salonika became battlegrounds between young political activists and riot police.

Such rapid developments, however, caught the EDA leadership unawares. Absorbed in a fierce, doctrinal intra-party debate with both the exiled and underground communists in charge of the party organizations which had begun earlier, the party remained disorganized and out of focus. The exiled leaders of KKE began to view their EDA counterparts as a dangerous faction capable of formulating serious theoretical questions and thus of challenging the legitimacy of their own authority. Anxious about losing control, the KKE leaders deliberately decided to organize cells within EDA, feeling that

if they allowed EDA to develop its own political potential and the 'interior' leaders to take on political functions and decision-making powers, they might sooner or later find themselves redundant. As a matter of fact conflicts of this kind were already taking place as a result of claims that the KKE leaders abroad had lost touch with reality. Thus, by making this move the 'exteriors' sought deliberately to consolidate their position in practice by dividing the militants into two classes: the chosen first-class Communists and the outcast second-class EDAists.[16]

Predictably, the move set up months of trench warfare between the 'interior' and 'exterior' leaderships which was to ensure that neither could pursue its goals effectively. The dispute reached its peak in February 1968 at the twelfth Plenary Session of the KKE's Central Committee with the party splitting into two: the

---

[15] Ibid.

[16] Kapetanyiannis, 'The Making of Greek Eurocommunism', p. 448; see also Panos Dimitriou, *I Diaspassi tou KKE, 2 Tomoi* [The Break-up of the KKE, 2 Vols.] (Athens: Politika Provlimata, 1975).

Moscow-oriented KKE, the so-called KKE of the exterior, and the KKE of the interior (KKE-es). The Russian invasion of Czecho-slovakia in August 1968 and the humiliation of its reformist lead-ers cemented the schism permanently with the 'interior' leadership severely criticizing the 'Brezhnev doctrine' and the Stalinist KKE giving its uncritical support to the Soviet Union.[17] In short, the break-up of the KKE can be seen as the

inevitable result of divisions on essential questions which had been maturing for years in the top party echelons. The party's long tradition of Stalinist political practice, its total dependence on the Soviet Union, its very structures, led inevitably to the choice between mechanical submission on the one hand and factionalism on the other. Unfortunately, there was neither a Gramsci nor a Togliatti in the Greek Communist tradition.[18]

However, sectarianism, ideological confusion and inertia within the traditional left had already opened the way for revolutionary radicalism.[19] Disillusioned defectors, who felt that the 'legitimate left' had not been sufficiently radical in its methods, aims and pol-icies, formed new rebel groups[20] turning to themes and issues that the party establishment had chosen to ignore: workers' control and human self-emancipation, university authoritarianism, oppo-sition to consumer society, social hierarchy and the decaying mechanisms of political control. Directly influenced by *gauchiste* ideological and organizational ecumenism, and protest events in

---

[17] Richard Clogg, *Parties and Elections in Greece: The Search for Legitimacy* (London: Hurst & Co., 1987), p. 177.

[18] 'The Making of Greek Eurocommunism', p. 450; see also Michalis Papayiannakis, 'The crisis in the Greek left' in Howard R. Penniman (ed.), *Greece at the Polls: The national elections of 1974 and 1977* (Washington, DC: American Enterprise Institute, 1981), pp.130–59; and 'Thirty Years after the Schism', *To Vima*, 17 May 1998, pp. 28–30.

[19] See Antonis Davanelos, *Noemvris 1973: I exegerssi* [November 1973: The Revolt] (Athens: Ekdosseis Ergatiki Dimokratia, 2nd ed. 1995), p. 7.

[20] Formed between 1964 and 1966, groups such as the *Ananeottiki Omada Dimokratikis Aristeras* (AODA), the *Enottiki Kinissi Dimokratikis Aristeras* (EKDA), *Anagenissi,* the *Panfoititikki Dimokratiki Kinissi Sotiris Petroulas* (PANDIK Sotiris Petroulas) and *Deltio Filon Neon Choron* (FNH), called for the Left's united exit from its political cul-de-sac and the establishment of an authentic popular democratic party. On the leadership, membership and ideology of the break-away groups and their publications see Panayiotis Noutsos, *I Sosialistiki Skepssi stin Ellada: 1875–1974* [The Socialist Thought in Greece: from 1875 to 1974] (Athens: Gnossi, 1994), pp. 430–7.

neighbouring Italy, these factions tried through theorizing and anti-regime polemical journalism to rearticulate left-wing principles and set in motion a mobilizing process.[21] Although they were very small, fringe minorities with no significant impact, their mere presence served to deepen the Right's paranoia about an imminent communist seizure of power. Before a new, more combative movement could give fresh impetus to further civil discontent, a military junta, composed of authoritarian colonels, quickly moved in to seize power and ensure that the door on democratic reform and pluralism was hermetically closed.

The Greek May: November 1973

The post-civil war period of socio-political and cultural change culminated in November 1973. National and international events fuelled a belief in direct confrontation with the ruling military regime. The Vietnamese victories against the US, the *événements de mai* in France and Italy's *Il Sessantotto* exercised a powerful ideological influence on Greek university student activists.[22] The Vietnamese example in particular had demonstrated that 'a people, however weak, when they have belief in themselves and follow the correct revolutionary strategy, can even defeat a superpower'.[23] Meanwhile, protest demonstrations in many European capitals (especially in West Berlin and Rome) against the Greek military junta exposed domestic public apathy. Fearing a generalized explosion, the dictatorial regime rushed through a number of educational and economic reforms in a final desperate attempt to de-radicalize the situation but this failed to placate university activists and the workers. A series of national strikes and student demonstrations increased tension. The occupation of Athens University Law School in March[24] and Athens Polytechnic in

---

21 See 'To thema tis Aristeras stin Ellada' [The Predicament of the Left in Greece] (Athens: *Ananeottiki Omada Dimokratitkis Aristeras* /AODA, 1965); *Anagennissi* No.1 (October 1964) and No. 23 (August 1966); *Antiimperialistis*, Vol. 3 (July 1965).

22 See Alkis Rigos, 'Foititiko Kinima kai Diktatoria' [The Student Movement and the Military Dictatorship], in *Anti* No. 344, (1987), pp. 54–5.

23 See EKKE in 'The left of the Left', *Eleftherotypia*, 18 June 1976; see also 'Vassika Politika Keimena, 1970–1974' [Essential Political Texts, 1970–1974], (Athens: *Epanastatiko Kommounistiko Kinima Elladas* [EKKE], 1974), pp. 46–7.

24 Stelios Kouloglou and Yiannis Floros, 'I Katalipsi tis Nomikis – Proagellos tou Polytechniou' [The Occupation of the Athens Law School – Prelude to the

November 1973 provoked a major crisis to the apparatus by ignit-
ing an apparent revolution. The Polytechnic events, in particular,
became the epicentre of student dissent and served as an effective
focus of opposition to the regime. Lasting for a mere three days
(14–17 November), the revolt not only challenged the military
regime but catalyzed popular mobilization in many sectors of
Greek society. What had begun as a student protest against an
authoritarian educational system escalated rapidly into a general
political uprising against the military dictatorship.[25] Demanding
'Bread, Education and Liberty' (the archetypal slogan of November
'73), the students provided anti-authoritarian ideology to a weak
and pathetically resigned populace and unsettled an imminent
deal between the conservative old-right and the military on 'a
stratocratic liberalization' based on the Chilean and Turkish
models.[26]

Between 1969 and 1973, the number of university students
rose significantly. In 1969, there were 12,175 new entrants, in
1972, 14,218 and in 1973, 15,389 out of a total 123,081 students
congested at the universities of Athens and Salonika.[27] Moreover,
the expansion of student numbers was not accompanied by the
necessary expansion of lecture rooms or hire of extra full-time
professors. During the 1970s, the number of full-time professors
increased by less than two-fold, resulting in 'the worst student-
teacher ratio in Europe'[28] (90:1 for the main teaching staff).[29] In
short, this new generation of students entered a university system
which was in an advanced state of malfunction. Student meetings,
strikes and demonstrations about the quality and organization of

Polytechnic], in *Anti* No.199, (1982), pp. 23–5.
[25] Stavros Lygeros, *Foititiko Kinima kai Taxiki Pali stin Ellada, Tomos 1* [The Student
Movement and Class Struggle in Greece, Vol. 1] (Athens: Ekdotiki Omada Ergassia,
1977), pp. 193–201, 204–9.
[26] Davanelos, *Noemvris 1973*, p. 4.
[27] See Georgia K. Polydorides, 'Equality of Opportunity in the Greek Higher Education
System: The Impact of Reform Policies' and Maria Eliou, 'Those Whom Reform
Forgot', both in Andreas M. Kazamias (ed.),'Symposium on Educational Reform in
Greece', in *Comparative Education Review* Vol. 22, No. 1 (February 1978), pp. 80–81 and
p. 67.
[28] Henry Wasser, 'A survey of Recent Trends in Greek Higher Education', in *Journal of the
Hellenic Diaspora*, Vol. 6, No. 1 (1979), p. 85.
[29] See George Psacharopoulos and Andreas M. Kazamias, Student Activism in Greece: A
Historical and Empirical Analysis' in *Higher Education*, No. 9 (1980), p. 130.

studies, the lack of dialogue between teachers and students, the petty regulations in student hostels, the nature of the teaching and the content of the courses, the lack of laboratories and inadequate welfare services and the links between university bureaucracy and the military regime were met with arrests and police violence leading to wider and more radical protests.

Meanwhile, economic recession and rising unemployment further polarized attitudes. By November 1973, the number of young people without a job had risen to 200,000.[30] As recession worsened and job competition increased, students came to accept that unemployment was not simply an ephemeral phase but the next step after university graduation and this realization took away any major sense of long-term planning. A sense of marginality and insecurity prompted highly politicized students with Trotskyist and Maoist affiliations to 'construct a critique of society, the role of family and the values and content of the education system itself'.[31] Exogenous factors also helped to shape such attitudes. Despite the fact that the ideas of May 1968 did not reach Greece until 1971, it nevertheless brought to

the surface not only the need for an incessant criticism of the old world, but also the urgency to prevent that need from being applied in a formalistic and impassable way. It questioned the economist and dogmatic 'hyperpolitical' way of viewing things, and with its theoretical, political and social weight, shifted the centre of debate.[32]

Faced with a massive budgetary crisis and losing credibility fast, the military regime sought to liberalize the system and preserve it at the same time. Many political prisoners in exile were allowed to return.[33] The limits of permissible debate in the media and political

---

[30] See Dionyssis Karageorgas, 'Oi Oikonomikes Synepeies tis Stratiotikis Diktatorias' [The Economic Consequences of the Military Dictatorship], in *Anti*, No. 1 (1974), pp. 41–46.

[31] See Tariq Ali and Susan Watkins, *1968: Marching in the Streets* (London: Bloomsbury, 1998), p. 57.

[32] Loukas Axelos, 'Publishing Activity and the Movement of Ideas in Greece', in *Journal of the Hellenic Diaspora*, Vol. 11, No. 2 (Summer 1984), p. 13; See also Petros Efthymiou, 'O Apoichos stin Ellada' [The After-effects of May '68 on Greece] in 'May '68: Thirty Years After', *To Vima*, Special supplement, 10 May 1998.

[33] Dimitris Haralambis, *Stratos kai Politiki Exousia: I domi tis exousias stin metemfyliaki Ellada* [Political Power and The Military: The Power Structure in post-Civil War Greece] (Athens: Exandas, 1985), pp. 296–302.

forums were expanded. Censorship was relaxed and this 'created a positive political and cultural climate that allowed comfortable margins for the pluralistic circulation of ideas'.[34] Publishers produced scores of new titles of all ideological trends and magazines devoted large space to Vietnam, the cultural revolution, the Sino-Soviet split, the death of Guevara, and the 1968 protest movements in France and Italy. Large sections of youth were 'brought into contact with the most significant works of historical and contemporary Marxist, anarchist, and bourgeois radical thought'.[35]

Student agitation began over long-standing, unresolved issues. Initial demands were for greater student participation in university and faculty governance, the democratization and modernization of the educational system and the abolition of legislation which restricted academic freedom. More specifically, the regime had instituted a commissar system under which they appointed retired or former military officers with wide powers of veto to 'supervise education and to see that every action of the university was in accord with the dictates of the government'.[36] It had also introduced in 1969 laws 93 and 180, which made provisions for harsh penalties for disciplinary offences and gave the commissioners 'the right to sit on all student meetings to guard over "national security interests"'.[37] As the liberalization experiment ran amok, the junta quickly returned to its old repressive ways invoking in 1973 law 1347 which gave the regime the power to 'revoke the deferment of students from national service because of wilful abstention from attendance at lectures and classes'.[38] From then onwards, protests against student conditions turned into mass actions against the oppressive and authoritarian character of the regime. One demonstration followed another. A series of savage student-police battles revealed the regime's barbarism and that encouraged extreme-left faith in violent action.[39] Violence against

[34] Axelos, 'Publishing Activity', p. 21.

[35] Ibid., p. 23.

[36] Wasser, 'A Survey of Recent Trends', p. 86.

[37] Ibid.

[38] Ibid., p. 87.

[39] See *Anakoinossi tis Antifassistikis Antiimberialistikis Spoudastikis Parataxis Elladas* (AASPE) [Announcement of the Antifascist Anti-imperialist Student Front of Greece (AASPE)], dated 27 November 1973; see also *Anakoinossi tou Epanastatikou Kommounistikou Kinimatos Elladas* (EKKE) *kai tis Antifassistikis Antiimberialistikis Spoudastikis Parataxis*

the regime came to be seen by some students as inevitable and justifiable and for some the campus itself became the battlefield. During the November events, ultra-militant factions adopted violent tactics which they hoped would awaken the majority to the barbarism and brutality of the regime.[40] Other factions saw such clashes as a tool to preserve and encourage political dissent. One group (Movement of 20 October or *Kinima 20is Oktovri*)[41] argued that armed violence was the only effective weapon students and workers had in their hands with which to respond to state repression.[42] The movement reached its zenith when it mobilized almost overnight thousands of previously non-political workers and students. For three days and nights, a worker-student alliance maintained permanent occupation of the Polytechnic building. Their uncompromising political language and heroic forms of action showed how vulnerable the regime could be to those who dared to challenge it.

Yet despite much agitation and blood, the November revolt failed to spark off a larger conflagration.[43] Although the protest quickly became political, there was neither coherent strategy nor strong leadership to take organizational command of the movement. Unable to recognize its nature and character, both KKEs saw the protest through 'the prism of a narrow student event with limited capabilities and potentiality',[44] thus declining to emerge as the 'avant-garde detonator'. Seeking short-term political gains, KKE student leaders went instead to great lengths to prevent all direct action.[45] However, November 1973 was clearly an important moment at which the course of Greek political and social history began to change in a concentrated and intense way.[46] The

Elladas (AASPE) [Announcement of the Revolutionary Communist Movement of Greece (EKKE) and the Antifascist Antiimperialist Student Front (AASPE)], dated 31 December 1973.

[40] See 'Polytechneio: Pera apo ton Mytho' [Polytechnic: Beyond the Myth], in *Anti*, No.6 (1974), pp. 14–16 and 24.

[41] The *Kinima 20is Oktomvri* [The 20th October Movement] was formed in 1969 from ex-EDA members with cells both in Greece and abroad.

[42] See for example, 'To Polytechneio mesa apo ta keimena tou' [The Polytechnic through its texts', in *Dekapenthimeros Politis*, No. 2 (19 November, 1983), p. 32.

[43] See Lygeros, *Foititiko Kinima*, T. 1, pp. 86–98.

[44] Olympios Dafermos, *To antidiktatoriko foititiko kinima 1972–1973* [the anti-dictatorial student movement, 1972–1973] (Athens: Themelio, 1992), p. 124.

[45] Ibid.

[46] See *Eleftherotypia* Special on the November '73 events, 15–16 November, 1976.

radicalism of November and the events at the Athens Polytechnic assumed symbolic significance and were ultimately seen

as the result of domestic and international political repercussions of the 1960s which retained their significance over the next decade and the expression of a long historical tradition of the Greek student movement which through its direct grassroots confrontation with a repressive dictatorship became the sole vehicle of collective expression of solidarity and public revulsion against oppression, injustice and limited freedom, gaining for itself autonomous political maturity and universal popular recognition. During the struggle, the student movement looked for the deeper reasons underlying the institutionalisation of an entrenched conservative political regime and demythologised the values, concepts and functioning base of the post-civil war state. In short, it learned how to act instead of simply reacting to events and to influence events through the collective and autonomous processes of direct democracy … thus inaugurating a novel and deeply libertarian conception of Greek politics and society.[47]

More crucially, November 1973 opened up a period of radical communist utopianism and heated political debate on conceptions of class, social structure and revolutionary strategy.

Junta by another name: Metapolitefsi and the extra-parliamentary left

November 1973 produced a new generation of political intellectuals and activists. The *Polytechneio* generation, as it came to be known, was a variety of non-conformist student leftism that appeared in Greece immediately after the collapse of the military junta. It was distinguished by its rejection of traditional patterns of authority, attention on new social and political issues, opposition to institutional forms of organization and hierarchy and a focus on youth as a social accelerator for change.

After 1974, the whole of the left experienced significant growth in political influence and membership. Although split into pro-Moscow (KKE) and Eurocommunist (KKE-es) wings since 1968, the two rival parties formed in 1974 an alliance with the pre-coup

---

47 Rigos, 'Foititiko Kinima kai Diktatoria', p. 55; see also Christos Lazos, *Elliniko Foititiko Kinima, 1821–1973* [The Greek Student Movement, 1821–1973] (Athens: Gnossi, 1987); Dionyssis Kapsalis, 'Anti-diktatoriko Kinima: istoria kai ideologia' [The anti-dictatorial student movement: history and ideology', in *O Politis*, No. 30 (November 1979), pp. 55–61.

EDA for the purposes of the first democratic elections. Despite winning 9.5 per cent of the popular vote,[48] the *Inomeni Aristera* (United Left) alliance soon dissolved into its constituent parts because of irreconcilable ideological differences. The 1974 and 1977 elections demonstrated that traditional working-class voters clearly preferred the pro-Moscow KKE and rejected Euro-communist renovation.[49] In the 1977 election, KKE fought as a separate entity (securing a 9.4% share of the vote and 11 seats), while the KKE-es found itself compressed between KKE and Andreas Papandreou's PASOK which, having electorally and ideologically absorbed the bulk of the centre and centre-left polit-ical forces during the 1970s, went on to capture the moderate communist vote and, ultimately, power in 1981. However, it was the far left which tried to recreate the conditions of November 1973. Before November 1973, the revolutionary left hardly existed in Greece, except for some Maoist break-aways from EDA. The post-1973 impetus gave the far left an opportunity to present a fresh, radical and autonomous form of activism. More specifically, the radicalization of November '73 and the general mood for fun-damental change that followed the collapse of the Colonels' regime reinforced their confidence and intensified their revolutionary uto-pianism.[50] While all mainstream left parties accepted the basic parameters of the post-1974 consensus, the far left tried to reshape protest and to foment an atmosphere of near-revolution. Although tiny in terms of membership compared with the parties of *metapolitefsi*, the extra-parliamentary left was able, through the fre-quent organization of demonstrations and strikes, to catch public attention and raise tension for the latter part of the 1970s.

Meanwhile, the post-1974 path to political pluralism and mod-ernization proved to be complex and difficult. Although Karamanlis commanded the popular assent of the country (54.4 per cent of the vote), he chose to adapt his ideas to the circum-stances rather than the circumstances to his ideas. The presence of

---

[48] The *Inomeni Aristera* alliance secured, in the first democratically elected parliament after the fall of the military junta, 8 seats, with 5 seats going to KKE, 2 to the KKE-es and 1 to EDA.

[49] See Vassilis Kapetanyiannis, 'The Communists', in Kevin Featherstone and Dimitrios K. Katsoudas (eds), *Political Change in Greece: Before and After the Colonels* (London: Croom Helm, 1987), pp. 153–155.

[50] Davanellos, *Noemvris 1973*, pp. 44–46.

ministers associated with the fascist period in the Karamanlis cabinet showed the premier's political elasticity and provoked strong resentment from the Athens press and intelligentsia.[51] At the same time, rumours and counter-rumours of aborted coups and assassination plots against Karamanlis abounded. Neo-fascist groups began a terrorist campaign with a series of bomb explosions and other attacks designed to create a climate of tension and instability. Cinema bombings became something of a neo-fascist hallmark. The years 1976 and 1978 were particularly critical. Faced with such challenges and uncertain of how far to go with the purge, the new regime did away with some regional state agencies[52] but the *modus operandi* of the main apparatus remained unchanged. Not surprisingly, the governmental attempts to placate both the army and the public led to half-measures with regard to reform legislation and *apohountopoiisi* (de-juntification).

Between 1974 and 1976, a plethora of groups from the revolutionary left appeared on the Greek post-junta political scene. Obsessed with the dynamics of November '73, these groups used violent rhetoric to denounce constitutional structures and justify the legitimacy of the revolutionary cause over the regime's legality, conservationist ethos and lack of structured political solutions.[53] Antipathetic to Karamanlis's gradualist approach, they advocated thoroughgoing political reform and the necessity of a viable democratic culture. Reflecting the ideological divides in the European revolutionary movement, these small but very active groups were anarchist, Maoist[54] and

---

[51] Yiorgos Votsis, *Se Mavro Fondo* [Against the dark background] (Athens: Stochastis, 1984), pp. 241–5.

[52] According to the *Eleftherotypia* of 29 July 1975, of the majority of the 100,000 junta sympathisers removed from their posts only a mere 200 were appointees and collaborators of the military with important positions in the state apparatus.

[53] See, for instance, *Kokkini Simaia* [Red Flag] No. 1 (October 1974) and Nos. 2–3 (November-December 1974); see also political announcements by *Epanastatiko Kommounistiko Kinima Elladas* (EKKE), dated 1, 28 March; 8, 21 April; and 16 May 1975.

[54] *Epanastatiko Kommounistiko Kinima Elladas* (EKKE) [Revolutionary Communist Movement of Greece]; *Organossi Marxiston Leniniston Elladas* (OMLE) [Marxist-Leninist Organization of Greece]; *Marxistiko Leninistiko Kommounistiko Komma Elladas* (ML/KKE) [Marxist-Leninist Party of Greece (ML/KKE)]; *Rixi yia mia Proleratiaki Aristera* (RIXI) [Rupture for a proletarian Left]; *Laiki Metopiki Protovoulia* (LMP) [Popular Front Initiative]; *Kommounistiki Organossi Machitis* (KO. MACHITIS)

Trotskyist[55]. Their distinguishing characteristic was an aggressive set of political attitudes and their principal enemy the regime itself. In spite of their size they tried in a number of ways to necessitate a fundamental re-analysis of the nature of society and class relations in post-dictatorial Greece. More precisely, the far left entered *metapolitefsi* with guilt for not having done enough in the past and the conviction that with strategic action, bolder tactics and a more aggressive political line, the time was ripe for revolutionary change. They believed that all the previous years of organizational lethargy, bitter defeat and political isolation were about to usher in a period of dramatic political developments. Little, of course, came of this. Intergroup competition and continual disagreements over strategy and methods of protest meant that groups did not remain united for long. Attempts to unify the many different ideological tendencies and temperaments only increased schisms. Divided into over two dozen more or less equal organizations, the revolutionary left lacked the resources to become what KKE already was: a single attraction pole for the working class.

The Maoists continually stressed the necessity of 'going to the people'.[56] They argued that even basic political and economic changes could not be brought about until the masses had been thoroughly permeated with true Marxist-Leninist principles. According to their analysis, since the working class cannot develop on its own a revolutionary state of consciousness that would liberate it from exploitation, a vanguard party was necessary. So long as Greece lacked a revolutionary party, it lacked a working class conscious of

[Communist Organization Machitis]; *Synepis Aristeri Kinissi Elladas* (SAKE) [Reliable Marxist-Leninist Movement]; *Kinissi Ellinon Marxiston Leniniston* (KEML) [Marxist-Leninist Movement]; and *Organossi Kommouniston Marxiston-Leniniston Elladas* (OKMLE) [Communist Organization of Marxist-Leninist of Greece].

55 *Ergatiki Diethnistiki Enossi* (EDE) [Workers' Internationalist Union]; *Organossi Kommouniston Diethniston Elladas* (OKDE) [Communist Organization of Greek Internationalists]; *Kommounistiki Diethnistiki Enossi* (KDE) [Communist Internationalist Union]; *Organossi Sossialistiki Epanastassi (*OSE) Organization Socialist Revolution]; *Epanastatiko Kommunistiko Komma (*EKK) [Revolutionary Communist Party]; *Sossialistiki Organossi Ergazomenon* (SOE) [Socialist Organization of Workers]; and *Kommounistiko Epanastatiko Metopo* (KEM) [Communist Revolutionary Front].

56 See front page text in EKKE's weekly newspaper *Laikoi Agones* entitled, '*I Enotita petychainetai mono meta apo ideologiko xekatharisma kai kato apo to elencho ton mazon*' [Unity can only be achieved through an ideological clean-up and under the control of the masses], dated 29 April 1975.

58 Europe's Last Red Terrorists

the necessity of revolution. Hence, the search for a Greek proletarian vanguard party 'becomes the principal strategic priority of today's revolutionary movement'.[57] The main Maoist groups were EKKE (*Epanastatiko Kommounistiko Kinima Elladas*) and OMLE (*Organossi Marxiston Leniniston Elladas*).[58] EKKE was founded in March 1970 by a group of Greek students based in West Berlin. In Greece it appeared in 1972, 'a period of intense political development and ideological confusion for the revolutionary movement'.[59] EKKE recognized state-monopoly capitalism and the foreign-led conservative élite as the two main sources for Greece's long-standing fascist and imperialist predicament. Strongly influenced by Mao's ideas, the group tried to base concrete political action on a model which totally rejected materialism and bourgeois values and which provided an ideological framework with which to complement traditional Marxism-Leninism. The launch issue of the group's journal *Kommounistis* in March 1972 contained a strong dose of Mao's texts and analyses. Drawing on his concept of 'configuration of the struggle', EKKE said that the people were fundamental to the struggle and planned a general war against capitalist exploitation. Although EKKE decided, in the group's words, to play the parliamentary game and join the electoral process, its political orientation pointed towards extra-parliamentary action. Despite contesting the 1974 election the group declared that it would fight both inside and outside parliament.[60] From 1975 to 1977, it undertook a series of mobilization campaigns,

[57] See *Epanastatiko Kommounistiko Kinima* (EKKE) leaflet entitled *Empros na xanactissoume messa ston agona tin epanastatitiki enotita tis ergatias kai tou laou* [Let's re-build through popular struggle the revolutionary unity of workers and the people'], dated 1 October 1975.

[58] Throughout June 1976, the *Eleftherotypia* newspaper published texts under the caption 'The left of the Left: Which are the extra-parliamentary left organizations in Greece?', by groups such as EKKE, OMLE, OSE, OMLE, KO MACHITIS, SAK, KES, KDE, EDE and KEM. The questions put by the newspaper to all the groups were: 1) What needs led to the formation of your organization?; 2) What are your aims and the methods of materializing them?; 3) What is your critical position against the country's current social structures?; 4) What is your position towards the Greek parliamentary parties?; 5) What is your position towards the United States, the Soviet Union, China and the European Community? and, finally, 6) What reasons underlie the fragmentation of the Left?

[59] See 'The left of the Left': Which are the extra-parliamentary left organizations in Greece?', *Eleftherotypia*, 18 June 1976.

[60] 'The left of the Left', *Eleftherotypia*, 18 June 1976.

each constructed around a single political theme.[61] In 1975, at a one million-strong anti-US protest march, EKKE activists broke into the US Embassy in Athens which led to a violent clash between police and protesters.[62] The group often directed its political slogans against Karamanlis. After a 'hot' military incident with Turkey in the Aegean, an anti-government editorial appeared in the group's newspaper *Laikoi Agones*, rhetorically asking Karamanlis 'to choose between the people and the imperialist superpowers'.[63]

Central to the group's electoral strategy was its aim to politicize the masses. EKKE used revolutionary language to attract workers and students disillusioned with KKE reformism but this strategy failed. In the 1977 national elections, EKKE received a mere 12,000 votes. At the same time, the KKE retained its hold on the working-class base which led EKKE leaders to the conclusion that 'the only way to bring the workers to their side was to go into the factories to establish contact'.[64] After Mao's death, the group had several ideologies and strategies. The majority now held the view that the cultural revolution was a totally negative episode, and that the radical policies of 1958–9 incorporated serious errors. Then in November 1979 the group split. After criticizing the EKKE

---

[61] See EKKE leaflets on the 1974 general election (dated November 1974); on the monarchy referendum (4 December 1974); on American Imperialism (21 January 1975); on the partition of Cyprus (25 January 1975); on political and syndicalist rights (27 January 1975); and on local elections (28 March 1975).

[62] In the '*Anakoinossi tou Kentrikou Symvouliou tou Epanastatikou Kommounistikou Kinimatos Elladas (EKKE)*' [Proclamation by the Central Committee of the Revolutionary Communist Movement of Greece (EKKE)], regarding the storming of the American Embassy, EKKE states that 'it showed once more the people's determination to fight with all their powers in order to live free from fascism and the American imperialists … The breaking of the police cordon and the storming of the embassy grounds by thousands of people … proves that the populace has recognized the real source of fascism in this country. It constitutes both a blasphemy and expression of a deeply rooted anti-democratization the fact that this outburst of accumulated anger by the people after a seven-year fascistic tyranny and after the carnage in Greece and Cyprus by the instruments of American imperialism has been deliberately presented by the authorities as a "suspect action" that "undermines our democracy" '. EKKE, Athens, 21 April 1975.

[63] 'Maoists: The Last of the Romantics' in *To Vima* Special on youth political movements in Greece, 23 July 1995.

[64] Ibid.; see also *Anakoinossi tou Kentrikou Organou tou EKKE: Schetika me ta apotelesmata ton koinovouleftikon eklogon* [Announcement of the Central Organ of EKKE: About the parliamentary election results], dated November 1974.

leadership for espousing too narrowly the official Chinese policy, 60 activists broke away and joined KKE (m-l).[65] Faithful to the Maoist quest for ideological purity, the KKE (m-l) went on to stridently denounce the new Beijing leadership as 'a revisionist clique'.[66] Despite much discussion and organizational planning, KKE (m-l) remained marginal and made little progress.

The second Maoist group, OMLE (*Organossi Marxiston-Leniniston Elladas*), initially emerged in 1964 as a small number of former *Lambrakis Movement* militants and dissident communist intelligentsia. OMLE was less rigid and confrontational than EKKE. It viewed issues in tactical rather than strategic terms. It tolerated factions and allowed public disagreement with majority decisions. Subgroups in factories and universities paralleled the main organization and made much of the running. The group tried to serve as the forerunner of a future communist movement by developing theory, programme and tactics, while waiting for the conditions for socialist revolution.[67] According to OMLE, 'the immediate duty of marxist-leninists as derived from a correct theoretical analysis of class thesis and antithesis and assessment of the current state of affairs in contemporary Greek society is the struggle for the political overthrow of American domination and the dissolution of foreign power subjugation'.[68] OMLE sought to transmit its message and project its image in numerous ways: posters, leafleting campaigns, public meetings and theoretical

65 Source: *Organosseis kai Exokoinovouleftika kommata*: Aporrito Enimerotiko Simeioma, Ypodiefthynssi Genikis Asfalleias Athinon/Ypiressia Pliroforion. [Extra-parliamentary organizations and parties: (Classified Report/Greek Intelligence Service), dated 29 March 1984, p. 7. The 56-page report is divided into seven main sections dealing with different types and organizations of extra-parliamentarism of the whole political spectrum. Pages 1–15 are devoted to pro-Chinese Maoist groups like EKKE; 16–24 to Troskyist organizations; 25–34 to revolutionary terrorist groups such as 17N, Group June '78, ELA, LEA, and October '80; 35–6 to anarcho-autonomous groups; and pages 37 to 56 deal with militarist, neo-fascist and pro-royal groups.

66 See 'Maoists: The Last of the Romantics'.

67 '*Thesseis tis K.E. tis OMLE yia ta 56 chronia apo tin idryssi tou KKE*' [Positions of the Central Committee of the OMLE for the 56 years since the formation of KKE] (Athens: 1975).

68 'The left of the Left', *Eleftherotypia*, 18 June, 1976; see also OMLE *Prokyrixi* [Proclamation], dated December 1973 and '*Oloi ston agona yia tin syntrivi tou Americanofassismou*' [All together in the struggle against American-Fascism], *Laiki Enotita* (No.22, December 1973), pp. 1–2.

discussions were all used as devices to build up membership. Obsessed by the November '73 events, it declared that the 'Polytechnic insurrection' was the first step towards the overthrow of the US-directed regime and 'the realisation of a democratic, anti-imperialist revolution in Greece'.[69] The group also believed that the Karamanlis government tolerated neo-fascist violence in the hope that extremism would mobilize public opinion behind the existing political arrangements. OMLE held the Karamanlis government solely responsible for 'the existence and actions of junta sympathisers and every other sort of fascistic elements', adding that 'such elements and their mechanisms would have never been able to survive and capitalize on the given situation without the government's undisguised tolerance'.[70] At the same time, OMLE relentlessly attacked the KKE for its 'revisionist and defeatist line and authoritarian and bureaucratic behaviour'.[71] OMLE believed that

since revisionism has pulverised the KKE, all marxist-leninist efforts should now need to concentrate and converge on the creation of the appropriate preconditions for the creation – re-establishment – of an authentic marxist-leninist KKE.[72]

However, antithetical fixations on the Shanghai Group and the Beijing new leadership fed a constant ferment of ideological debates. In 1976 the group split into two competing factions[73] each pressing for different policies.

Trotskyists were equally fractured and varied between three main organizations: OSE, OKDE and KEM. Belief in the inevitability of a world communist revolution did not prevent Trotskyist organizations from frequent schisms and departures over 'abstruse theoretical disputes and historical hair-splitting'[74] which neutralized much of their original appeal to the youth. OSE (*Organossi Sossialistiki Epanastassi*), the strongest and most experienced group,

[69] 'The left of the Left', *Eleftherotypia*, 18 June 1976; see also *Laokratia*, (No. 9, December 1973), pp. 1–2 and *Laikos Dromos* (No. 17, October 1973).
[70] 'The left of the Left', *Eleftherotypia*, 18 June 1976.
[71] Ibid.; see also *'Empros sto dromo tis epanastatikis palis'* [On the path of revolutionary struggle], *Laiki Foni* [Popular Voice], Nos. 35–36 (February-March 1974), pp. 1–2.
[72] 'The left of the Left', *Eleftherotypia*, 18 June 1976.
[73] KKE/m-l and M-L/KKE.
[74] See Willie Thompson, *The Left in History: Revolution and Reform in Twentieth-Century Politics,* (London: Pluto Press, 1997), p. 170.

believed that post-junta Greece could only be reshaped by audacious proletarian action. It viewed rapid industrial development as a pre-condition for revolution and stressed the need to develop a strategy for the achievement of socialism in Greece that rejected both reformism and Stalinism.[75] OSE also argued that 'the problems which confront the workers and farmers today (unemployment, poverty, state terrorism and civil-liberties infringements) can only be tackled when the working class achieves power and abolishes the power structures upon which the bourgeois society functions'.[76] Radicalizing the masses through the transformation of their attitudes towards the existing authority relationships became the group's overriding strategic priority:

Unless the working masses generated revolutionary discontent and consciously stormed into the foreground of history through their struggles, the smashing of the existing capitalist state apparatus and liquidation of the exploiting classes – would never occur.[77]

The group polemicized endlessly against the Karamanlis regime. In OSE's eyes, the July 1974 transition was merely a device designed to re-shape the system's power-structure and deradicalize the masses:

Karamanlis and his government, in a desperate attempt to gain time and thus consolidate their position, appeared initially anti-dictatorial and anti-American, distributed a plethora of promises to workers and farmers and, generally made sure not to fuel political tension. But it quickly metamorphosed into a government: which systematically undermined the movement's democratic gains; which methodically protected the junta's personnel and institutions; which introduced a constitution no different from that of the dictators; which readily accepted the imperialists' demands for a bizonal status in Cyprus; and which restored diplomatic relations with Washington by making humiliating concessions.[78]

Like other Trotskyist groups, OKDE (*Organossi Kommouniston Diethniston Ellados*) and KEM (*Kommounistiko Epanastatiko Metopo*) supported all challenges to the socio-political system through disruptive forms of collective action. Following extreme-left political

[75] 'The left of the Left', *Eleftherotypia*, 17 June 1976.
[76] Ibid.; see also *Sossialistiki Epanastassi* (No.1, September 1974).
[77] 'The left of the Left', *Eleftherotypia*, 17 June 1976.
[78] Ibid.

traditions, KEM and OKDE did their utmost to encourage workers into a radical state. They organized political demonstrations, occupations, strikes and other actions. 'Raising the level of consciousness of the working class' was an essential precondition, OKDE argued, since a national socialist revolution had to be consciously constructed through workers' actions.[79] Both KKEs were seen as 'degenerative working-class parties which now play a political role, already being played by social democracy. Having abandoned their historic responsibility of organizing class struggles, their sole aim now is electoral compromise'.[80] At the same time, OKDE explained that 'the mushrooming of revolutionary groups was due to the political confusion which KKE reformism had inflicted upon the workers' movement'.[81] In the 1977 elections, the group went as far as to advise its followers to vote – 'just once' – for the KKE 'since a KKE parliamentary presence would expose its reformism and that would wrest workers' loyalties away from the KKE. In fact, it will help the workers to fully realise what kind of role the reformists play within the movement'.[82] Contacts with the French OCI and the Italian Lotta Continua became increasingly numerous after 1977.[83] This coincided with debates within OKDE about the use of violence, semi-legal political action and internal democracy. The 'dominance of reformism over the working movement' had finally convinced OKDE that 'unity on the far left and of the entire working-class movement could only be brought about through the trial of ideas, political evaluations and programmes, within the process of class-struggle'.[84] OKDE remained convinced that 'only through struggle, could a vehicle

---

[79] 'The left of the Left', *Eleftherotypia*, 21 June 1976; see also the proclamation in the newspaper *Ergatiki Pali* [Workers' Struggle] (OKDE's monthly organ), announcing the re-emergence of OKDE, 21 November 1975. According to the 1984 Intelligence Report on the Extra-parliamentary organizations, OKDE originally emerged in May 1967 with 'a diaspora of duplicating communiqués'. In August 1968, the OKDE founding members (Panayiotis Doumas, Theodossis Thomadakis, Sofronios Papadopoulos and Eleni Doumas) were arrested, which led to the organization's postponement of activities until the *metapolitefsi*. In '*Organosseis and Exokoinovouleutika kommata*', Greek Intelligence Service/ Classified Report, 29 March 1984, pp. 17–18.

[80] 'The left of the Left', *Eleftherotypia*, 21 June 1976.

[81] Ibid.

[82] Ibid.

[83] Source: *Organosseis kai Exokoinovouleftika kommata*, p. 18.

[84] 'The left of the Left', *Eleftherotypia*, 21 June 1976.

emerge with the needed prestige to rally around it the main working class and put an end to sectarianism and diaspora'.[85]

Similarly, KEM focused on reformulating 'a united revolutionary pact between all the Trotskyist forces in Greece'.[86] A splinter group itself,[87] it posed awkward but familiar questions about the movement's self-destructive sectarian tendencies. Stressing the intellectual and political imperative for a permanent shift away from the 'constant doctrinal faction fights, splits, anathemas, expulsions, recombinations',[88] KEM argued that 'the emancipation of the working class from the bourgeois state and its institutions … involves waging a struggle against the oppressive incorporative structures (family, church, military service, sexual discrimination) created by bourgeois ideology.'[89] KEM also argued that the regime's legislative attack on trade union rights (law 330/1976) and other such measures (banning of strikes) was a design 'to paralyze the labour movement and crush revolutionary syndicalism'.[90] Such belief was based in the group's rejection of *metapolitefsi* which KEM saw as a mere change of guard in which 'the Karamanlist regime simply took over from the stratocrats and consolidated its grip on power through the daily blackmail of "Karamanlis or the tanks" '.[91]

Overall, between 1974 and late 1979, Trotskyist, Maoist and other extra-parliamentary extreme leftist groups constantly sought to transmit their specific messages, ideas and perspectives to 'the proletarian masses'. Despite their organizational defects and fragmented nature, all sections of the movement dreamed of a modern-day Bolshevik revolution. When it became clear that the political ground was infertile, some fanatical Marxist militants broke away from the movement and behind organizational acronyms such as ELA, Group June'78 and 17N sought to impose 'deep and wholesale revolutionary change' through small-group urban terrorism.[92]

---

85 Ibid.
86 Ibid.
87 Formed in December 1975, KEM was the result of a merge between the groups *Kommounismos and Sossialistiki Epanastatiki Enossi.*
88 Thompson, *The Left in History,* p. 168.
89 'The left of the Left', *Eleftherotypia,* 21 June 1976.
90 Ibid.
91 Ibid.

ELA (Epanastatikos Laikos Agonas)

ELA argued that meaningful revolutionary change needed strategic direction from an armed vanguard of professional revolutionaries since 'the conflagration that will eventually lead to the overthrow of the capitalist regime will be a long, hard and violent armed struggle'.[93] As a result, it set out from the start to form an operational vanguard to educate the 'passive' masses and convert them to the cause. ELA viewed itself as a part of the international revolutionary movement and thus counted imperialism, capitalism and fascism in all their various forms as its enemies. The group carried out hundreds of non-lethal, low-level bombings aimed at symbolic material targets, ranging from US military and business facilities (such as IBM, American Express), to EC and United Nations offices and foreign embassies. The group also used propaganda and factory management targets to increase tension between strikers and the employers since it believed that conditions in the workplace are specifically designed by the capitalist bosses to dehumanize and isolate the working-class population.[94]

ELA tried to present its violence as a way of responding to material restraints and the need to form a united command structure for the revolutionary forces. Rejecting completely the possibility of building socialism from within the existing system, ELA argued that

there have been plenty of dramatic examples in the past which demonstrate the illusion of power-seizure through peaceful parliamentary transition: the Greek civil war, Allende's Chile, the fascist Greece of 1967 and November 1973 – all prove that the only path to the establishment of a dictatorship of a proletariat is the path of popular and revolutionary violence.[95]

Clearly aware of the fact that the objective conditions for a revolution did not yet exist in Greece, ELA said that its prime goal was to establish a concrete strategy of attack and a political line which would facilitate the total unity and consciousness of all forces confronting the capitalist order. At the same time, ELA attacked KKE

---

92 ELA manifesto: *'Yia tin anaptyxi tou Ellinikou Laikou kai Epanastatikou Kinimatos'* [For the development of the Greek Popular and Revolutionary Movement], dated June/July 1978, p. 12.

93 Ibid., p. 16.

94 Ibid., pp. 10–11.

95 Ibid., p. 3.

for making a valuable contribution to the consolidation of the bourgeois social order. Ever since 1974, it maintained, KKE had placed its whole political weight on the side of accommodation and settlement.[96] ELA argued in its 48-page manifesto that 'KKE's acceptance of the idea of playing by the bourgeois political rules' made the need for 'a coherent revolutionary socialist leadership' all the more imperative.[97] 'Despite lip-service to the contrary, KKE', the group added, 'has done absolutely nothing to organize and advance the proletarian class struggle'.[98]

ELA advocated revolutionary violence as an ideological response to declining radicalism and reformism. The group believed that the working class had been very poorly served by the KKE. It also believed that far from being prime agents of the dissemination of radical value systems, KKE party leaders had turned themselves into opponents of any such system 'weaning organised labour and the working class away from anything that could be called socialist revolutionary consciousness'.[99] ELA asserted that the KKE

has abandoned illegality and underground activity – the methods of political practice which support and strengthen the development of the popular movement. By abandoning the organisation and exercise of revolutionary violence, it has effectively deprived the popular movement of the two most essential preconditions for the seizure of power and the creation of socialism in Greece. Instead, KKE insists on organizing and promoting a political struggle that is reduced to a legally accepted bourgeois framework, cultivating the illusion that only gradual and peaceful protest can lead to revolutionary change and a fundamental break with advanced capitalism – something which historically has proved to be unrealisable.[100]

One of ELA's earliest acts was the firebombing of eight cars belonging to US servicemen in the military base of Elefsina on 29 April 1975. The group promised more attacks against the military forces of American imperialism because it was:

US imperialism that partitioned Cyprus and turned the island into a Natoist military base. And it is US imperialism which tries now through

96   Ibid., p. 6.
97   Ibid., p. 1.
98   Ibid., p. 6.
99   Ibid., p. 5.
100   Ibid.

its agents (CIA, its Athens Embassy, ITT and other multinationals) to control and exploit everything that there is on Greek soil, ranging from our oil resources in the North Aegean to the country's entire politico-military machinery.[101]

Although the number of attacks increased as promised, the group seemed reluctant to escalate its military methods and strategy. Despite its violent rhetoric, ELA continued to concentrate on the same type of targets and it soon became clear that its actions were primarily intended to publicize its political message rather than cause bloodshed. ELA gradually abandoned its original image of an organic military vanguard and began to see itself more as an educational service for the proletariat. The regular publication of the group's underground journal *Andipliroforissi* (counter-information) became a propaganda channel for ELA to communicate with its supporters and sympathizers and other like-minded groups of the revolutionary left. In 1978, however, an ELA breakaway hardline group called *Group June'78* began independent operations.[102] Frustrated with the nugatory sentences which many fascists and their accomplices in the police and security services received in 'the farce-trials'[103] of *metapolitefsi*, the new group set itself up as judge, jury and executioner. On 31 June 1979, in a 17N-style sophisticated attack, *June'78* assassinated Petros Bambalis, a retired intelligence officer and junta-torturer. Though the group polemically stated in the follow-up communiqué that more operations were to follow and urged the whole revolutionary left to raise the level of violence,[104] it mysteriously vanished from the scene. ELA violence did not fluctuate after that perplexing episode. As before, the group continued through sporadic, low-level, non-lethal tactics, to pursue its own agenda of armed struggle.

Like the Italian BR and the French AD, ELA believed that 'Western Europe was the cardinal point in the conflict between the international proletariat and the imperialist bourgeoisie'.[105]

---

101 Ibid., p. 44.

102 ELA admitted thus in 1989. See Mary Bossis, *Ellada kai Tromokratia: Ethnikes kai Diethneis Diastasseis* [Greece and Terrorism: National and International Dimensions] (Athens: Sakkoulas, 1996), p. 237.

103 *Group June'78* attack communiqué on Petros Bambalis, reprinted in Yiorgos Karambelias, *To Elliniko Andartiko ton Poleon, 1974–1985* [Urban Guerrilla Warfare in Greece, 1974–1985] (Athens: Roptron, 1985), p. 142.

104 Ibid., p.145.

Given Greece's peripheral status, ELA saw the country becoming a permanent part of an imperialist chain constructed by the US and maintained through political-military-economic structures such as NATO and the European Community. Strongly internationalist, ELA shared RAF's view on the need for the formation of a West European revolutionary militant front against 'American-led NATO imperialism'. ELA claimed that an intense revolutionary war against imperialism was already taking place simultaneously in other parts of the world such as 'Chile, Argentina, Turkey, Iran, Palestine, Lebanon and Angola and with some positive results'.[106] Domestically, November 1973 played an important role in ELA's thinking. References to the early 1970s student movement and the 'spontaneous Polytechnic uprising' increased sharply after new left groups were voted down heavily in the 1977 elections. ELA argued that

> it was the political effectiveness of student radicalism in raising the fundamental political issues of the time that helped the post-civil war social struggle to reach its zenith in November 1973. Having produced a genuine revolutionary crisis that smashed the Junta's normalisation efforts the movement proved to all revolutionary forces the necessity of fundamental political change.[107]

ELA viewed the November events as a revolution largely unfulfilled and took up arms in an attempt to complete it.

However, Greece, in the late 1970s, was not on the verge of a revolution. Revolution, in fact, was the last thing in the minds of ordinary Greek people. Seven years of military dictatorship had a dramatic impact on national political values and attitudes. All Greek society wanted after 1974 was political calm and long-term institutional stability.[108] Only the highly ideological militant left interpreted the dynamics of *metapolitefsi* differently. Their Marxist-influenced definition of democracy drove them to the radical rejection of *metapolitefsi* as 'junta by another name'.[109] Moreover,

---

[105] Yonah Alexander and Dennis Pluchinsky (eds), *Europe's Red Terrorists: The Fighting Communist Organizations* (London: Frank Cass, 1992), p. 24.

[106] ELA manifesto: '*Yia tin anaptyxi tou Ellinikou Laikou*', p. 45.

[107] Ibid., pp. 35–36.

[108] See Ch. 2.

[109] See George Kassimeris, 'The Greek State Response to Terrorism', in *Terrorism and Political Violence*, Vol. 5, No. 4 (Winter 1993), p. 307.

BR terrorist spectaculars in neighbouring Italy and Baader-Meinhof prison heroics in West Germany encouraged them to believe that violent action could be the most effective way of talking to the masses and 'achieving the revolutionary change of Greek society'.[110] When violence shifted from junta-related revenge attacks to hard-core political terrorism, the majority of the Greek extra-parliamentary left distanced itself.[111] Unwilling to assume the role of fellow travellers with paramilitary terrorist organizations such as ELA and 17N, they reacted by characterizing the militants as 'comrades who erred'.[112] Having rejected their logic as 'avantgardist, dogmatic and militaristic',[113] the extra-parliamentary left argued that 17N's analysis of Greek society was false.

Those comrades who, in such an early stage of the new revolutionary movement, take a short cut and choose the path of militarism are all wrong. When class struggle and the logic behind it are not the products of the maturation of the revolutionary process (within the popular movement), then militarism, a general desire for unlimited violence, élitism, sectarianism and the contempt of the masses becomes inevitably the order of the day. [114]

For a brief period, ELA and 17N engaged in a war of words and symbols with organizations of the extra-parliamentary left. 17N, in particular, attacked them as 'petit-bourgeois groupscoules incapable of expressing the people's will'.[115] However, revolutionary

---

[110] '*Yia tin anaptyxi tou Ellinikou Laikou*', p. 9; see also *To Elliniko Antarktiko*, p. 23.

[111] See Mary Bossis, *Ellada kai Tromokratia*, p. 120.

[112] See Yiorgos Karambelias, *Enopli Pali kai Enallaktiko Kinima* [Armed struggle and the Alternative movement] (Athens: Kommouna, 1986), p. 15; see also *Kinima Neas Aristeras – Apantissi sto Manifesto tis 17Noemvri* [New Left Movement – A Response to the 17N Manifesto], in *Eleftherotypia*, 9 May 1977.

[113] See 'Enopli Pali kai Tromokratia' [Armed Struggle and Terrorism] by *Omada yia mia Proletariaki Aristera* (OPA) [Group for a Proletarian Left] (Athens: Kommouna, 1985), p. 28; see also *Antiparathesseis*, No. 8, 1985.

[114] *Enopli Pali kai Tromokratia*, pp. 53–54.

[115] Ibid., pp. 29–30; In its April 1977 manifesto, '*Apantissi sta Kommata kai tis Organosseis*' [A Response to Parties and Organizations], 17N used EKKE's April 21, 1975 storming of the American embassy, which the group called 'an action of mass popular violence against American imperialism', to attack the organizations of the extra-parliamentary left for not being 'on the frontline to embrace and support the popular initiative of mass violence', pp. 15–16. On page 18, 17N mockingly refers to the extra-parliamentary leftist organizations as 'revolutionary organizations' and states that all their activities 'are centred on the publication of a weekly or monthly newspaper and

politics never gained popular sympathy in post–1974 Greece.
Realizing that guerrilla struggle would lead them nowhere, most
of the extra-parliamentary left abandoned revolutionary militancy. Only ELA and 17N remained committed to a full-blooded
communism in Greece and held on to their belief in November
1973 as the first stage of a revolution waiting to happen.

two to three ludicrous demonstrations in theatres or *Propylaia* [downtown Athens]
where the police can have a laugh at their expense'.

4

THE HISTORY OF RO-17 NOVEMBER

TACTICS, TARGETS AND OPERATIONAL
EVOLUTION, 1975–2000

An examination of RO-17N's campaign of violence clarifies its political physiognomy and operational development. It also provides an outline of attacks and explains the logic behind the group's selection of targets. 17N was strongly influenced by national and international political events as well as West European revolutionary groups such as the Italian Red Brigades and the German Baader-Meinhof Group which became active between 1968 and the early 1970s. A closer examination of 17N's campaign, however, reveals imprecise politico-military goals and priorities. Despite a strong and, at times, clear sense of national history and political tradition, 17N misinterpreted the post-1974 political realities which pertained during the initial period of its activity.

17N was heavily influenced by the ideology, leadership and methods of the communist-led EAM/ELAS (*Ethniko Apeleftherotiko Metopo/Ethnikos Laikos Apeleftherotikos Stratos* or National Liberation Front/Greek People's Liberation Army). One of the largest and most impressive Resistance movements in Nazi-occupied Europe, EAM/ELAS aimed at the creation of a new and modern nation-state before its crushing defeat in the 1946–9 civil war.[1] Both EAM/ELAS wartime radicalism and the

---

[1] Mark Mazower describes EAM/ELAS, in his book on wartime Greece, as 'something unprecedented in modern Greek history – a mass ideological movement in a country of clientelistic factions and charismatic leaders. It was, in fact, one of the most startling manifestations of the radical break with established political traditions that the Second World War inspired inside and outside Europe (the resistance movements in Yugoslavia, Italy, French Indochina and the Philippines provided parallels)', in

decades of right-wing authoritarianism which followed the civil war linked 17N to modern Greek political history and formed its ideological ethos. November 1973, however, influenced 17N more directly and more profoundly than any other event. Indeed, the *Polytechneio* student rebellion of November 1973 and the subsequent massacre became the defining formative feature in the group's violent behaviour and political radicalism.

17N engaged in an armed struggle because it viewed itself as the vanguard of the working class and the last-ditch defender of Greek national independence. Yet throughout its campaign, the group never broadened its message to become a popular movement and, inevitably, never won the support needed for the revolution. This chapter outlines the group's different operational phases (1975–80; 1983–90; and 1991–2000) and analyses how 17N corresponded to national and international political developments and how great an impact its actions had on Greek public life.

Phase One: 1975–80

Unlike most European urban guerrilla groups, 17N did not begin as a loose network of minor groupings which shared general extreme-left orientations. For example, both the Italian Red Brigades and the French *Action Directe* originally emerged from various groupuscules with names such as CPM (*Collettivo Politico Metropolitano*) and Clodo (*Comité liquidant ou détournant les ordinateurs*).[2] 17N, in contrast, never attempted to expand its sphere of influence on the national territory which explains the organization's operational continuity and remarkable resistance to infiltration.[3] Another equally striking difference between 17N and other European extreme-left groups was its tactical strategy. Most Marxist terrorist groups on the European scene followed a common pattern: a gradual transition from low-level bombings to

M. Mazower, *Inside Hitler's Greece: The Experience of Occupation 1941–44* (New Haven: Yale University Press, 1995), p. xviii.

[2] See Michael Y. Dartnell, *Action Directe: Ultra-left terrorism in France, 1979–1987* (London: Frank Cass, 1995), pp. 73–7; and Vittorfranco S. Pisano, 'A Survey of Terrorism of the Left in Italy: 1970–78' in *Terrorism: An International Journal* (Vol. 2, Nos. 3 & 4, 1979), pp. 171–213.

[3] George Kassimeris, 'Two decades of terrorism in Greece', in *Jane's Intelligence Review*, (Vol. 8, No. 3, March 1996), pp. 117–18.

more lethal attacks. *Action Directe*, for example, waited four years before it moved from a low-level bombing campaign to political assassinations.[4] The Belgian CCC (*Cellules Communistes Combattantes*) carried out 26 bombings before it even considered a lethal attack and Italy's Red Brigades went through seven years and two major operational phases before they started killing their victims.[5] 17N adopted a radically different approach: they started off by killing their targets.

The group appeared for the first time at Christmas 1975. On 23 December, three unmasked terrorists stalked Richard Welch,[6] the CIA's station chief in Athens, shooting him down at point-blank range in front of his wife and Greek driver. By choosing such a high-profile target, 17N aimed to put itself immediately on the map and establish credibility as a revolutionary group. However, this strategy produced the reverse effect. Because the operation was conducted with high precision and efficiency, the Greek authorities dismissed the responsibility claims of a previously unknown organization calling itself *Revolutionary Organization 17 November* as the work of cranks. Police officials believed at the time that both the extreme left and right were trying to embarrass each other by sending fraudulent communiqués to the media. Without solid leads and given the vicious atmosphere of the period, the police imposed a ban on publicizing reports in the press 48 hours after the assassination, which only served to exacerbate media speculation.[7]

---

4   AD commando Elisabeth-Von-Dick assassinated French General René Audran on 25 January 1985.

5   See Yonah Alexander & Dennis A. Pluchinsky (eds), *European Terrorism: Today & Tomorrow* (McLean,VA: Brassey's, 1992), p. 94.

6   US officials blamed the English-language *Athens News* paper for identifying Welch and eight other embassy employees as CIA operatives in an anti-CIA article published on November 25. Welch's cover in Athens was, in fact, extremely thin. He lived in a house known by many to have been used by CIA station chiefs for years. His function was hardly secret. See *International Herald Tribune*, 9 January 1976.

7   Until the police imposed the ban, there was wild speculation in the Greek press with stories ranging from open warfare between major intelligence services and CIA-FBI score-settling to Carlos-led Palestinian terrorist operations on Greek soil. A sample of front-page titles in the Greek press will suffice: 'CIA assassinates Richard Welch'; 'Double-agent Welch executed by the CIA'. See *Eleftherotypia* and *International Herald Tribune*, 21 December 1976.

At the time of 17N's appearance, Western Europe was the most active terrorist scene in the world.[8] From 1970 to 1978, 47 per cent of all significant terrorist incidents occurred on West European soil.[9] This was a period of Red and Black terror, state-sponsored political assassinations, kidnappings and indiscriminate public bombings on an almost daily basis. The climate of political extremism was typified by the fact that the Welch assassination took place only hours after the eleven OPEC ministers kidnapped by Carlos the Jackal in Vienna were released. In Greece, during the same period, groups of politically frustrated youths were regularly attempting to provoke chaos and violence. Demonstrations were frequently held in both Athens and Salonika with thousands of young activists chanting anti-Franco slogans and burning American and Spanish flags. The US Embassy in Athens was stormed twice by extreme-left demonstrators and home-made bombs regularly exploded outside ministries and offices of international organizations. Arson was, in fact, the most widespread form of action and the targets were all in one way or another connected to *metapolitefsi*. According to the US Embassy in Athens, nearly 200 cars belonging to US military and affiliated personnel were firebombed in 1975, 120 in 1976 and 84 in 1977.[10]

Twelve months after the attack on Welch, 17N killed Evangelos Mallios, a former police captain during the Colonels' junta. Before new conspiracy theories began circulating in the press, a publicity-hungry 17N sustained the momentum with a publicity coup. Ten days after the murder, the left-wing Parisian daily *Libération* published a 17N communiqué in which the group claimed credit for the attack and explained – in vivid detail – how it carried out the Welch operation.[11] The *Libération* publication together with the assassination of Pandelis Petrou (deputy

---

[8] Peter Chalk, *West European Terrorism and Counter-Terrorism: The Evolving Dynamic*, (London: Macmillan, 1996), pp. 52–65.

[9] During that decade, a total of 3,498 terrorist operations was registered in Europe, out of 8,114 incidents worldwide; See Charles A. Russel, 'Europe: Regional Review', in *Terrorism: An International Journal*, Vol. 3, Nos. 1–2, (1979), p. 158.

[10] *New York Times*, 17 December 1979.

[11] *Libération*, 24 December 1976. Although the editor of *Libération*, Serge Zuly, never said it outright, the 17N communiqué is believed to have come through Jean-Paul Sartre. See Nikos Konstandaras, Dark Star: The Story of November 17, *Odyssey*, (February–March 1994), pp. 28–34.

commander of MAT riot police and, like Mallios, a former security officer during the military junta) and his driver in January 1980 gained the group national recognition, if not public sympathy.[12] All four victims were shot with the same .45-calibre weapon which was to become the group's signature weapon. By using the same weapon 17N ensured that no other group could take credit for its operations. At the same time, the limited number of operations carried out by the 17N in this initial phase mirrored the insecurities and organizational dilemmas of a terrorist group in a preparatory stage. Yet the choice of targets and their symbolism showed 17N's desire to link themselves – albeit from a distance – to the broader socio-political protest movement of the period. By the end of the decade, Greek public opinion and the media came to accept 17N as an ephemeral group of ultra-left militants who, outraged by the new regime's lenient treatment of the fascists in the courts, simply took the law into their own hands and sought retrospective justice.

Phase Two: 1983–90

When Andreas Papandreou's Panhellenic Socialist Movement (PASOK) came to power with an electoral landslide in October 1981, it seemed that any remaining motives for extreme-left political violence were removed. Indeed, there was no action by the 17N until late 1983. Papandreou, like François Mitterrand in France, had promised to regenerate the country through a full-blooded socialist programme and this produced an instant sense of national vigour and purpose. The number of acts of violence drastically declined: from 56 in 1980 to 4 in 1983 and 3 in 1984.[13] Despite protestations by the right-wing opposition, PASOK abolished the anti-terrorist legislation introduced by the Karamanlis administration back in 1978. The New Democracy party said that this showed laxity on the part of the Socialists with regard to law and order. However, Papandreou's peculiar brand of socialism combined with deepening economic malaise soon deflated the huge popular expectations. The drachma was devalued overall by

---

[12] Mary Bossis, *Ellada & Tromokratia: Ethnikes kai Diethneis Diastaseis* [Greece & Terrorism: National and International Dimensions] (Athens: Sakkoulas, 1996), p. 120.

[13] Source: Ministry of Public Order, (Athens: 1989).

64 per cent, unemployment continued to rise affecting 8–10 per cent of the urban labour force and a policy of gradual austerity began to be introduced. At the same time, persistent public protest against Papandreou's foreign policy U-turns, especially the renewal of the US bases agreement in 1983, intensified tensions. After 23 months of socialist government, opinion polls in the main Greek cities confirmed a rapid decline in the government's popularity.

Almost three years after its last attack on Mallios, 17N was back in business. On 15 November 1983, when it was widely thought that the group had been auto-dissolved, 17N stunned the country by assassinating US Navy Captain and head of JUSMAGG[14] naval division George Tsantes and his Greek driver.[15] 17N explained the attack as a response to the continuing US military presence in Greece. The group also explained the reasons behind its 3-year operational silence and launched a vitriolic attack against the Papandreou government. The group believed that PASOK not only had betrayed the trust of the electorate but had also abandoned socialism. At the same time, 17N threatened all Greek personnel working in the US bases. It warned that like Tsantes's driver, all Greek driver-bodyguards of CIA, DIA and JUSMAGG agents, embassy officials and US base commanders would be targeted without warning. Once again, sections of the Greek press fictionalized the murder case. Unconvinced that an indigenous terrorist group could carry out such daring and clinically planned operations, they printed numerous stories about Turkish agents and contract killers.

The Tsantes attack heralded the transition of 17N revenge terrorism to a full-scale terrorist campaign. In fact, the group used the assassination as an occasion to declare war against the Americans, inaugurating a campaign of violence to remove them from Greece. Less than five months after the Tsantes operation, in April 1984, 17N attacked but failed[16] to assassinate JUSMAGG

---

[14] JUSMAGG = Joint US Military Advisory Group in Greece.

[15] Tsantes was shot and killed as he was being driven to work. Two 17N commandos on a motorcycle pulled alongside Tsantes's car while it was stopped at a traffic light and shot him with the .45-calibre signature weapon.

[16] The operation against Judd was carbon-copy of the Tsantes attack. Judd was attacked by two men on a motorcycle at a traffic stop as he was driving a shipment of diplomatic mail to the US Air Force base at Athens Hellenicon airport. The attackers pulled

M. Sergeant Robert Judd in a fresh attempt to draw attention to the continuing function of the American bases in Greece.[17] In fact, both the Tsantes and Judd communiqués opened with identical paragraphs: 'The bases will not leave with either elections or parliamentary methods . . . Only dynamic mass struggle and justified popular revolutionary violence will force them out'.[18] Commenting on its first operational failure, 17N said that it merely demonstrated that they were not a group of professional assassins as portrayed by sections of the press but 'simple, popular fighters with simple means and rudimentary organization'.[19]

17N attacked Papandreou for renewing the US base agreement and for breaking his pledges to pull out of both NATO and the EC. Papandreou's 'betrayal' was a strong and sufficient justification for terrorism in 17N's eyes. It actually became the ideological catalyst which confirmed the group's view that 'popular revolutionary violence' and not parliamentarism was the only road to socialism.[20] Outraged that PASOK was pursuing economic austerity, EC integration and closer NATO ties, 17N saw PASOK-type socialism and US imperialism as the two major enemies of the revolutionary cause. A communiqué depicted the Papandreou-led government as a committee managing the affairs of the 'lumpen big bourgeois class', that is the Greek oligarchy. This also meant that what was initially a military campaign against US imperialism became also an attack against perceived servants

---

    alongside Judd's car and fired with the trademark-weapon five rounds against him. Judd, instinctively, accelerated, jumped the median strip, and sped away.

[17] The bases were installed after Greece and the United States signed a bilateral defence agreement in 1953. Since then, the US has developed a sophisticated network of military installations on the mainland and in the island of Crete. Although the four major bases and several smaller installations functioned within the Greek-US defence agreement they came under the NATO umbrella since they were considered important in maintaining the East-West military balance in the Mediterranean.

[18] 17N communiqué taking credit for attack on Judd, dated April 1984.

[19] In a communiqué sent to satirical weekly *To Pontiki* (20 July 1984), three months after the unsuccessful attempt against Judd, 17N argued that 'no professional killer would have missed at a distance of 1 to 2 meters while the car was stationary'. The communiqué to *Pontiki* was the third since the group's emergence that did not follow an assassination.

[20] 17N communiqué taking credit for attack on Tsantes and his driver, dated October 1983.

of the Greek political establishment. From now on, 17N would be systematically killing on those two fronts.

In February 1985, 17N killed in central Athens Nikos Momferatos, publisher of the country's biggest-selling conservative newspaper *Apogevmatini* together with his driver-bodyguard. Momferatos was targeted because, as the president of the Association of Athens Newspapers Publishers, he was held responsible for the press campaign of 'misinformation and systematic distortion of the truth' against the Greek people.[21] Describing Momferatos as a fascist-junta man[22] and CIA agent, 17N attacked the entire Greek press for poisonous sensationalism. Papandreou condemned the murder as the work of 'dark forces serving foreign interests'.[23] Meanwhile, new austerity measures introduced by the socialists aiming to bring the runaway public sector and current account deficits under control provoked huge public dissatisfaction and massive nationwide labour unrest.[24] Having been voted back to power for a second four-year term on a platform promising the Greeks 'better days to come', Papandreou explained his abrupt U-turn in economic policy as a necessary attempt to rescue the country from bankruptcy.[25] In June 1985, soon after a TWA hijacking, the US State Department advised Americans to avoid Athens airport for the summer, which strained relations between Athens and Washington and cost the Greek tourism industry $300 million in foreign exchange. A second hijacking of an EgyptAir plane within months of the TWA incident placed Athens

[21] 17N communiqué taking credit for the attack on Momferatos and his driver, undated.
[22] Momferatos was a close personal friend of Konstantinos Karamanlis and had served as a Minister of Industry in the short-lived Markezinis government during the military junta.
[23] *New York Times*, 22 February 1985.
[24] Strikes in 20 cities paralyzed commercial and civic life disrupting basic services both in the private and public sector. These included banks, civil air and Olympic Airways personnel, electricity, telecommunications, the Post Office, urban transport, schools and hospitals.
[25] Greece's external debt amounted to more than $14 billion, 36 percent of the GNP. Under the new austerity regime, the socialist government substantially remoulded the system of wage indexation which it first introduced when it came to power in 1981; it also imposed a two-year freeze to the end of 1987 on any other salary and wage increases. An import deposit requirement was introduced for a little under half of the products coming to Greece and the drachma was devalued by 15 per cent to boost exports.

alongside Lagos and Bogota as airports with the worst security in the world.[26]

In November of the same year, 1,000 left-wing extremists barricaded themselves in Athens Polytechnic in protest at the killing of a 15-year-old demonstrator, Michalis Kaltezas, by a stray police bullet during a march to the US Embassy to mark the anniversary of the November 1973 *Polytechneio* student revolt. Both the Minister of Public Order, Menios Koutsogiorgas, and his deputy, Thanassis Tsouras, submitted their resignations but Papandreou refused to accept them. 17N reacted to the Kaltezas incident almost immediately with a further escalation of violence. A week after the incident, on 26 November, the group detonated a remote-controlled car bomb against a Greek MAT police bus fatally injuring one of the 22 officers inside and wounding another 14. The attack, the bloodiest on the force for 40 years, shocked the authorities and indicated that 17N was determined not only to raise the level of its tactical sophistication but also to carry out attacks which resulted in mass casualties.[27] The car bomb was to become an operational model for future 17N attacks. From this point on, 17N activity increased in number, frequency and lethality.

Throughout 1986, the Papandreou government fought a two-front war. In addition to the anti-austerity protests and labour walkouts which had become a daily sight, there was also dissent inside PASOK. Several grass-roots activists left the party protesting that such tough austerity measures mainly hit the disadvantaged classes.[28] In April, 17N carried out its tenth political assassination since its Christmas 1975 debut. Leading industrialist Dimitris Angelopoulos, chairman of Halivourgiki Steel company and close friend of the Greek premier, was shot dead in a central Athens street. During the

---

[26] Jean-Luc Steiger, president of France's Air Pilots' Trade Union, described Athens airport as 'the one where arms are passed the most easily'. See *The Guardian*, 25 November 1985.

[27] The bomb was placed in a parked Volkswagen van and was detonated by remote control as the police bus passed by. The area where the attack took place near the Hilton and Caravel hotels was devastated with buildings damaged up to 80 yards away and glass shattered over a larger area. Police said that the casualties could have been much higher but a petrol tanker parked nearby which 17N chose to take no notice of failed to ignite. It was the first time the group used a car bomb. Up to the Momferatos attack it had only used its .45-calibre signature pistol.

[28] *Financial Times*, 4 February 1986; *The Guardian*, 2 April 1986; *Newsweek*, 20 October 1986.

incident, witnesses saw a young man pull a pistol from a travel bag and fire five times before escaping on a motorcycle in the dense morning traffic.[29] Angelopoulos, aged 79, had played a prominent role in Greece's steel industry and Halivourgiki, which he founded in the early 1950s, accounted for 60 per cent of the country's production. 17N said that Angelopoulos was targeted because, like a typical big Greek capitalist, while he deliberately let his state-aided Greek business go bankrupt, he smuggled out massive funds to make investments in the UK.[30] Papandreou cut short an official visit to China and returned to Athens. Pledging that police would find the killers Papandreou named an ex-army general to take charge of the Public Order Ministry, replaced the chief of EYP (National Intelligence Service) and dismissed both the national police chief and his chief of order and security.[31] Soon after, a team of British experts arrived in Athens on a six-month stint to train Greek police officers in anti-terrorism techniques.[32] In the same year, 17N targeted for the first time governmental property. In October, powerful blasts rocked four separate tax-revenue offices around Athens. The bombs were placed at office entrances and were set to go off before dawn.[33] Denouncing the country's taxation apparatus, 17N stressed that the bombings in no way indicated a change in the group's strategy, tactics or type of actions.[34] At the same time, the group issued specific threats against all individuals

---

[29] In the Angelopoulos operation, 17N introduced the use of .38-calibre weapon instead of the .45-calibre signature-weapon used for the all previous assassinations. Source: Angelopoulos File, Ballistic & Graphologic Analysis, DAA/YKA [Criminal Division], Ministry of Public Order, 10 December 1995.

[30] 17N communiqué claiming the attack on Angelopoulos, undated.

[31] Within hours of the assassination, Papandreou gave a press conference in the Greek Embassy in Beijing where he cryptically stated that his government would go to great lengths to bring these executioners-instruments as well as the intelligentsia that ideologically directs them to justice. Papandreou also said to an already astonished group of journalists that 'we in PASOK have supposedly betrayed its ideological principles and 17N tries now through violence to put us back on track'. Source: Alexis Mardas, *Pisso apo ton Ilio: Andreas Papandreou, Oramata kai Efialtes*, [Behind the Sun: Andreas Papandreou, Visions and Nightmares] (Athens: Gnossi, 1995), pp. 315–16.

[32] See *Daily Telegraph*, 26 November 1985.

[33] It was the first time 17N carried out ELA-style simple bombings designed to cause only property damage. In fact, before 17N claimed responsibility for the attack police thought that the explosions were the 'work' of ELA which had actually bombed two government offices only five days before the 17N attack.

[34] 17N communiqué taking credit for the attack on the tax offices, dated 3 October 1986.

(from the Minister of Finance down to inland revenue directors) involved in the organization and operation of such apparatus.[35]

The first major 17N action of 1987 was the deliberate wounding in February of well-known Greek neurosurgeon and owner of the private *Engefalos* Medical Clinic, Zacharias Kapsalakis. Two 17N commandos shot Kapsalakis several times in the stomach and legs outside his clinic in a BR-style kneecapping attack which was clearly designed to only wound him.[36] 17N chose Kapsalakis because, in their eyes, he was one of the leading big-doctors[37] responsible for 'the degradation of the country's national health services'.[38] In March, Greece and Turkey came to the brink of war over oil rights and territorial limits in the Aegean. Papandreou gained considerable national prestige[39] when the Turkish oil research vessel, *Sismik One*, finally decided against exploring in disputed waters and staying within Turkey's own territorial waters. A month later, 17N carried out its fourth attack against a US target. On 24 April, a roadside bomb exploded in front of a military bus en route to the American base at Hellenikon injuring 16 US servicemen and the Greek driver.[40] Although the explosive device was wire, rather than radio, detonated it still illustrated the group's new logistical sophistication. The group began to worry about Papandreou again breaking his electoral pledge to close the American bases when the current agreement expired at the end of

---

35 Ibid.

36 The choice of a .38-calibre handgun, which would do less damage instead of the deadly .45-calibre pistol, clearly indicates that the group had no intention of killing Kapsalakis.

37 In the communiqué, 17N actually uses the Greek term *megalogiatros* – which literally means big-doctor – to mean wealthy, corrupt and exploitative.

38 17N communiqué taking credit for the attack against Kapsalakis, dated 1 February 1987.

39 Faced with the prospect of immediate war with the militarily far superior Turkey, Papandreou did not turn for help, or even moral support to NATO, the EEC or the United States. Instead, Papandreou sent his foreign minister to Sofia for consultations with President Zhivkov of Bulgaria – a Warsaw Pact country and one which, like Greece, has a common border and mutual historical animosity with Turkey. Standing up to the Turks went down very well in Greece and enhanced Papandreou's stature as the defender of the nation. On the *Sismik One* crisis see: *The Independent*, 27 March 1987; *The Times*, 28 March 1987; *The Sunday Times*, 29 March 1989 and *International Herald Tribune*, 30 March 1987.

40 The bus passengers belonged to an artillery unit at Elefsina assigned to guarding US nuclear warheads in Greece.

1988. 17N, in fact, warned that unless the PASOK government closed all American bases and got rid of the nuclear weapons it would continue its campaign of violence against US servicemen stationed in Greece.[41]

In June, the long-awaited diplomatic confrontation between Athens and Washington over the issue of terrorism finally erupted when Robert Keely, the US Ambassador to Athens, confronted Greek Foreign Minister Karolos Papoulias with 'evidence' that the Greek government had made a deal with Abu Nidal which would exempt the country from terrorist activity during the tourist season.[42] A month later, Greek police captured a Red Brigade terrorist, Maurizio Follini, after a tip-off from Interpol. In the same month, on 10 August, a second US military bus was targeted. Like the MAT bus attack in 1985, 17N detonated a car bomb by remote control against a US military bus wounding 11 people. 17N was reacting to Papandreou's two-day official talks in Athens with US under-secretary of state Michael Armacost over the future of the US bases in Greece. Instead of closing the bases down without any discussion, 17N declared, the government had already started negotiations with Washington for an extension of the bases agreement.[43]

In 1988, the group targeted American agents, Turkish diplomats, a leading Greek industrialist and the police. In January, an attempt to assassinate George Carros, head of DEA (Drug Enforcement Agency) in Athens, with a remote-detonated bomb, failed when the 17N commando responsible for detonating the device was frightened away by a security guard.[44] Once again, 17N attacked the Papandreou government for lying to the

[41] 17N communiqué on the military bus attack; In 1987, there were 3,500 US military personnel and their 3,000 dependants at the four American main bases in Greece.
[42] *Financial Times*, 29 June 1987; *The Times*, 29 June 1987; *The Sunday Telegraph*, 5 June 1987 and *International Herald Tribune*, 16 July 1987; Since the Athens airport TWA hijacking in 1985 and the five-week US State Department travel advisory notice that followed, Greece had lost an estimated $700 million over a two-year period.
[43] 17N communiqué taking credit for the attack on the US military bus, dated 5 August 1987.
[44] The attack was carried out on 22 January. The device was placed in Carros' trash bin, some three metres away from the front door of his house. When the attack was aborted, the group notified the police through a phonecall to the *Eleftherotypia* newspaper where they could find and de-activate the device so there would be no innocent casualties.

Greek populace over the US bases issue and revealed that Carros was actually a CIA agent working behind the cover of a narcotics expert.[45] In a communiqué sent to the media a week after the incident, it explained why the operation failed and made clear that the type of device used in the Carros operation would from now on be the preferred mode of attack against targets travelling in bullet-proof/armoured cars.[46] At the end of January, Papandreou met his Turkish counterpart Turgut Özal in Davos, Switzerland, for face-to-face talks in an effort to define 'problem areas' and encourage the development of closer political and economic relations.[47] Although the Davos meeting, the first summit between Turkish and Greek leaders in ten years, marked a dramatic improvement in bi-lateral relations, 17N was outraged that Papandreou[48] was pursuing *rapprochement* with Ankara.

In that year, 17N attacked, for the first time, twice in the same month. On 1 March, 17N in an operation almost identical to the Tsantes attack in 1983 killed Alexandros Athanassiadis-Bodossakis, general director of both Larco, a company involved in mining, and Pyrkal, Greece's largest arms company. Like Angelopoulos who was murdered in 1986, 17N placed Athanassiadis-Bodossakis in the same group of LMAT (lumpen big bourgeois class) who,

---

[45] 17N communiqué on the Carros attempt, dated 15 January 1988.

[46] 'These type of actions', the 17N communiqué said, 'that is, with bombs against the agents of the CIA become necessary from the minute that all of them – the most important ones who like the real bosses lead the Greek police, the Greek armed forces and the Greek security services – circulate with bullet-proof cars. These cars are easily discernible to anybody because of their thick windows. Each person should avoid being exactly next to such cars to the maximum degree possible. Of course, there is always a very small risk, even though we take all possible measures to avoid hitting a third party seriously', dated 22 January 1988.

[47] *Financial Times*, 3 February 1988; *The Guardian*, 4 February 1988 and *The Times*, 5 February 1988.

[48] Since he first came to power in 1981, Papandreou had steadfastly maintained a tough and uncompromising stance towards Turkey, refusing to open a dialogue unless all Turkish troops were withdrawn from Cyprus and the dispute over the Aegean continental shelf was settled through the International Court in the Hague. When Turkish President Özal soon after the *Sismik One* crisis expressed a desire for dialogue Papandreou refused, insisting that he would not deal with a 'militaristic' regime. In Davos, Papandreou effectively abandoned this policy of 'no dialogue' and embraced Ozal's long-standing proposal that Greece and Turkey should seek to ease tension through a gradual rapprochement. See: *The Times* 1 February 1988; *The Guardian*, 2 February 1988 and *The Independent*, 4 April 1988.

according to the group, enriched themselves at the expense of the Greek working-class people. Twenty-two days later, the group placed bombs under four cars used by Turkish diplomats. Two of the four devices went off causing minimal damage and no injuries.[49] 17N timed the attacks to coincide with the arrival of the Turkish Foreign Minister, Mesut Yilmaz,[50] for a three-day official visit to Athens. A communiqué condemned the Davos initiative, the 'fascist Turkish government' and its US backers.[51] At the same time, the group accused the Papandreou government of trying to turn the Turkish military occupation of northern Cyprus into a secondary issue.[52] 17N's hatred of both Turkey and its 'US backers' deepened when Turkish president Turgut Özal came to Athens in mid-June for a three-day summit with Papandreou. Papandreou dubbed the visit as historic but opposition leaders accused him of secret diplomacy. One Athenian newspaper carried the headline: 'Welcome Attila' and groups of Greek-Cypriots erected banners in front of the Greek Parliament (where Özal laid the customary wreath at the tomb of the Unknown Soldier) demanding an end to Turkey's 14-year occupation of northern Cyprus.[53] In the same month, 17N assassinated the US Embassy's military attaché in Athens, Navy Captain William Nordeen. Driving to work in his bullet-proof limousine, Nordeen was hurled 50 feet from the roadside when a car bomb parked on his route exploded by remote control.[54] The operation was conducted with such precision and efficiency that the 17N terrorists had even piled bags of cement against the pavement side of the vehicle to ensure that the full force of the detonation tore into their

---

[49] Two devices were discovered and defused. It was the first time 17N carried out an attack against a Turkish target.

[50] Yilmaz, the first Turkish foreign minister to visit Athens since 1952, had made himself highly unpopular in Athens with a series of hawkish statements on Cyprus. More specifically, he had said that the Cyprus issue was unrelated to the Davos process of Greek-Turkish rapprochement. Yilmaz had also declared that Turkey would not withdraw its troops from the island, and that he intended to visit the self-styled Turkish Cypriot state in northern Cyprus. See: *The Independent* and *Financial Times*, 24 May 1988.

[51] 17N claiming credit for the attack, dated 20 May 1988.

[52] Ibid.

[53] *Financial Times*, 10 June 1988; *The Independent*, 14 June 1988 and *International Herald Tribune*, 16 June 1988.

[54] Knowing that Nordeen's car was armoured, 17N packed the car bomb with significantly more explosives than used in any previous attack.

target.[55] Soon after, an FBI team arrived in Athens to investigate the murder and Washington offered a $500,000 for information leading to a 17N arrest while urging the Papandreou government to accept 'all technical expertise' the US had to offer.[56]

In July, Abu Nidal terrorists attacked the Greek-owned-and-operated cruise ship *City of Poros*, killing nine passengers and wounding nearly 100. When two French passengers were wrongfully implicated in the attack, the Parisian *Le Monde* devoted its front-page editorial to the incompetence of Greek anti-terrorist police and stressed that the whole episode showed that Greece, despite the efforts it had made, remained 'the soft underbelly of Europe'.[57] This incompetence was further exposed in mid-August when an Athens suburban police station was taken over by 17N commandos. Without firing a single bullet, six commandos tied up the police officers, locked them up and after 20 minutes of search, made off with a number of weapons and other police paraphernalia.[58] In a communiqué accompanied by a photograph of the stolen arms under the group's red flag and portraits of Karl Marx and Aris Velouchiotis,[59] 17N said it raided the police station

55 17N communiqué claiming the attack on Nordeen, dated 14 June 1988. Since the communiqué was dated 14 June 1988 and the attack was described in the text as the second of a two-part operation against Turkey [the first part being the bombing of the four diplomatic cars during the Yilmaz visit], it is assumed that the attack on Nordeen, which took place a fortnight later, was planned to coincide with Özal's visit, but was postponed due to either operational difficulties or possible danger of injuring bystanders.

56 *International Herald Tribune*, 13 July 1988 and *Daily Telegraph*, 17 July 1988.

57 See Nathan M. Adams, 'Greece: Sanctuary of International Terrorism', in *Reader's Digest*, (June 1989), p. 199–208, and *International Herald Tribune,* 8 August 1988. In a desperate damage-limitation effort, Greek police had initially named (without consulting the French authorities before making the accusations) two young French tourists as members of the commando team.

58 A 17N terrorist dressed in a policeman's uniform and pretending to hold a suspect, approached the entrance of the Vyron police station and overwhelmed the guard on duty. The two terrorists were then joined by four others wearing masks who entered the station and caught the police staff by surprise and locked them in the station's detention cell. The terrorists left the station with two revolvers, two automatic weapons, six long-barrelled guns, six portable radios, four police officers caps and the station's seals.

59 Velouchiotis' real name was Thanassis Klaras. He was a member of the Greek communist party as well as a journalist for the *Rizospastis* newspaper before earning a reputation as an intrepid hero of the resistance against the Nazi occupation. Klaras assumed the *nom de guerre* Aris Velouchiotis in May 1942, when he took to the mountains as a guerrilla fighter and the leader of ELAS (the Popular Liberation Army).

to gather 'more weapons and material' for its struggle 'against the rotten and corrupt regime of scandals and dependency'.[60]

Meanwhile, the political landscape began to change dramatically. Papandreou fell gravely ill with heart disease and ran the country for six weeks from a London hospital bed. During the same period, media baron and owner of Greece's largest private bank, the Bank of Crete, George Koskotas[61] absconded to America, leaving behind unaccounted-for debts of $230 million and a host of allegations of corrupt dealings with senior ministers of the Papandreou government. Although the government rejected the charges and set up a parliamentary fact-finding committee to look into the case, the Koskotas affair plunged the country into political turmoil.[62] Amidst a political frenzy of accusations and counter-

[60] 17N communiqué claiming the attack on the Vyronas police station, dated 16 August 1988.

[61] The 34-year-old banker, George Koskotas, rose from obscurity to power between 1982–7, during which time he acquired control of the Bank of Crete and set up a press conglomerate comprising six magazines, three daily newspapers and a radio station.

[62] Konstantinos Mitsotakis, the conservative opposition leader, described the Koskotas affair as 'the biggest financial and political scandal Greece had ever known' and added that 'it was certain that ministers and persons close to the Prime Minister were implicated', see: *Financial Times*, 3 November 1988; *The Guardian*, 3 November 1988 and *The Independent*, 4 November 1988. The governing PASOK party was divided between those who believed that the individuals named in the corruption allegations should be asked to step aside, pending the outcome of parliamentary and judicial inquiries; and those who argued that no action should be taken which might in any way be construed as an admission of guilt or responsibility. Papandreou, still recovering from heart surgery and at the centre of an extra-marital scandal, chose the latter course. In a cabinet reshuffle in November, he promoted the two ministers who were alleged to have taken bribes from Koskotas. Agamemnon Koutsogiorgas, the Minister of Justice, was made number two in the cabinet as minister to the Prime Minister, while George Petsos, former Minister of Transport and Communications, became the Minister of Public Order. The move caused several resignations of junior PASOK ministers, and Papandreou was only able to restore order to party ranks by declaring the forthcoming December budget vote to be a matter of confidence. The socialists' credibility was further undermined in March 1989 by an interview with Koskotas in *Time* magazine [which ran a front-cover entitled *The Looting of Greece*] in which the former banker alleged that he had been blackmailed into a scheme to systematically siphon funds from the Bank of Crete in order to finance PASOK. He claimed that public enterprises and industries deposited money with the bank but received only a fraction of the interest due while the balance was diverted to the party. Koskotas further alleged that, when the scheme began to unravel, he had paid Koutsogiorgas $2 million to introduce legislation which would inhibit investigation. Yiannis Matzouranis, the former secretary to the cabinet who had become legal adviser

accusations between government and the entire opposition, 17N intervened by issuing a communiqué-commentary on the crisis. The group castigated the political system for the Bank of Crete scandal which had pulverized the Greek economy.[63] As a hint of the sustained and wide-ranging campaign of violence that would follow, the group also charged the Greek judiciary with 'failing to move against' industrialists involved in financial scandals.[64] At the beginning of 1989, 17N targeted two public prosecutors in the space of eight days. On 10 and 18 January, the group knee-capped prosecutors Costas Androulidakis and Panayiotis Tarasouleas.[65] The shootings had such an impact on the Greek judiciary that two Supreme Court justices resigned shortly after the incident. A fortnight later, the group resumed its bombing campaign against three unoccupied luxurious residences in Kolonaki, Vrilissia and Chalandri belonging to Greek businessmen.[66] Apart from making a social commentary on the

to Koskotas was arrested and admitted to having deposited $2 million in a Swiss bank account. The PASOK government survived an opposition censure motion, but three former ministers abstained and were expelled from the party. Koutsogiorgas was forced to resign the day after the vote, claiming he had been exonerated by the House. Petsos was sacked in a new cabinet reshuffle. Both men were subsequently denied places on the PASOK list of electoral candidates, but the political damage had been done and PASOK was eventually voted out of power. See Robert McDonald, 'Greece's year of political turbulence' in *The World Today* (November 1989) p.195; Stavros Lygeros, *To Paichnidi tis Exoussias* [PowerGames], (Athens: Nea Synora, 1996), pp. 49–59; *Time*, 13 March 1989; *The Times*, 15 March 1989 and *The Guardian*, 16 March 1989.

63 17N communiqué-commentary on the Koskotas scandal, dated 11 November 1988.

64 Ibid.

65 17N accused Androulidakis of proposing the acquittal of the Tsatsos family, former owners of the Aget-Heraklis cement company, and Tarasouleas of the Andreadis family, former owners of a commercial bank and shipyards. Both families were accused of large-scale fraud and malfeasance, similar to the charges against Koskotas. 17N communiqué claiming credit on the kneecappings, dated 22 December 1988; Androulidakis, after being on a critical list for three weeks in a public hospital for treatment, had to have both legs amputated. Androulidakis's wife accused the doctors of negligence and the health minister ordered an official inquiry. On 3 February, 17N sent to *Eleftherotypia* a communiqué criticizing public health service in Greece. 'If proper medical treatment was given to Androulidakis, he would be at home in 4–5 days'. Androulidakis died on 10 February 1989, from complications resulting from his injuries. Like Kapsalakis in 1987, both prosecutors were shot not with the signature weapon .45 but with a .38 handgun.

66 The 17N communiqué, dated 22 February 1989, said that the residences were bombed because 'they were kept deliberately unoccupied by their owners or rented at

question of rents, the group also promised to 'intervene' in the forthcoming June election.

Despite the introduction of new anti-terrorism measures[67] and the astronomical rewards[68] offered by both the Greek and US authorities, 17N kept up a steady pace of attacks. In 1989, a US State Department official declared that while considerable advances against urban terrorist groups had been made throughout Europe, 17N and the IRA continued to give a particular cause for concern.[69] In May, a month before the general election, 17N attacked former Minister of Public Order, George Petsos, because of his alleged involvement in the Bank of Crete scandal and alleged corrupt practices in arms procurement when he was deputy Defence Minister. In a carbon-copy of the 1988 Nordeen operation, a massive bomb in a parked car exploded as Petsos was en route to work, severely damaging his car but only slightly injuring the ex-minister and his bodyguards. The attack on Petsos failed because the terrorists underestimated the speed of Petsos's limousine and thus detonated the bomb a fraction of a second too early before his Mercedes was parallel with it. The blast destroyed two vehicles parked nearby, broke windows, cut electricity and phone lines and shattered trees over a 300-yard radius. In the follow-up communiqué, 17N called on the electorate to boycott the 'farcical parliamentary elections' in June.[70] A week before polling day, 17N brazenly dropped hundreds of leaflets in several Athens suburbs asking voters to cast invalid votes![71]

In September 1989, 17N shot and fatally wounded Pavlos Bakoyiannis, chief parliamentary spokesman of the conservative

---

exorbitant prices' at a time when 'thousands of Greeks are searching for houses at affordable rates'. 'All this happens', 17N went on, 'when corruption is rampant and taxpayers' money is wasted'.

[67] See *Mesimvrini* 28 January 1989; *Kathimerini*, 29 January 1989; *To Vima*, 29 January 1989 and *Acropolis*, 29 January 1989.

[68] 200 million drachma the Greeks and $500,000 the Americans.

[69] The speech was given at a conference on European terrorism in Washington on 22 May 1989 by State Department official Alvin Adams. Cited from Control Risks/Threat Assessment Update, Country: Greece, May 1989.

[70] 17N communiqué claiming responsibility for the attack on Petsos, dated 25 April 1989.

[71] The leaflets were 8 × 12 cm in size and were printed on one side with the offset method, meaning that the group had access to a printing press. The leaflet consisted of the group's five-pointed star with the letters 17N in the centre and also the words 'blank' and 'invalid'.

New Democracy party and son-in-law of its leader, Kostantinos Mitsotakis, who became Prime Minister in April 1990. The attack came two hours before the start of a parliamentary debate to decide whether Andreas Papandreou, and four of his ex-ministers – including Petsos – should stand trial on bribery charges in the Bank of Crete scandal. Bakoyiannis, the first active politician to be targeted, was shot seven times with the group's .45 signature weapon at point-blank range in the chest and stomach, as he entered his office about ten blocks from the Greek Parliament in central Athens. During the incident, eyewitnesses said the three killers walked casually away from the scene of the murder before speeding off in a waiting yellow Fiat.

Apart from horrifying the entire nation, the Bakoyiannis assassination had a terrorizing effect on the country's political establishment. Several leading politicians were immediately placed under 24-hour armed guard. For 17N it was the greatest political propaganda victory to date. The timing of the Bakoyiannis assassination placed the group in the centre of the political debate. Soon after, the Cabinet, in an emergency session, increased the reward for information to 200 million drachma, changed the entire police leadership, announced a new set of counter-terrorism measures and a serious hunt for 17N militants began.[72] While public opinion was still under the shock of the Bakoyiannis incident, 17N sent to *Eleftherotypia* newspaper a 15-page communiqué-response to its media and political critics with regard to the killing. Written in polysyllabic jargon the text attacked the national media while at the same time containing lengthy diatribes against the entire body politic which it dubbed as 'parliamentary social fascism'.[73] The group also said that they originally planned to kill Bakoyiannis some ten days before the actual assassination took place, but cancelled after the attack on Petsos failed.

Since the November 1989 general election again failed to produce a majority government, the three major parties agreed to form another temporary coalition government headed by an 85-year-old former central banker, Xenophon Zolotas, until a new election – the third in ten months – could be held in April 1990. In an attempt to divide public opinion further, 17N said that the

---

[72] *International Herald Tribune* and *The Times*, 28 September 1989.
[73] 17N communiqué, dated 9 October 1989.

worsening parliamentary instability crystallized the political and social ills of the last two decades. Despite police pressure, the tempo of 17N attacks increased and operations became more spectacular. In February 1990, four 17N commandos entered the National War Museum in broad daylight and stole two bazookas. Astonished guards and visitors said that the terrorists calmly left the museum and went to a waiting car.[74] On 5 February, *Epikairotita* published a lengthy 17N communiqué in which the group said, among other things, that it entered a military warehouse near Larissa back in December 1989.[75] Once more, the communiqué was accompanied by photographs of the stolen weapons along with photos of Karl Marx, Che Guevara and the Greek Resistance leader Aris Velouchiotis. On 16 May, 17N launched its first attack against the 35-day-old New Democracy government. Twenty-eight devices went off in the exclusive area of Ekali causing no injuries and minimal property damage. 17N said that the bombings were a protest against all-party hypocrisy on tax

[74] The four 17N commandos entered through the museum's main entrance a few minutes after the doors had been opened. They went directly to the reception area where there were two guards and ordered them at gunpoint to stay put while one commando left a package at the entrance warning that it was a bomb which would activate in case of any movement. One commando remained on the ground floor to keep an eye on the guards while the other three went up to the first floor where the bazookas were exhibited. After neutralizing the guard, they put the bazookas in a sack but just before going back down to the reception area, another guard came out of the elevator. Reacting immediately the three commandos levelled their guns at him and ordered him to sit in an armchair. They went down to the ground level and before making off they said to the guards and visitors that the bomb would go off if they moved. The 'bomb package' left by the 17N commandos at the museum's entrance turned out to be a box filled with paper and pieces of cable. Source: National War Museum File, DAA/YAEEB/Tmima Erevnon, Criminological Services Directorate, Anti-Terrorism Branch, Ministry of Public Order, (13 December 1995).

[75] In the communiqué dated 4 February 1990, 17N provided details of both operations. Referring to the military warehouse operation, 17N said that 'although the storage rooms were guarded our commandos remained undetected. In total we stole a large number [60] of rockets of 2.36 and 3.5 inches, also bullets 0.45, 0.38, and 7.62. Also grenades, explosives and other useful material'. On the War Museum raid, the group said that 'we attacked the museum, neutralised guards and visitors and stole two launchers of bazookas 2.36 and 3.5. The operation took place calmly without any guards or visitors feeling any particular anxiety. Contrary to what has been written, the launchers function properly'. The communiqué ended with 17N stressing the fact that the acquisition of the weapons had considerably expanded the group's arsenal and therefore strengthened its operational capabilities: 'It would go without saying that they [the bazookas] can launch rockets of 2.36 and 3.5 inches identical to those we took from the Larissa warehouse on December 24'.

evasion. The group also said that New Democracy's Thatcherite economic model with its emphasis on competitiveness, privatization of loss-making state companies and public spending cuts meant fresh austerity measures and deepening social inequality.[76] On 10 June, 17N responded to the government's privatization programme ('the policy of selling out Greece', in 17N's words) by firing its first rocket[77] against the offices of multinational Procter & Gamble. The group maintained that the sale of profitable industrial units and public enterprises constituted stealing from the Greek people.[78]

Meanwhile, the Greek authorities, under pressure and increasingly frustrated at the lack of any breakthrough, went to extraordinary lengths in seeking out 17N. An EYP-led 17N was set up in a desperate attempt to wrong-foot the terrorists. The experiment backfired with humiliating consequences for the security apparatus when a very obviously fake communiqué-announcement of 17N's 'break-up due to disagreements' reached *Epikairotita*, which the newspaper initially refused to publish.[79] After a four-month silence, 17N returned to action with a multi-rocket attack against the Greek shipping magnate Vardis Vardinoyiannis who miraculously escaped death. As Vardinoyiannis was en route to work his armour-plated Mercedes was hit by three 2.36 mm rockets. The rockets were concealed inside the boot of a car parked along his route. The first rocket hit the rear of his Mercedes, then went up and over the car, and exploded in an apartment house, injuring one woman. The second rocket glanced off his car and went down the street without exploding and the third got hung up in the launching tube.[80] Responding to the Minister of Public Order,

---

[76] 17N communiqué claiming responsibility, dated 14 May 1990.
[77] Soon after the rocket attack, the then public order minister Ioannis Vassiliadis confirmed that the missile used in the attack was one of those stolen from the Larissa military warehouse and it was fired with the bazooka stolen from the War Museum in December 1989 and February 1990 respectively. See *Eleftherotypia*, 13 June 1990.
[78] 17N claiming credit for the Procter & Gamble rocket attack, dated 10 June 1990.
[79] The newspaper eventually printed the communiqué after it received a second copy which it consented to publish it with reservation.
[80] According to US Department of State intelligence specialist, Andrew Corsun, the rockets did not detonate because the distance between Vardinoyiannis and the car containing the rockets was too close to allow the rockets sufficient time to arm and detonate. Source: Andrew Corsun, 'Group Profile: The Revolutionary Organization 17 November in Greece (1975–91)', in *European Terrorism Today and Tomorrow*, pp.

Yiannis Vassiliadis, who called the 17N attack 'a fiasco which put the lives of 15–20 people at great risk', the group stressed that it postponed the attack on two separate occasions precisely to avoid hurting innocent people.[81]

On 13 December, the Greek Parliament passed a new draconian anti-terrorist law which split Greek society down the middle. Government circles and some leading writers and academics hailed it as the first serious step in countering terrorism, but it was labelled by the opposition and in prominent legal circles as 'an abrogation of the fundamental provisions of the constitution' and 'the beginnings of a police state'.[82] 17N ended 1990 with another rocket attack three days after the introduction of the new legislation, when two missiles smashed through the empty European Community offices across one of Athens' main boulevards, causing extensive damage. Two women who were standing at a nearby bus stop were slightly injured by flying glass. Again the group stressed in the follow-up communiqué that before the attack it warned the police 'to block off the street in front of the offices and halt the traffic both vehicular and pedestrian, to prevent any possible wounding by fragments … The police did absolutely nothing either through incompetence or deliberately so.'[83]

113–14; The 2.36 mm rockets were part of the military equipment stolen from the Larissa military warehouse and the number of 17N commandos seen in the get-away car was four. Indicative of how meticulously planned the whole operation was, police found inside the white Mitsubishi get-away car (stolen a month before the operation) three boxes with fruits and a large quantity of cotton fabrics which did not belong to its owner and probably served to ward off any suspicion. Source: Vardinoyiannis File, Ballistic and Graphological Analysis, DAA/YAEEB/Tmima Erevnon, Criminal Intelligence Directorate, Anti-Terrorism Branch, Ministry of Public Order, No. 727 656.3/172 (17 February 1992).

[81] According to 17N, 'the rocket did not hit any passer-by, exactly as we had foreseen. Furthermore, our action could have taken place last week, but it was cancelled twice, because the first time some truck drivers were holding discussions nearby and the second time there were two passers-by at the car bomb exactly the minute Vardinoyiannis went by'.

[82] See *New York Times*, 21 January 1990.

[83] 17N taking credit for the attack, dated 17 December 1990.

Phase Three: 1991–2000

1991 was packed with violence. Turkey, France, British and American banks, the Greek police and German companies were 17N's main targets in that year. The group no longer acted in accordance with a coherent political strategy. Between 24 January and 8 December, the group, in a barrage of murders, bombings and rocket attacks, struck 16 times. Eleven of the attacks occurred in just 12 days[84] and were made against Western targets involved in the US-led military coalition against Iraq. Although 17N had never joined the Euro-terrorist Anti-Imperialist Front in the 1980s (German RAF, French AD, etc.), the sudden 'international-ization' of its struggle reflected 17N's attempt to mimic other West European terrorist groups by trying to integrate present-day national and international issues into a single revolutionary perspective.

On 24 January, the offices of the French military attaché and Barclays and Citibank offices were bombed in protest against Operation Desert Storm. On 28 January, a bomb shook the Inter-American Insurance Company office and twenty minutes later a rocket hit the Athens branch of American Express causing serious damage but no casualties. Less than 24 hours later, 17N fired a rocket against the main British Petroleum offices. Thousands of extra policemen were called in from other parts of the country for round-the-clock protection of foreign firms and embassies; and military patrols were also introduced around oil refineries, ports and Athens airport. On 11 March, a series of pre-dawn explosions damaged five tourist coaches (requisitioned by the authorities during an Athens public transport strike) in protest against Mitsotakis's privatization plans. Twenty-two hours later, 17N detonated a massive remote-controlled bomb which killed US Air Force Sergeant Ronald Stewart as he entered the apartment build-ing where he lived. Placed behind some bushes nearby, the bomb caused serious damage to buildings and cars in the immediate area. The major theme of the group's communiqué was the Gulf War. 17N blamed the US-led alliance for the extermination of 130,000 Iraqi civilians on the pretext of liberating Kuwait and promised more attacks against US forces on duty in Greece or

---

[84] Between 25 January and 7 February 1991.

holidaying on Greek islands.[85] The Greek government, the US
State Department and private individuals offered a total of $4.6 mil-
lion for information leading to the arrest of a 17N terrorist.

Having lost its central rationale of action, 17N's attacks made
less and less sense. On 31 March, at 10:20 pm, 17N fired a 3.5 inch
rocket at the luxury-class Pentelikon Hotel which on its way hit a
tree and detonated harmlessly in the hotel garden. Attacking such
an exceptionally soft target made anti-terror chiefs believe that
17N was seeking either a major city-centre atrocity or a high-profile assassination.[86] Police also said that, by pure coincidence, the
Education Minister and the chairman of Public Power Corporation were dining in the hotel's French restaurant, popular with
Greek officials, foreign diplomats and wealthy holidaymakers. On
the same night, ELA bombs exploded at two branches of Citibank.
On 25 April, 17N sunk the Karapiperis 6 tugboat at the Perama
pier because of 'strike-breaking manoeuvres' in the Piraeus port!
In May, the group fired rockets at the offices of DEI[87] (Public Power
Company), Siemens,[88] Halyps[89] and Löwenbräu[90] companies. The

[85] *Eleftherotypia*, 14 March 1991.
[86] Confidential Report: *I Ideologiki, Politiki kai Epicheirissiaki Physiognomia tis E.O 17Noemvri* [The Ideological, Political and Operational Physiognomy of R.O 17November], Criminal Intelligence Directorate, Anti-Terrorism Branch, dated May 1995, pp. 21–4.
[87] On 2 May, at 12:35 am, a rocket was fired at the offices of DEI. The rocket exploded inside the offices causing significant damage. A tripod was not used and the rocket was attached to the scaffolding with a wire. The rocket was fired from a building under construction, opposite the DEI offices. The firing system was an automatic ignition system.
[88] On 7 May, two 3.5-inch rockets were fired at the offices of Siemens in Maroussi, eight minutes after a telephone warning to *Eleftherotypia* newspaper. The rockets were fired from two plastic tubes from the roof of a building under construction across the road from the Siemens offices. The rockets hit the ground and first floors of the building. When police responded, they found that the walls of the fourth and fifth floors of the building were spray painted with the 17N logo.
[89] On 16 May, a man called the *Eleftherotypia* switchboard and said: 'This is 17 November, the cement plant will be struck in 13 minutes from now. Their telephone number is 5572109, call them'. There were 26 people working in the plant at the time. Two 3.5-inch rockets placed in an abandoned building 150 yards from the plant were fired. One rocket hit the evacuated building causing minor damage. The second device malfunctioned. Halyps, one of the four major cement companies in the country was controlled by the Bank of Greece until 1990 when it was sold to a subsidiary of the French multinational firm, Ciments Français.
[90] On 31 May, 17N launched two rockets at the Löwenbräu brewery in Atalanti (160 kilometres from Athens), causing a fire but no casualties. The rockets were fired from

German Löwenbräu brewery, in particular, was targeted because of Second World War reparations. An attack communiqué declared that 'verbal condemnation of Nazi crimes by the present German leaders has absolutely no value so long as it is not accompanied by practical condemnation. Not paying war reparations means not acknowledging these crimes'.[91]

Concern over 'the Cyprus issue' was re-stimulated when US President George Bush came to Athens in July 1991 for an official visit. On the eve of Bush's arrival, 17N tried but failed to kill Turkish embassy chargé d'affaires, Deniz Bolukbasi and administrative counsellor, Nilgun Kececi, when a remote-controlled bomb exploded next to their car. In October of the same year, in a follow-up attack, the group did not fail when it shot dead the Turkish embassy's 28-year-old press attaché, Cettin Gorgu. 17N claimed that Gorgu was targeted because he was using his position to promote the interests of Turkish expansionism and to prolong the occupation of northern Cyprus.[92] Soon after, the Greek police came face to face with a 17N commando unit in Sepolia but a combination of amateurism and panic allowed the terrorists to escape in a taxi, leaving behind four wounded policemen.[93] The group ended its 1991 high-level activity with a double rocket attack on a police bus parked outside the PASOK headquarters in central Athens which left one officer dead and seven others injured.

In March 1992, 17N barely eluded a police drag-net. Acting on a tip, a 30-strong EKAM team (police special unit) set up an ambush in Louisa Riankour Street during a 17N 'dry run'[94] but

---

an olive grove some 120 metres away from the brewery. The Löwenbräu attack was the first 17N operation outside the capital.

[91] 17N communiqué claiming responsibility for the Löwenbräu attack, dated 4 June 1991; Over the May 25–6 weekend, the island of Crete hosted a celebration party attended by hundreds of German and allied veterans of the battle, as well as several political figures including German Chancellor Helmut Kohl.

[92] 17N communiqué taking credit for the attack on Gorgu, dated 7 October 1991.

[93] The shoot-out began when a police patrol spotted three men around midnight trying to steal a Toyota mini-van in Sepolia district, a mile away from the centre of Athens. The two police officers left their automatic weapons in the patrol car as they jumped out to arrest the three suspects. But within seconds a fourth commando emerged from a parked car and opened fire with a pistol. Two more patrol cars were quickly on the scene, but were met with a barrage of hand grenades as the four commandos made their getaway in a commandeered taxi.

lost the terrorists in the chase. A week later, in a letter to the media, the group explained how its five-man unit slipped through the fingers of EKAM and claimed that the police officers deliberately gave up the chase when they realized that several weapons were pointed at them from inside the stolen Mitsubishi van.[95] This close call did not affect the group's operational confidence. The next attack in July against the Finance Minister, Yiannis Paleokrassas, in the afternoon rush hour in down-town Athens, confirmed 17N's departure from any rational application of their original objectives. The group's indifference to the risk of inflicting random civilian casualties became apparent when the 3mm rocket glanced off the minister's armour-plated Mercedes and exploded on the pavement killing a 20-year-old university student and injuring five passers-by.[96] The explosion created a one-metre crater and destroyed two vehicles.[97] Initial anti-terrorist police suggestions that a hardline 17N breakaway was behind the attack were quashed when the group claimed full responsibility. The kneecapping of a little-known New Democracy backbencher in December also indicated that 17N's mindset was changing and that the leadership's cool analytical logic had been displaced by a more emotional and nihilistic rationale. Even a 'relaunch' document of new political objectives was released which the group called 'Manifesto 1992'. Security was dramatically stepped up

---

[94] Soon after the Louisa Riankour incident, the group issued a communiqué-commentary (dated 8 May 1992) on the encounter, and said among other things that it frequently carried out 'dry runs' – that is, practising a planned hit.

[95] The Greek police never fully explained why their ambush collapsed. The public order minister, Theodoros Anagnostopoulos, admitted in a press conference that the 'EKAM unit involved in the operation did not do its job well' and the police officer who headed the EKAM squad, US-trained Michalis Mavrouleas, somewhat inevitably, became the scapegoat and was transferred to the remote Aegean island of Samos. 17N said in its post-Louisa Riankour communiqué, that Mavrouleas 'acted calmly and prudently, and drawing on his experience realized that had the police made a move against the 17N van, the five commandos would have sprayed them with bullets'. On the aftermath of the Louisa Riankour Street aftermath see also *Athens News*, 6 May 1992; *Eleftherotypia*, 9 May 1992 and *To Vima*, 10 May 1992.

[96] 'They could have activated the device at some other time and even at some other place but not in the afternoon rush hour in the heart of the city-centre when they knew in advance that there was certain danger of inflicting civilian casualties'. Unattributable interview with a security expert at the US Embassy in Athens, October 1995.

[97] Paleokrassas File, Ballistic and Graphological Analysis, DAA/YAEEB, (No. 2329.F.656.3/172), Ministry of Public Order, dated 30 September 1993.

with high-visibility police presence and authorities publicly accepting that a most militant and fundamentalist faction within 17N was in command of the operations.[98]

In 1993, security authorities expected yet more serious and callous violence, but 17N carried out instead a series of sporadic, low-level bombings against tax offices and vehicles.[99] Communiqués, at the same time, became more bombastic, less jargonistic and made little sense.[100] However, the assassination of the former National Bank of Greece governor, Michalis Vranopoulos, in January 1994, marked a temporary return to more traditional targets. Vranopoulos, when still the governor in 1992, presided over the controversial sale of 70 per cent of the AGET-Heracles state-owned cement company to the Italian Calcestruzzi consortium for 124 billion drachmas ($650 million), a deal which soon became entangled in allegations of bribery and corruption in Greece and Italy. All nine police eyewitnesses described the two gunmen as middle-aged, with dark complexions, in business suits, who after pumping four bullets into the 48-year-old banker sped off on a stolen Honda motorbike.[101] After the attack, the public prosecutor, Christophoros Tzanakakis, investigating the allegations of irregularities in the Heracles deal in Milan, was given special police protection. In a six-and-a-half page communiqué-exposé of corruption in Greek politics, 17N characterized the Heracles sale as 'criminal' and named along with Vranopoulos, the outgoing premier Konstantinos Mitsotakis and his Finance Minister Stephanos Manos as primarily responsible for the disintegration of the Greek cement industry. The group also said that the attack had to be postponed on three different occasions (June, July and September), something which demonstrated

---

[98] 'We deduce from the increasing callousness of the group's operations that a second generation has now taken over' said Minister of Public Order, Theodoros Anagnostopoulos in an interview with the *Sunday Times Magazine*, 10 May 1993.

[99] Throughout 1993, 17N carried out bomb and bazooka attacks against tax offices in Moschato, Haidari, Petroupoli, Peristeri, and Kaminia and firebomb attacks against tax officials' cars in Illisia, Pangrati, Patissia, Aghia Paraskevi and Galatsi. Responsibility for the attacks was claimed in the Vranopoulos communiqué, dated June 1993. The Vranopoulos operation, in fact, took place on 24 January 1994.

[100] *I Ideologiki, Politiki kai Epicheirissiaki Physiognomia tis E.O 17 Noemvri*, pp.4, 14.

[101] Vranopoulos File: Ballistic and Graphological analysis, DAA/YAEEB/Tmima Erevnon, No. 2566.F.656/172, Ministry of Public Order, dated 1 October 1994.

once again 17N's penchant for well-planned and perfectly executed operations.

Meanwhile, Papandreou's emphatic prime ministerial come-
back made little impression on the group. Despite the trade block-
ade on Macedonia, attacks against the ailing Socialist leader and
criticism over Greek foreign policy *vis-à-vis* the EU, Washington
and Ankara continued. This motivated several rocket attacks
against British, Dutch, German, Turkish and American firms.
Throughout 1994, powerful blasts devastated the Athens
branches of Alico, Nationale Nederlanden, Mille and IBM in the
pre-dawn hours causing extensive material damage but no injuries. Although the choice of targets was by now typical, the attacks
nevertheless seemed mechanical and lacked symbolic force. The
abortive missile attack on April 11 against the British aircraft carrier HMS *Ark Royal*[102] under NATO command and temporarily
docked at Piraeus also demonstrated logistical gaps in the
group's operational planning.[103] The media covered the failure
exhaustively and some newspapers even argued that 17N had
become arthritic and was drifting into operational decline.[104] Realizing that the *Ark Royal* failure had placed them at centre-stage in
the media, but for the wrong reasons, a publicity-conscious 17N
turned again to political assassinations to restore its organizational
prestige. On 4 July, Omer Haluk Sipahioglou, a senior Turkish
diplomat, was shot dead in a 17N ambush outside his home as he
got into his car to drive to the embassy.[105] The three-man hit squad
pumped six bullets into Sipahioglou with the familiar .45 calibre
semi-automatic pistol and drove away casually into the heavy
morning traffic. In a ferociously worded four-page communiqué
that was signed '17 November – *Theofilos Georgiadis Commando*',[106]

---

[102] The British carrier had been serving in the Adriatic Sea as part of NATO's operations
in Bosnia.

[103] *Eleftherotypia*, 12 April 1994, *Athens News*, 13 April 1994 and *Kyriakatiki Eleftherotypia*, 30
April 1994.

[104] The Greek press devoted much space to 17N's failure and began questioning the
group's tactical and operational sophistication. Citing security sources, *Eleftherotypia*
(the newspaper to which 17N preferred to send its communiqués) pointed out on 30
April 1994 that the group seemed to be becoming operationally rusty and less daring
since it started using rockets against 'easy and safe targets', that is, attacks against empty
offices of foreign firms, such as IBM and Alico earlier in the year.

[105] *Ta Nea*; *Avgi*; *Apogevmatini*; *Eleftherotypia*; *Ethnos* and *Kathimerini* 5 July 1994.

the group attacked the Ciller government for practising ethnic cleansing against the Kurds and the Greek-Cypriot community in northern Cyprus.[107] Although Ankara handled the incident with moderation, the Turkish press accused Greece of tolerating terrorism. Anti-terrorist detectives believed that Sipahioglou, the fourth Turk to be targeted, had been under 17N surveillance for some time because the group chose to carry out the attack on a day that he was unguarded.[108] Such tactics were also employed for the Bakoyiannis and Vranopoulos attacks in 1989 and 1994 respectively. For the first time since the mid-1980s, Greek police did not release photographs of how the three terrorists might have looked and a new manhunt began. [109]

Between July 1994 and 15 March 1995, the group undertook no acts of terrorism, but several other incidents occurred. Firebombs were planted in banks, public buildings and vehicles. On 19 September 1994, the ELA group, always operating in the shadow of 17N, captured nationwide attention when, in its most audacious, important and tactically sophisticated operation since its emergence in April 1975, it detonated a remote-control device in front of a police bus.[110] The explosion, which came as a shock to

---

[106] Although European groups such as the RAF in Germany and Action Directe in France would almost always name the attack unit after a dead terrorist or a special date, 17N never before dedicated an attack to somebody. Theofilos Georgiadis was a Cypriot human rights activist allegedly assassinated by the MIT Turkish secret service for his pro-Kurdish political activities in March 1994 in Nicosia.

[107] 17N communiqué claiming credit for the attack on Sipahioglou, dated 4 July 1994.

[108] Sipahioglou File, Ballistic and Graphological analysis, DAA/YAEEB, No. 5/112/851, Ministry of Public Order, dated 10 December 1995.

[109] *Athens News*, 6 July 1994 and *Eleftherotypia* 6 July 1994.

[110] ELA is the second most prominent urban guerrilla group operating in Greece. It first emerged in 1975 and is still active on the terrorist scene. Rooted in the anti-junta student protests of the early 1970s, ELA set out, almost from the start, to form an armed, clandestine vanguard to educate and lead the proletariat towards revolution. The group views itself as a part of the international movement and, therefore, counts imperialism/capitalism and fascism in all their various forms as its enemies. As a result, all ELA terrorist attacks have been directed at targets which symbolized one or more of these enemies. Since its initial appearance in April 1975, the group has carried out more than 250 attacks. Before February 1992, all attacks had been non-lethal, low-level bombings aimed at property damage, ranging from US military and business facilities to EU and UN offices, as well as foreign embassies. From 1986 onwards, the group became very critical of successive Greek governments for introducing austerity measures against the working class and thus expanded its campaign to Greek government targets. Organizationally, the

the security services, fatally wounded a senior police officer, injured
ten policemen and three passers-by. In an attack communiqué, in
which the word *kathestos* (present political regime) appeared 52
times, ELA explained that it carried out the attack because of the
socialist government's rejection of its short-lived truce offer back in
November 1993.[111] ELA signed off with a promise of future no-
warning indiscriminate attacks against the Greek police.[112]

> group bears little resemblance to 17N. It is a bigger, multi-levelled organization whose
> hard-core members, according to US intelligence sources, are estimated between 20 and
> 30 and it has a network of sympathizers. Since no group member has ever been arrested,
> little is known about its internal decision-making process. However, as with other
> European leftist groups, operational decisions are most likely to be taken on a collective
> rather than a personal basis. One major difference, however, between 17N and ELA is that
> the latter is a less 'closed' group. Unlike 17N which issues only communiqués, ELA also
> uses an underground publication, namely *Andipliroforissi* (Counter-information) to outline
> its politico-military strategy and to educate its sympathizers. *Andipliroforissi* is distributed
> through some clandestine channels and the state-run Greek mail (EL.TA). Since the first
> issue which came out shortly after the first attack, ELA has published up to 50 more, the
> most recent one being dated May 1990. That issue of 23 closely typed pages entitled
> 'Disinformation, Propaganda, Ideological Agitation' was of particular interest because ELA
> announced its alliance with the Revolutionary Organization 1 May. The most striking fact,
> however, about that issue was ELA's call to sympathizers to strengthen the merger by
> subscribing to the publication. The partnership with 1 May was to have a dramatic effect
> on ELA operational strategy. After almost 18 years of bloodless bombings, the group
> suddenly escalated to lethal attacks. On 26 February 1992, ELA, in a joint operation with 1
> May, detonated a remote-controlled device against a Greek police bus causing serious
> injuries to 18 riot (MAT) policemen. Before February 1992, ELA had never used remote-
> detonated devices, never expanded its tactics beyond low-level bombing and never
> attempted to cause casualties. The most significant sign that ELA might be entering a
> strategic and operational metamorphosis came on 22 November 1993 when the group
> sent to Athens daily newspaper *Eleftherotypia* a communiqué in which it took the 'political
> initiative', making an offer to the newly installed socialist government to suspend its
> campaign against the Greek state until the summer of 1995. In return, the government was
> expected to release within the next 100 days people who were in prison 'because of their
> anti-capitalist and anti-imperialist stand'. Given the government's refusal to enter any
> form of dialogue, the 22 November communiqué signalled that ELA was determined to
> strike at its authority. And after 11 months of intermittent low-level bombings, ELA, on 19
> September 1994, detonated the remote-controlled device which devastated the police bus
> in Perissos. Source: George Kassimeris, 'Greece: Twenty Years of Political Violence', in
> *Terrorism and Political Violence*, Vol. 7, No.2 (Summer 1995), pp. 79–83.

111 ELA communiqué claiming responsibility for the attack on the police bus, dated 16
September 1994.

112 'All police employees are the local representatives of the CIA … and we will strike
against these forces of repression in the future, without warning … regardless of sex or
age'. And since the communiqué was dated four days before the actual attack, it must

Governmental reaction was swift and emphatic. Pushing terrorism to the top of his agenda, Papandreou announced the country's most ambitious campaign since 1974 to tackle the problem. A crack commando force and a specialist think-tank were set up as part of a 6.5 billion drachmas package of counter-terrorism initiatives.[113] The security and intelligence forces were upgraded and co-ordination between the two increased. Public order minister, Stelios Papathemelis, also announced a 500 million drachmas reward for information and revealed to the Greek and foreign press that 3,000 possible targets were given round-the-clock police protection.[114]

Despite massive security activity, 17N attempted a fresh strike. In March 1995, two rockets hit the Mega TV network studios during the channel's 8.30 main evening news bulletin. Although the explosion created a one-metre hole in the wall and destroyed a newsroom, miraculously, no one was killed. Since there were more than 100 people in the studios at the time of the attack a national media outcry followed.[115] Claiming responsibility for the attack on Mega TV, 17N argued that the intent was never to cause mass casualties but its 15-minute-warning to *Eleftherotypia* newspaper was deliberately ignored.[116] The group also said that there was a CIA-FBI-Greek media conspiracy to misrepresent them and specifically attacked the management of *Eleftherotypia* and *To Vima* newspapers. The mortaring of Mega TV confirmed the group's obsessive hunger for publicity and emphasized its clouded strategic thinking. Its once impenetrable Marxist diatribes on crucial social issues were replaced by conspiracy-theorizing and political paranoia.

follow that the group expected casualties from the bombing.

[113] See George Kassimeris, 'Two decades of terrorism in Greece', in *Jane's Intelligence Review*, Vol. 8, No.3 (March 1996), pp. 118–9; see also *Eleftherotypia*, 21 September 1994.

[114] See public order minister, Stelios Papathemelis, in an interview with *The Guardian*, 30 September 1994; see also *Ethnos; Ta Nea; Apogevmatini*, 21 September 1994.

[115] *Eleftherotypia*; *Ta Nea*; *Ethnos*; *Athens News* and *Kathimerini* 16, 17, 18 March 1995.

[116] 17N claimed in the Mega TV attack communiqué (dated 27 March 1995) that it had called *Eleftherotypia* informing them that two bombs were to go off in 15–20 minutes and asked them to contact the TV station so that the building would be evacuated. *Eleftherotypia*, the group argued, being part of a CIA-FBI-Greek press conspiracy against 17N, ignored the warning – a deliberate attempt to provoke casualties and consequently public outrage against them.

One-year-long lulls between one action and another continued. Eleven months after the attack on Mega, 17N marked its 20
years anniversary of violence with an IRA-style mortar attack
against the heavily guarded American Embassy in Athens.
Although the attack was designed to provide high-profile evidence of the group's undiminished penchant for prestige targets,
the operation failed disastrously as the rocket rammed into a security wall and exploded 100 metres from the embassy compound.
The group did not claim responsibility for the attack until May
1997, when it ambushed and killed shipowner Costas Peratikos in
broad daylight in a busy Piraeus street.[117] In its first attack communiqué in over two years, 17N said that Peratikos was targeted
because he was responsible for the 'fraught' privatization of the
Elefsis shipyards, which his shipping group bought in 1992 and
closed three years later with around $17 billion of accumulated
debts. At the same time, 17N began systematically to attack the
new socialist premier, Costas Simitis, for his attempts to normal-
ize relations with Turkey and bring Greece closer to the Euro-
Atlantic community. Simitis outraged 17N in 1996 when, in a
speech in the Greek Parliament, hours after the Imia crisis[118] was
defused, he thanked the US government for their diplomatic
intervention. 17N saw the Imia incident as a disgraceful politico-
military defeat for Greece ('the Greek Waterloo', in the group's
words) and denounced Simitis for his handling of the episode.
The group portrayed the Greek premier as a stooge of the Americans, the EU and the LMAT – 'the best available after

---

[117] The operation did not go according to plan as the three 17N commandos were briefly
stranded. After shooting Peratikos, the commandos walked away from the scene of the
killing towards a Mitsubishi van that was parked there. They had wired the van in such
a way that when the accelerator was stepped on the engine would engage – without
having to use a key. Apparently, the wiring didn't work, so they left the van, walked
down to the main street and hijacked a taxi, pulling out both the passenger and the
driver.

[118] In January 1996, Greece and Turkey almost went to war over the Aegean islet of Imia
and it was only the intervention of US President Clinton and his assistant secretary of
State, Richard Holbrooke, that actually prevented armed conflict between the two
NATO allies. What began as jingoistic flag-waving, first by the mayor of a
neighbouring Greek island and then by Turkish journalists, rapidly deteriorated into
an international crisis with both sides landing troops and warplanes and frigates
shadowing each other off-shore. See *Sunday Telegraph*, 4 February 1996 and *The
Guardian*, 10 February 1996.

Papandreou's resignation'.[119] With the Imia episode still in mind, the group in 1998 bombed three General Motors car dealerships, two McDonald's fast-food outlets and mortared a Citibank branch in central Athens. 17N explained the attacks as a response to 'US and Western nationalist and geopolitical designs' and blamed the Americans for allegedly siding with Turkey in disputes over sovereignty in both the Aegean and Cyprus.[120]

In 1999, the abduction of the Kurdistan Workers' Party (PKK) leader Abdullah Ocalan and the NATO air strikes against Serbia motivated a series of rocket attacks against the PASOK party headquarters in downtown Athens and three branches of American, English and French banks (Chase Manhattan, Midland Bank and the Banque Nationale de Paris) in the space of 35 days.[121] The capture of the Kurdish rebel leader by Turkish agents while supposedly being escorted[122] across Nairobi by Greek diplomats infuriated 17N. A communiqué expressed the group's 'deep regret' and accused the Simitis administration of betrayal for colluding in the rebel Kurd's capture. In May, 17N fired, as a

[119] 17N communiqué claiming responsibility for the Peratikos assassination, in *Eleftherotypia*, 30 May 1997.

[120] Communiqué taking credit for the General Motors, MacDonald's and Citibank attacks, dated 4 October 1998.

[121] The only rocket to explode hit the Chase Manhattan Bank, on the ground floor of the Handris Shipping office building, where it shattered windows and wrecked wall fittings. Police confirmed that all the rockets used were from the same batch of anti-tank rockets stolen from the Sykourio army base in Larissa in the mid–1980s. The age of the missiles could be a contributory factor in their failure to detonate.

[122] The precise details of Ocalan's capture are not clear but what is incontrovertible is that Ocalan was abducted in Nairobi, Kenya, where he had taken shelter in the Greek ambassador's residence for almost two weeks. Ocalan had been on the run ever since Turkish sabre-rattling forced him from his hideout in Syria in October 1998. First he fled to Russia, then to Italy, where he was arrested. Two court cases and two quashed arrest warrants later, he set off for a new refuge chased by the Turkish secret service. With Russia, the Netherlands, Switzerland, and Germany all unwilling to harbour him, he found himself on a plane above Europe with nowhere to land. The Greek authorities allowed him to refuel in Corfu before smuggling him onwards to the Kenyan capital, Nairobi. There, on 16 February, as he drove to the airport, apparently under the impression that he would be travelling to the Netherlands, the Turkish government somehow managed to lay its hands on him. Source: *The Economist*, 20 February 1999. See also Takis Michas, 'How the PKK took an Embassy' in The *Wall Street Journal Europe*, 10 March 1999 and Michael Howard, 'A Kurdish Adventure: Greece & the Ocalan Affair' in *Odyssey* (March–April) 1999.

retaliation against NATO's continuing bombardment of Yugoslavia, a rocket attack on the German ambassador's residence in Athens which hit the roof but failed to detonate. The attack (the fifth in a fortnight)[123] was designed to intensify pressure on a Greek government struggling to balance its obligation as a NATO member with its reluctance to put pressure on Milosevic given the overwhelming opposition of public opinion to NATO's campaign. Police found a bloodstained cap close to the scene of the rocket launching and began searching hospitals and doctors' surgeries but failed to find evidence of anyone who had been treated for a suspicious injury. However, the discovery of drops of blood inside 17N's getaway car a few days later gave the authorities their first potential lead to the elusive group in two-and-a-half decades.[124]

17N's reaction to NATO's strategy towards the Balkans led to further violence in 2000. On 8 June, the British embassy military attaché in Athens, Brigadier Stephen Saunders, was shot dead in an ambush as he drove to work. In heavy morning rush-hour traffic, two 17N commandos wearing crash helmets and riding a powerful Enduro motorbike drove up to the passenger side of the British diplomat's near-stationary car. Before Brigadier Saunders could react, the man riding pillion opened fire with 17N's trademark .45 calibre revolver, firing at least four bullets into his head and chest from a range of three feet. Witnesses said that as the terrorists drove away at high speed weaving their way through the traffic, Saunders stumbled out of the car door calling for help, only to collapse in a pool of blood and glass fragments. Timed to coincide with the first anniversary of NATO's operations in Kosovo, the attack was intended as a reminder that 17N remained lethal. Both site and method were selected by the group to provide evidence of its undiminished capacity to mount high-profile military operations. Saunders, who had been based in Athens for nearly two years, was ambushed at almost exactly the same point – the highway intersection in Kifissias Avenue where commuter traffic invariably grinds to a halt – at which 17N had killed twice already. The motorcycle

---

[123] Few days before the attack on the German ambassador's residence, on 8 May, 17N also detonated a bomb outside the Dutch embassy.

[124] Greek Police announced that blood analysis indicated that only one 17N commando was injured and that the terrorists' DNA information will be used for comparison with that of future suspects. See *To Vima*, 18 May, 6 June and 14 August 1999 and *Athens News*, 18 May and 19 September 1999.

team took exactly the same escape route into a nearby suburb as in the Tsantes and Athanassiadis-Bodosakis operations. Under heavy international pressure to be seen to be doing something, the Greek government doubled its reward to 1 billion drachmas (£1.75m, $2.9m) for information on the assassination and promised to make more intense efforts to end the terrorist attacks, but this time investigators even failed to find the assassins' motorbike which could have provided critical DNA evidence.

Since its emergence in December 1975, 17N tried purposely to cultivate an image of itself as a revolutionary group engaged in a protracted struggle against domestic and foreign enemies of the Greek populace. Openly defying both the Greek and the US security services, the group from 1975 to 2000 carried out 106 attacks and killed 23 people by striking at will against carefully and most heavily protected targets. Although the group has become, mainly due to police ineffectual efforts, almost an accepted part of Greek national life, it never held the country to ransom by terror in the way the Red Brigades did in Italy back in the early 1980s. Soon after the 1974 transition to a multi-party democracy, 17N called the quality of this democracy into question. Stepping forward as the defender of the oppressed and the abused it initially sought, through revenge terrorism, domestic popular support. The group's failure to attract support was largely because their politico-military rationale had little connection with contemporary political and social realities. Although *metapolitefsi* was not a product of a clear and sharp break with the Colonels' regime, it still offered a serious opportunity for the country to develop a viable, long-term national plan. At the same time, the extra-parliamentary left decided that the events of November '73 belonged to a historical moment that had irrevocably passed. Ignoring these facts, 17N continued to fantasize about a return to the radical street politics of 1973. The failure to ignite serious revolutionary activity deepened its avant-gardism and led 17N to proceed in an élitist fashion. With no clear avenue of progress visible and receiving media coverage on an extraordinary scale the group gradually drifted into self-admiring exhibitionism, theatricalities and purposeless violence. The following chapter, which focuses on the ideology of the group, shows how they justified the strategy and direction of their campaign.

5

THE IDEOLOGY AND STRATEGY OF
RO-17 NOVEMBER

This chapter focuses on the ideology of 17N and the strategic approach the group developed throughout the years to achieve its political aims and objectives. The following analysis traces the different phases of ideological change the group went through between 1975 and 2000 and specifies the links between 17N's ideology, the Greek political system and the European neo-Marxist revolutionary tradition. Further, it defines the group's place in Greece's left-wing political culture and explores a number of ideological themes from which 17N drew inspiration and motivation for its terrorist campaign. At the same time, a close examination of the connection between ideology and military strategy reveals the group's intellectual structure and helps to explain why 17N chose and organized certain modes of action to affect its host political environment. Although the group initially had rational political motives and raised important questions, its Marxist-Leninist analysis of political and cultural conditions in post–1974 Greece was ultimately expressed through brutal terroristic violence which deprived 17N of any public endorsement or legitimacy.

17N's main aim was to change the pattern of Greek society and move it towards a revolutionary situation. Like the Red Army Faction in Germany, Action Directe in France and the Red Brigades in Italy, 17N also used the argument that 'if violence constitutes the most efficient and essential instrument without which the revolution cannot succeed, then it is desired, rational and justified'.[1] An examination of more than 55 17N attack communiqués,

---

[1] Raphael Cohen-Almagor, 'Foundations of Violence, Terror and War in the Writings of Marx, Engels and Lenin', in *Terrorism and Political Violence*, Vol. 3, No. 2 (Summer

commentaries and letters to the media shows the organization's constant search for an issue which would serve as the basis for winning public sympathy and support for its strategy. This led to frequent changes and variations in methods, tactics and language.

The texts outline 17N's political positions and purposes and offer a commentary on domestic and international conditions. From the beginning, the group recognized that a well-defined clear strategy and 'proper' justification of its actions served as an indicator of political effectiveness and ideological cohesion. However, although prolific in issuing commentary-communiqués, 17N never produced strategic resolutions to outline its politico-military strategy in the manner of other well known European Marxist-Leninist organizations. The Red Brigades, for example, when active used to issue *Resolutions of the Strategic Directorate* or *Strategic Directives* twice a year providing theoretical guidelines or changes in strategy and tactics to group supporters and sympathizers.[2] In Germany and France, similarly, the RAF used the underground publication *Zusammen kaempfen* for its strategic resolutions and Action Directe the ultra-leftist journal *L'Internationale*.[3] The majority of 17N texts have been long, polemical and self-defensive. At the same time, 17N writers, in their attempt to display intellectual depth and increase the group's respectability, always presented their case in abstract, jargon-ridden Marxist language which often undermined their general point. The enemy was defined in different terms at different chronological periods: *metapolitefsi*, the Greek political world, US imperialism and NATO, Greek plutocracy, the European Union, Turkish expansionism, the Greek police and the national media.

Despite 17N's attempts to legitimate and moralize its actions as both an extension of a historically defined Greek communist tradition and a quest for independence and nationhood, its entire ideological trajectory suggests that it is less of an authentic

---

1991), p. 2.

[2] Yonah Alexander and Dennis Pluchinsky (eds), *Europe's Red Terrorists: The Fighting Communists Organizations* (London: Frank Cass, 1992), pp. 35–40.

[3] Dennis Pluchinsky, 'An Organizational and Operational Analysis of Germany's Red Army Faction', in Yonah Alexander and Dennis A. Pluchinsky (eds), *European Terrorism: Today and Tomorrow* (McLean, VA: Brassey's, 1992); Michael Dartnell, 'France's *Action Directe*: Terrorists in Search of a Revolution', in *Terrorism and Political Violence*, Vol. 2, No. 4, (Winter 1990), pp. 457–88.

revolutionary group and more of a clandestine band of armed radicals with a flair for revolutionary rhetoric and symbolism. Although the early years of *metapolitefsi* were particularly volatile and produced an unusual political situation, no conditions for a guerrilla insurrectionist war ever existed. Moreover, the scale of Papandreou's victory in the 1981 general election shifted the national debate, moving the focus of attention away from the political indecision of the mid-1970s to the construction of a new society and governing culture. 17N never posed a serious threat to the Greek establishment simply because it was neither a guerrilla force nor an effective political movement. Thus, even if a revolutionary situation had arrived, the group would have lacked the organizational strength to exploit it.

17N had hoped that its extreme tactics and early revenge-motivated attacks would attract and radicalize a militant minority willing to engage in urban guerrilla warfare. In their attempts to articulate their goals and strategy, 17N leaders ignored the fact that there was little enthusiasm among the people for the organization's theoretical models of revolution and root-and-branch critique of Greek parliamentary democracy. 17N's refusal to acknowledge this and its belief that ordinary people would eventually be converted to the revolution through an escalation of violence alienated almost every level of Greek society. 17N leaders believed that the group was destined to become a symbol of defiance and play a historic role, but it never really managed to affect Greek political and social structures. This disjunction between 17N's political analysis and actual conditions derived from a large admixture of utopianism, militarism and revolutionary romanticism.

The ideological trajectory of RO-17 November

In the years following *metapolitefsi*, a marginal but vocal and persistent ideological current developed which favoured confrontational anti-regime rhetoric and radical forms of action. As the student movement began to disintegrate, a number of new extra-parliamentary left-wing groups emerged to participate in protest events. Political activists viewed the process of constitutional change and democratic consolidation with deep scepticism. Many of them did not accept the legitimacy of the transfer of power and saw *metapolitefsi* as nothing more than a brief and cynical interlude before a new military intervention.[4] At the same time, the far-left took a stand against Karamanlis and his government's style of political authority. Between 1975 and 1977 protest spread and became more radical as the new regime resisted extra-parliamentary demands for fundamental change in the socio-political structures.[5] During the same period, electoral failure for the far-left effectively cancelled out any likelihood of its recognition and institutional integration into the political mainstream.

Soon after the 1977 general election, small group violence increased. Street clashes between police and youth militants and subsequent police heavy-handed tactics exacerbated extremist attitudes.[6] 17N recognized this and tried to use these protest groups to further radicalize the political situation. Influenced by the *autonomia* movement in Italy,[7] 17N leaders thought that the more radical fringes of the Greek extra-parliamentary left could become 'springboards for revolution'[8] in an explosive situation. Because of its ideological élitism, 17N did not follow the French *Action Directe* in setting up 'a network structure to attract autonomist support',[9] even though it believed that such groups, however peripheral and heterogeneous, could 'through the correct choice of targets and type of action'[10] exercise political influence and strengthen the armed initiative against the regime.

17N used its early attacks to gain sympathy and galvanize left-wing extremists into action. 17N attacks were deliberately

4 'Laiki Etymigoria pano se pseudonymous stochous' [Popular verdict on spurious aims], in *O Politis*, (October 1977, No. 13), pp. 2–4; Angelos Elephantis, 'I Politikes dynameis tis exoussias' [The Political Forces of Power], in *O Politis*, No. 14 (November 1977), pp. 11–16.

5 See Ch. 3.

6 Yiorgos Votsis, *Se Mavro Fonto* [Against the dark background] (Athens: Stochastis, 1983), pp. 23–56, 82–96.

7 See '*Yia tin anaptyxi tou epanastatikou kai laikou kinimatos*', [For the development of the revolutionary and popular movement], 17 November communiqué released in the summer of 1981, undated; For an analysis on the Italian *autotomia* see Federico Orlando, *P 38* (Milano: Editoriale Nuova, 1978), pp. 49–112; Giorgio Bocca, *Il terrorismo Italiano 1970/1978* (Milano: Rizzoli, 1978), pp. 87–98.

8 Michael Y. Dartnell, *Action directe: Ultra-left terrorism in France, 1979–1987* (London: Frank Cass, 1995), pp. 98–9; Edward Moxon-Browne, 'Terrorism in France', in William Gutteridge (ed.), *Contemporary Terrorism* (New York: Fact on File, 1986).

9 Dartnell, p. 98.

10 '*Yia tin anaptyxi tou epanastatikou kai laikou kinimatos*'.

designed to identify the group with the concerns of the Greek masses and to capitalize on public perceptions of US complicity in the emergence of the military dictatorship and the Turkish invasion of Cyprus.[11] After killing Welch, 17N declared that the 'CIA was responsible for and supporting the military junta' and that this was the 'first time in Greece that it paid for its contribution to the events in Cyprus'.[12] 17N writers tried to link American hegemonism to long-standing domestic political problems. Exploiting endemic local prejudice, the Welch communiqué charged that 'US imperialism is the Number One enemy of the people' and held the Americans responsible for 'decades of innumerable humiliations, calamities and crimes'[13] inflicted upon the Greek people:

> wherever you turn your eyes, there is the finger of the CIA that you find behind each event: behind the execution of heroic [communist activist] Beloyiannis, behind the Zurich and London treaties, behind the 1961 election of rigging and violence, behind the apostasy and the overthrow of George Papandreou in 1965, behind the 1967 military coup and the seven-year tyranny and, most recently, behind the betrayal of Cyprus with the resultant rivers of tears, blood, pain and 200,000 refugees and with Kissinger expressing his 'humanitarian concerns'.[14]

Resentment of American power and influence also meant that the group placed strong ideological emphasis on the impact of imperialism on national socio-political structures. 17N argued that American presence on national soil was the root cause of Greece's underdevelopment and was responsible for its perpetuation. It believed that the continuing US presence humiliated Greek

---

[11] See Andrew Corsun 'Group Profile: The Revolutionary Organization 17 November in Greece' in Yonah Alexander & Dennis A. Pluchinsky (eds) *European Terrorism: Today & Tomorrow* (McLean, VA: Brassey's, 1992), pp. 93–8.

[12] 17N communiqué sent to the French daily *Libération* reprinted in Philip Agee and Louis Wolf (eds), *Dirty Work: The CIA in Western Europe* (London: Zed Press, 1978), pp. 95–7; see also 17N commentary-communiqué entitled *Anakoinossi pros ton Typo* (Announcement to the Press), 26 December 1975, reprinted in Yiorgos Karambelias, *To Elliniko Antartiko ton Poleon* [Urban Guerrilla Warfare in Greece, 1974–1985] (Athens: Roptron, 1985), pp. 31–2; In *Anakoinossi pros ton Typo*, 17N attacked the Athenian press for deliberately distorting the truth with regard to the Welch attack. 17N sarcastically said that certain political correspondents were metamorphosed or transformed overnight into crime writers filling in stories about Arab-looking assassins, Turkish provocateurs and foreign secret services.

[13] Welch communiqué, dated December 1975, reprinted in *To Elliniko Antartiko*, p. 29.

[14] Ibid.

people and disfigured all aspects of life in the country. Conveying its rage through the dramatized style of the text 17N declared that

enough is enough. The American imperialists and their domestic agents must understand that the Greek people are not a flock of sheep. They must also understand that this time the people won't swallow their lies, provocations and poisonous propaganda; they have realised that the Americans have tied the government's hands behind its back so it has no independence of action and thus can do absolutely nothing. The main slogan of the 1973 Polytechnic uprising 'out with the Americans' remains today unfulfilled. The Americans are not out and what is worse, the government allows even more to come on national soil: multinational monopolies have moved here from Lebanon and the CIA moved its Middle East headquarters from Beirut to Athens. For the Americans, Greece continues to be a *xefrago ambeli* like it was throughout the dictatorship. A Latin American Banana Republic in the Southern Mediterranean.[15]

Seeking to link political activism, class conflict and the armed struggle, the group released in April 1977 its *'Apantissi sta Kommata kai tis Organosseis'*[16] manifesto. The 28-page-long text presented the group's analysis and interpretation of Greek political circumstances in the late 1970s. As its title indicated, *'Apantissi sta Kommata kai tis Organosseis'* was a polemical response against mainstream political parties, extra-parliamentary organizations of the left and the intelligentsia. The text was also concerned with the prospects and obstacles of democratization in post-junta Greece. The timing of the text's release and its five-part publication in a national newspaper[17] ensured an immediate impact on Greek

---

15 Ibid.
16 17N sent *'Apantissi sta Kommata kai tis Organosseis'* [A Response to Parties and Organizations] to the editor of the Athens daily *Eleftherotypia* with a cover letter stating: 'We are aware that your newspaper barely agrees with our positions but we're sending it to you for two reasons: 1) Yours was the only newspaper that did not try to distort the truth in relation to our actions. 2) your newspaper has been the only one which, in the past, has published a number of texts by the extra-parliamentary left whose positions it doesn't accept either, Last summer, it was the only newspaper that published a text written by the German fighter Rolf Pole. Our text, surely, is long. Yet, it could be published in two or three parts. We have sent this text to your newspaper only. We shall wait one week. In case some pressures prevent you from publishing it, we shall then send it elsewhere. Signature: Revolutionary Organization 17 November, April 1977'.
17 *'Apantissi sta Kommata kai tis Organosseis'* was published by *Eleftherotypia* in five parts, between 27 April and 4 March 1977.

society. 17N offered an analysis of a society that required violence in order to be changed. The group, in fact, saw its violence as a logical and inevitable political consequence of national and constitutional processes. 'Greece's historical experience', 17N explained, 'had very clearly shown that there could be no peaceful transition to socialism'.[18] Further, the group argued that there was nothing in the recent past to indicate otherwise: the 1967 military coup, democratization and *apochountopoiisi* (dejuntification), the new institutional framework of the 1975 Constitution, 'all have incontrovertibly shown that to even mention transition to Socialism via peaceful, parliamentary, democratic means is, for Greece at least, both an idiocy and a dangerous cultivation of legalistic illusions'.[19]

'Apantissi sta Kommata kai tis Organosseis' ferociously attacked all political parties and in particular the communist KKEs. Referring to the killing of former police torturer Evangelos Mallios and the subsequent party political reaction, the group said that it highlighted the wide chasm which existed between ordinary Greek people and their political leaders: 'Although the majority of people approved enthusiastically of our just action, all parties rushed instead to condemn it. This deep gulf between popular base and political power, between the people and the ruling class is nothing new. It is, in fact, the main feature of the present political situation which our action has demonstrated in a crystal-clear way'.[20] The group claimed that both communist KKEs were far more revisionist than their 'revolutionary phraseology'[21] suggested. 17N rejected what it saw as an extreme element of flexibility which the KKEs showed in applying their ideological principles. The text charged that Greek communist parties had become fully reconciled to the political institutions and practices of the post–1974 regime. In this light, 17N argued that both KKEs were continuing the work of the Karamanlis government by effectively sabotaging the dynamics of class struggle:

On 21 April, 1975, thousands of demonstrators stormed the den of American imperialism [US Embassy] to burn it down. Both KKEs gave

18 Ibid., p. 27.
19 Ibid., p. 10.
20 Ibid., p. 1.
21 Ibid., p. 2.

them neither support nor political cover and, what is worse, labelled them as provocateurs. On 24 July, thousands of demonstrators battled against police riot vehicles, guns and tear-gas. The KKEs, again, did nothing to stand behind them and attacked their actions as provocations. On the 25 May general strike, thousands of workers demonstrated against the 330 anti-labour law. And although this was a strike with specific political aims and purposes and it could have gone the workers' way, KKEs political apathy undermined the strike and the workers' struggle as a whole.[22]

In an attempt to discredit the two KKEs further, 17N provided a wider historical perspective which compared them with the KKE of the 1940–4 period. Historically sensitive and anxious to stress certain ideological differences, the group made effective use of wartime history to anathematize today's KKE and prove that the party of that period was an authentic

revolutionary party. It might have made political and military mistakes but it carried out a revolutionary armed struggle for the purpose of winning power, something that could and should have been achieved. Whereas present-day KKE are consciously revisionist and reformist parties which have no aims at seizing power through armed violence.[23]

Looking back to the seven years of military junta, 17N said that KKE resistance against the dictators was non-existent. Condemning the KKE's feeble resistance to the Colonels, the text charged that between the military *coup d'état* of 1967 and July 1974 'not only did they not carry out a single act of resistance but at the same time they continued at every opportunity to denounce all those who did, which explains why Karamanlis legalised them'.[24] The fact, 17N added, that the communist left declined to use violence 'during a phase of open military dictatorship, when popular armed struggle is universally acceptable, *shows in an incontrovertible way that it has no intention to use violence ever*'.[25]

At the same time, 17N attacked the extra-parliamentary left for uncompromising ideological myopia. Commenting on the fact that various extreme-left organizations had been critical towards the group's methods, 17N asserted that distortion came before

[22] Ibid., p. 4.
[23] Ibid., p. 5.
[24] Ibid., p. 6.
[25] Ibid.; this sentence is, in fact, the only one underlined by the 17N writers throughout the 28-page manifesto.

criticism. The main charge was that in making their case against 17N these groups 'attempted no serious criticism on our writings, never treated our acts of guerrilla warfare as such, but went instead straight for the good, old-fashioned recipe of preposterous dogmatism, opinion-twisting and labelling (atomised terrorism, anarchists etc.)'.[26] The group devoted 13 of the 28 pages of *Apantissi sta Kommata kai tis Organosseis* to challenging the extra-parliamentary left's notion of them as utopia-driven militants. The main criticism by the extra-parliamentary left was that 17N-style terrorist violence was counterproductive: it could only provoke stronger state repression and have damaging consequences for the movement. Predictably, 17N dismissed that as 'a classic revisionist argument'[27] and argued that their actions 'shouldn't be seen as isolated acts of violence but as parts of a long-term, multi-faceted revolutionary process'.[28] The group advocated revolutionary violence as a response to right-wing pressure and declining working-class radicalism. A belief in the ability of the organized proletariat to shape history allowed 17N to view violence as legitimate, heroic and politically effective and thus the most vital instrument of social war against bourgeois democracy. At the same time, the group repudiated suggestions of 'atomised terrorism', made in some left-wing quarters, which drew on general '19th-century Leninist theories of terrorism'.[29] The fact, 17N trenchantly declared, that 'they unhesitatingly pulled bits and pieces of Lenin's general views against terrorism together' in an attempt to 'pass 17N activism as terrorism is both indicative and revealing of the politico-ideological disintegration afflicting those self-proclaimed "revolutionary" organizations'.[30]

The text further affirmed that 'present-day Greece is no 1906 Russia' and that 17N aims and practices 'had absolutely nothing to do with Narodniks and 19th-century anarchism'.[31] Moving back to the ground of contemporary political violence, 17N writers denied the accusations of terrorism and sought to show that 'if

---

[26] Ibid., pp. 12–13.

[27] Ibid., p. 13.

[28] Ibid., p. 15.

[29] Ibid., p. 16.

[30] Ibid.; For Lenin's writings on Revolution, the State and 'Left-wing' communism see David McLellan (ed.), *Marxism: Essential Writings* (Oxford: Oxford University Press, 1988), pp. 150–3, 163–77 and 177–84.

[31] '*Apantissi sta Kommata kai tis Organosseis*', p. 18.

anybody, today in Greece, routinely practices terrorism, that is the ruling class together with imperialism seeking to perpetuate the system of working-class exploitation'.[32] The group accepted that it was necessary to analyse 'terrorism', although it had its own definition, namely 'the use of violence deliberately designed to foment greater fear, insecurity and panic in a wider target audience'.[33] Seeking to prove that 'not every use of violence is terrorism'[34] 17N offered particular instances of what it considered as terrorist behaviour: Terrorism, 17N declared

is when tanks and riot vehicles are mobilised against the people. Terrorism is the use of thousands of tear-gas against street demonstrators and by-standers, against men on strike in factories and farmers in rallies, in a deliberate attempt to terrorise the whole population. Terrorism is when fascists in Italy blow up railway stations and public squares. Terrorism is when journalists are beaten and fighters are tortured, not just for information, but in order to break their will and induce terror and despair in others.[35]

In that respect, 17N rhetorically asked whether the killing of 'a terrorist-torturer [Mallios] was terrorism' and who exactly did 'the just execution of the head [Welch] of the criminal and terroristic CIA in Athens terrorize?'[36]

In addition, 17N recognized that 'the fascistic mechanism and its interventionist violence' made the 'long-term development of the popular movement' extremely difficult.[37] The group insisted that the pre–1974 'fascistic state mechanisms' have remained intact:

All the parties of the left agree that there was no catharsis which basically means that the fascistic state mechanisms remain intact …The fascistic state mechanism did not suddenly emerge during the seven-year dictatorship. In fact, it existed well before the military junta. It made open and violent interventions against the people, and organized the then Karamanlist campaign of terrorism which culminated in the assassination of the parliamentarian Lambrakis. In co-operation with the CIA it organized electoral violence and widespread rigging in the election of 1961 in an attempt to keep the Greek Right in power. Again,

32 Ibid., p. 16.
33 Ibid.
34 Ibid.
35 Ibid. p. 17.
36 Ibid.
37 Ibid., p. 9.

in 1965, in co-operation with the CIA and the Palace it toppled the George Papandreou government … and in 1967, again with the CIA's help, had no qualms in staging a military coup which, incidentally, did not take place because of some anti-imperialistic or anti-capitalistic elements in Papandreou's political programme but to prevent him – as he was under immense popular pressure – from going ahead with any modest purges in the armed forces, the security services and the state apparatus which if materialized would then throw the whole system into question.[38]

Confronting such mechanism, the group maintained, was the prime challenge facing the movement today and that 'cannot be done with pleadings and prattles in parliament nor with political confetti and declarations but with the legitimate application of popular militant violence'.[39]

Beyond that, the 'fascistic mechanism' was seen as a vehicle serving American imperialism. As is the case in other capitalist, US-dependent peripheral societies, the group argued, the 'fascistic mechanism has been an essential part of the political supremacy and operation of imperialism in Greece and … the same forces unleashed in the past against the popular movement were bound to be unleashed again in the future'.[40] 17N contended that this phenomenon was evident 'in most western European imperialist metropoles whereby liberal democracies in the early stage of capitalist development had given way – in most cases – to authoritarian democracies which are now moving in the direction of what many have termed "fascism with a human face"'.[41] These charges expressed 17N's conviction that the 'fascistic mechanism' was a permanent feature of Greek political life: 'the most decisive factor of parliamentary political culture which has … dictated everything, from the 1974 election result and the composition of Parliament to what kind of Constitution we have'.[42]

Throughout *'Apantissi sta Kommata kai tis Organosseis'*, 17N remained very critical of Karamanlis. The group, in fact, used Karamanlis to attack the model of parliamentary politics and 'the compliant, politically apathetic culture' which he had created.[43]

[38] Ibid., pp. 7–8.
[39] Ibid.
[40] Ibid.
[41] Ibid.
[42] *Apantissi*, p. 10.
[43] Ibid., p. 9.

17N saw authoritarianism in every action of the Karamanlis government. The Greek premier was portrayed as a bigot, an opportunist and a dangerous despot cut off from daily political reality largely because of his political arrogance. Karamanlis, the group claimed, in his determination to consolidate and perpetuate the regime, used his authority to supersede the normal functioning of a parliamentary democracy. Employing the coercive apparatus of the state, 17N argued implicitly, Karamanlis sought to weaken the political basis of a broad communist alliance and crush working-class challenges to the existing system.[44] Karamanlis was also accused of 'selling Greece's national interests to the US' and turning the country into an American 'lackey'.[45] The group said that the November 1974 electoral slogan '*Karamanlis or the tanks*' had confirmed its fears that Karamanlis had 'sold out'.

In the final section of '*Apantissi sta Kommata kai tis Organosseis*', 17N stressed its determination to foment revolution. At the same time, the group denounced finance capital, the consumer society and parliamentary democracy. Lauding trade-unionism and left-wing political activists for seeking to promote greater social justice through the dominant bourgeois culture, 17N made it clear that socialist reformism and old-style Marxist internationalism were completely discredited. The text charged that the two KKEs and a large section of the self-described 'revolutionary' organizations had no revolutionary part to play. 17N added that such disjunction between armed revolutionary activism and the lack of revolutionary resistance had automatically initiated a 'clearing up process within the popular movement'.[46] Arguing that the essence of a communist revolution was based on a wide-ranging assault on the dominant political culture of the age, the group confidently promised to provide the autonomous groups and the working masses with intellectual leadership. In combative tone, 17N claimed that 'the junta years, the Polytechnic uprising, and the violence and repression of July '75 and May '76 were useful reminders of the imperative need for strategy and organization, if armed struggle were to be sustained and waged more effectively'.[47]

---

[44] Ibid., p. 10.
[45] Ibid.
[46] Ibid., p. 28.
[47] Ibid., pp. 21–2.

Although 17N saw itself as a fomenter of revolution, it still recognized that a lot of ground had to be made up and thus prescribed patience in the present political circumstances. Drawing on ideas associated with French traditions of protest and violence, 17N believed that a new approach was needed which 'had to be created, combining imaginative visions of revolution, rituals of political behaviour and ideological analyses'.[48]

In *'Yia tin anaptyxi tou epanastatikou laikou kinimatos stin Ellada'*[49] which appeared in the summer of 1981, 17N again stressed the need for armed struggle but attempted at the same time to elucidate ambiguities in the relationship between revolutionary organization, the pursuit of political ends and armed intervention in daily life. Reacting to recent abortive attempts at arson in several supermarkets and the destruction of the Minion and Katrantzos department stores in the centre of Athens by firebombs, the text raised the question of whether certain 'acts of popular violence' by extreme-left groups could eventually prove to be politically counterproductive. A highly idiosyncratic essay, *'Yia tin anaptyxi tou epanastatikou laikou kinimatos stin Ellada'* concentrated on three sets of military-ideological themes:

- revolutionary strategy and selection of targets
- political propaganda
- the initiation of armed struggle.

The group tried to explain to the extreme-left groups exactly what violence was meant to achieve politically. Although the group in the Petrou communiqué in 1980 had congratulated ELA and other groups[50] for 'promoting violence at the grassroots level in the five years of "democracy"'[51] through numerous bombings and arsons, it now doubted the political efficacy of such 'easy, risk-free'[52] and 'militarily spontaneous actions'.[53] 17N said that 'violence was necessary for the popular movement to defend itself against the violence of the

[48] Robert Tombs, *France 1814–1914* (London: Longman, 1996), p. 8.
[49] 'For the development of the revolutionary popular movement in Greece'.
[50] Maj. Gen. Pandelis Petrou was deputy commander of MAT (the Athens Riot Police) and former intelligence officer during the military junta; The other groups mentioned in the text were: *Kanaris, Laiki Sispeirossi, LAS, Omada Christos Kassimis,* and *LEA Salonika.*
[51] 17N attack communiqué on Petrou and his driver Stamoulis, undated, in *To Elliniko Antartiko,* p. 68.
[52] *'Yia tin anaptyxi tou epanastatikou laikou kinimatos stin Ellada',* p. 69.
[53] Ibid., p. 80.

regime today and in the future,'[54] but it was not 'a panacea which would resolve every single problem'.[55] In this light, the group saw violence as a 'form of struggle that should never replace other forms nor be confused in any way with them'.[56] The group used the Minion-Katrantzos arsons to argue that military actions of that type were uncoordinated, unsuitable and politically futile. 17N held that the 'use of violence against a capitalistic target did not automatically make it a politically anti-capitalistic action and therefore a revolutionary one, for the simple reason that we are not in a phase of generalised use of armed violence and full-frontal working-class assault against the regime when any kind of blow would weaken the class enemy and aid both the struggle and the revolution'.[57] The group also said that the selection of a target must be as such that 'it spoke for itself . . . one that ordinary people would immediately understand and identify with'.[58] Military actions, 17N added, 'must stem from within the social movement itself and be directed against major, strategically important carriers of anti-popular violence'.[59] 17N used the assassinations of Welch, Mallios and Petrou as prime examples to assert that only such acts of violence reflected public opinion and 'expressed Greek antiamericanism-antiimperialism and popular demands for catharsis'.[60] 17N believed that the groups behind the supermarket and Minion-Katrantzos attacks behaved opportunistically. Although 17N was inclined to view military action in functional terms to a certain degree, it argued that such operations were inappropriate to the attainment of the popular movement's political objectives. 17N insisted that 'the selection of a target must be such that there are no politically or materially negative consequences for the workers and the mass movement'.[61] According to the group, the Minion-Katrantzos firebombings were motivated by a military imperative instead of a politically conscious strategy. If the central purpose of these acts, 17N further argued, 'was to suit the prevailing political circumstances they failed' since the blaze left 600 people

---

[54] Ibid., p. 73.
[55] Ibid., p. 80.
[56] Ibid.
[57] Ibid., p. 87.
[58] Ibid.
[59] Ibid., p. 88.
[60] Ibid.
[61] Ibid.

without a job[62] and 'alienated the popular opinion that they sought to stimulate and reflect'.[63] The text also drew attention to the abortive supermarket arsons and charged that technical shortcomings and neglectful preparation left the image of the revolutionary struggle severely tarnished. Distancing itself from the attacks, 17N diagnosed an 'underestimation of the political and operational difficulties' which proceeded from 'excessive militarism and the absence of a well-developed organizational strategy'.[64]

The final section of *'Yia tin anaptyxi tou epanastatikou kai laikou kinimatos stin Ellada'* concentrated on a probable Socialist victory in the forthcoming 1981 general election. 17N said that in both ideological and political terms, a Panhellenic Socialist Movement (PASOK) electoral triumph would inaugurate a 'crucial and decisive period for the revolutionary forces and the popular movement itself'.[65] At the same time, PASOK's calls for 'national independence, popular sovereignty and democracy in all phases of public life',[66] its anti-Americanism and Third-World Trotskyism[67] appealed to 17N. Although 17N did not believe that a Papandreou government would open a simultaneous struggle on every front, it believed that since PASOK 'is not a social-democratic party managing the affairs of imperialism and the ruling classes'[68] it would attempt to shift the terms of political debate and reorganize the political terrain by changing the balance of political forces in favour of the socialist left and the working-class movement. At the same time, 17N predicted, this would result in PASOK's overthrow. As the group explained, even if PASOK failed to move forward with its pre-election promise of the nationalization of certain sectors of the economy, 'it would still feel obliged to (1) withdraw the country from NATO and deal decisively with the American military bases, (2) clean up the police and military apparatus and (3) take minimal measures against the impunity of big capital'.[69] PASOK, the group

---

[62] See *The Times*, 20 December 1980 and the *Daily Telegraph*, 4 June 1981.

[63] *'Yia tin anaptyxi'*, p. 89.

[64] Ibid., p. 83.

[65] Ibid., p. 91.

[66] Panhellenic Socialist Movement (PASOK), International Relations committee, '3rd of September Declaration' (1974).

[67] See Donald Sassoon, *One Hundred Years of Socialism: The West European Left in the Twentieth Century* (London: I.B. Tauris, 1996), pp. 627–35.

[68] *'Yia tin anaptyxi'*, p. 91.

added, would have no option but to go ahead with this 'minimal package of measures since it is essential and without it, it is pointless discussing socialism and democratisation of the state mechanisms; and also because PASOK will find itself under pressure from a polity thirsty for substantial and radical social change'.[70] In so doing, 17N said, Papandreou, like his father George back in 1964,[71] would only be threatening privileges which the *katestimeno*[72] had always considered automatic and 'strategically important'[73] and thus his government would also be brought down. Given these political realities, 17N concluded that the challenge confronting the revolutionary movement was how best to 'combat complacency in case of a PASOK victory, and at the same time prepare the people politico-ideologically, mobilize them … and organize their potential for popular auto-defence'.[74]

Following PASOK's electoral triumph, 17N did not carry out any acts of terrorism and did not release any kind of document or political commentary for the next two years. The assassination of Tsantes propelled the group into its second phase of violence (1983–90). After the attack, 17N went to some lengths to justify the military action and explain why it had disappeared. The group ridiculed Papandreou's governmental policies as 'right-wing policies' and damned him for 'violating his electoral mandate and burying long and painful years of popular struggles (EAM and the Polytechnic events, etc.) for national independence'.[75] In October 1981, the text charged

at least a 65 per cent majority, for reasons much related to history and the popular movements' past experiences, voted in favour of a platform which may, of course, not have been socialist, but it was undoubtedly and beyond details and verbalistic demagogy, in its basic lines, anti-monopolistic, anti-imperialist and democratic. For this reason our organization, even though it does not believe in the success of this platform, nevertheless respecting the people's mandate for its

[69] Ibid.
[70] Ibid.
[71] On George Papandreou, see Ch. 2.
[72] *katestimeno* = present political regime.
[73] '*Yia tin anaptyxi*', p. 91.
[74] Ibid., p. 93.
[75] 17N communiqué taking credit for the attack on Tsantes and his driver, dated October 1983, reprinted in *To Elliniko Antartiko*, p. 101.

enforcement along parliamentary legitimate guidelines decided to postpone its activities temporarily so that it would not create additional obstacles. Two years later the situation has entirely cleared up. This platform has been tattered.[76]

17N used the attack to denounce Papandreou for renewing the US base agreement permitting the Americans to operate them for another five years and for breaking his 1981 pre-election pledge of taking the country out of both the European Community and NATO. Papandreou's media statements that the renewal agreement was an 'indication that Greece had regained its national sovereignty to a great extent'[77] enraged the group further. The group's savage attack on the PASOK administration rested upon the plain fact that

the anti-imperialist, anti-monopolist, democratic change which the people had voted for, changed into a policy which differs only in details from that of New Democracy ... But where mockery has surpassed every boundary is in the implementation of the anti-imperialist pre-election platform. The breaking of the bonds of dependence, the 'No' to the EC, withdrawal from NATO and kicking out the bases changed to the exact opposite, and to an agreement that the bases stay. Here the first deceit of the violation of the platform is changed into a second one, that is the false promise that the bases are going to leave in five years time.[78]

By 1984, it was clear that 17N was determined to use any operational tools and military tactics to achieve a complete removal of the 'US occupation forces'[79] in Greece. 17N strategy was premised on the prototype guerrilla assumption that a sustained rate of small-scale military operations could generate a degree of coercive psychological pressure disproportionate to their destructive consequences. Having studied recent conflicts in Angola, Central America and Salvador, 17N believed that sustained guerrilla campaigns had succeeded in altering perceptions in the Western metropolitan centres of imperialism. It became convinced that a constant level of military activity would eventually lead to 'the complete paralysis of the US occupation forces' in Greece.[80] Following the basic mechanisms of the Provisional IRA strategy in Northern

[76] Ibid..
[77] *The Times,* 16 July 1983.
[78] Tsantes communiqué, pp. 96–7.
[79] Ibid., p. 98.
[80] Ibid., pp. 98–9.

Ireland and the RAF in Germany, 17N attempted 'to use its limited resources to wage a war of psychological attrition'[81] against Americans stationed in Greece. Taken together the Tsantes and Judd[82] communiqués defined 17N's political-military orientation in the coming years and set the ground for a systematic campaign of terrorist violence. The core argument of these two communiqués was that of 'imperialist dependence being the main problem of the country'.[83] 17N argued that decades of Western imperialist exploitation and oppression had deformed Greek political life and blocked the country's economic system. Adapting a classic Marxist-Leninist analysis of imperialism, the group pointed out that this 'specific model of economic development imposed by the American-led western imperialist *katestimeno* (establishment)' had durable consequences for the development of both social relations and the productive forces in the country.[84] At the same time, 17N placed particular emphasis on PASOK's ideological betrayal and its retreat from traditional socialist objectives. Reaching the conclusion that Papandreou was happy to manage the system rather than transform it, the group said that it made his government look nothing less than 'a committee managing the affairs of the lumpen big bourgeois class and imperialism'.[85]

17N also used high-profile assassinations to connect traditional institutions (i.e. the Greek press) and establishment operational codes to American hegemony in Greece. After killing Momferatos, the group claimed that the CIA in its attempt to condition domestic affairs and control information used

a fascist, a junta minister, who instead of being in jail because as a minister he is jointly responsible for the junta's crimes, is so brazen that he wants to guide the people. In addition to this newspaper, Momferatos, with the power he has as a chairman of the Association of

---

[81] See M.L.R. Smith, *Fighting for Ireland? The Military Strategy of the Irish Republican Army* (London: Routledge, 1995), p. 97; D.A. Pluchinsky, 'An Organizational and Operational Analysis of Germany's Red Army Faction Terrorist Group (1972–1991)', in Yonah Alexander & D. A. Pluchinsky (eds), *European Terrorism: Today and Tomorrow* (McLean, V A: Brassey's 1992). pp. 43–93.

[82] US Army Master Sergeant Robert Judd also a JUSMAGG officer was attacked by 17N commandos almost five months later than Tsantes on April 1984.

[83] Judd attack communiqué (dated April 1984), reprinted in *To Elliniko Antartiko*, p. 102.

[84] Ibid., p. 103.

[85] lumpen big bourgeois class = the Greek oligarchy.

Athens Newspapers Publishers, passes on various foreign confidential and secret publications of Western imperialism to other newspaper owners. Thus, he shows the line to be followed by the rest of the press on all fundamental issues …[86]

Although in the communiqué the group did not deal with the 1974 political changeover at length, it still made clear its disgust with the transition and hoped that the Momferatos attack would show how Karamanlis's *metapolitefsi* 'had metamorphosed a fascist-junta man into a democrat' and also 'how this kind of metamorphosis had taken place in all key sectors: the army, police, judiciary, civil service and the press'.[87]

At the same time, polemical attacks on the PASOK government continued unabated. 17N charged that in spite of their messianic rhetoric the Socialists in office had come to emulate New Democracy governmental ethics and practices. For the group, the shift from 'Karamanlist democracy to Papandreou-ite socialism'[88] over the past three years had conclusively

proved not only that reformism is condemned but also that its practice invariably converts naive, well-intentioned armchair socialists, in the eyes of the people, into vulgar politicos who in parliament have sold out all their principles and contracts with the people [Papandreou's pre-election campaign slogan]; have colluded with the people's enemies, the Americans and the Western imperialists; have signed the agreement on the retention of the bases; have concluded the deal of the century [the purchase of 80 fighter planes]; have remained in the EEC; and by refusing to open the Cyprus dossier have effectively sold out the Cyprus issue altogether.[89]

In this context, 17N raised another issue: the relation of the Greek state and security authorities to the US intelligence agencies and, in particular, to the CIA. Focusing on recent events, the group said that it was difficult to avoid the impression that the police 'are tools of US imperialism … acting under CIA orders'.[90] More specifically, 17N denounced the Papandreou administration for allowing

---

[86] Momferatos attack communiqué reprinted in *Europe's Red Terrorists*, p. 96.
[87] Ibid., p. 97; Momferatos had served as minister of industry in the short-lived Markezinis civilian government during the dictatorship.
[88] Tsantes communiqué reprinted in *To Elliniko Antartiko,* p. 101.
[89] Momferatos attack communiqué, pp. 97–8.
[90] Ibid., p. 95.

groups of CIA killer-agents with previous criminal service in Vietnam and El Salvador to roam Athens in armoured cars bearing Greek license plates in search of the 17 November organization. They were thereby allowed to supplant the Greek police, to act without control, to search homes, and to make arrests, such as that of last March involving a purported Arab terrorist, and not only without first notifying Greek authorities, but with the assistance of Greek central intelligence agents and police under their orders, as if Greece were simply a US colony. This was a total violation of state authority on Greek soil, an absolute humiliation and a case of complete servility. Is this our national independence, and how does this reflect the [Pasokite] slogan 'out with the Americans'? [91]

At the same time, 17N attacked a MAT police bus to display an allegedly 'dynamic reaction' and 'a militant response to police violence'.[92] The group justified the car-bomb attack by explaining that 'the violence of the regime, the MAT in this case, cannot be met with an ideological fight but with a popular violence instead'.[93] According to 17N, the MAT 'plays the same role played by the torturers during the dictatorship, by intimidating a broad strata of people with the fiercest and most ruthless form of open terrorism'.[94] Police brutality, it added, showed 'the tragic reality of contemporary Greek society' and unmasked 'its political and social anaesthetisation'.[95] Drawing a parallel with Pinochet's dictatorial regime in Chile and the South African apartheid state, 17N claimed that 'murders like that of a 15-year-old schoolboy', Michalis Kaltezas, were not accidental but reflected instead a deepening ideological process of 'social fascistization' which the Socialists inspired, instrumentalized and for which they were 'directly responsible'.[96] The group bitterly damned the 'PASOK government and Papandreou' for preserving and perpetuating 'a purely fascistic system of police methods and practices'.[97] The communiqué affirmed that 17N saw itself as the only credible

---

[91] Ibid.
[92] 17N communiqué taking credit for the attack on the police bus, dated 26 November 1985.
[93] Ibid.
[94] 17N attack communiqué claiming responsibility for the 16 January 1980 assassination of MAT chief Petrou, undated.
[95] 17N attack communiqué, dated 26 November 1985, on police bus.
[96] Ibid.
[97] Ibid.

instrument of popular mobilization and resistance against state brutality. The group said that the Greek state not only failed to protect its citizens from police forces with paramilitary tendencies but 'it orders them to shoot at innocent children …'.[98]

Convinced that PASOK was 'now working for the Right, which explains why it has yet to be overthrown'[99] and having realized that Greek society was incapable of fighting PASOK-sponsored fascistization, 17N took the view that there was no alternative but to widen the struggle through a maximum coercive pressure on the Greek government.[100] The group saw the Kaltetzas incident as an opportunity to generate armed struggle propaganda and gain public sympathy. By using 'in the name of the people' military effort 'to respond, punish and retaliate against organized state violence', 17N hoped to establish a dialogue with the community and justify its existence as 'the military extension of the movement'.[101] Beyond this, the attack signalled a change in the group's strategic emphasis and this was reflected in both the pattern of its military activity and its choice of targets. Trying to function with 'the rationale of a political party', 17N began to take a single-issue approach in an attempt to exert direct influence on Greek political life.[102]

17N's determination to 'participate' in the political process culminated in the assassination of industrialist, Dimitris Angelopoulos[103] and bombings of government offices[104] within the same year. 17N attacks were intended to highlight the severity of Greece's accumulated economic and social problems arising from a conflict of interests between 'dominant groups and exploited classes' within society.[105] In a text which read more like an academic

---

[98] Ibid.

[99] Ibid.

[100] Confidential Report: *I Ideologiki, Politiki kai Epicheirissiaki Fysiognomia tis E.O. 17 Noemvri* [The Ideological, Political and Operational Physiognomy of R.O. 17 November] Criminal Intelligence Directorate, Anti-terrorism Branch, Athens, dated May 1995, pp. 11–12.

[101] 'I nea phassi tis 17 Noemvri' [The new phase of 17 November], in *Anti*, No. 305 (1985), p. 24.

[102] 'I periptossi tis 17 Noemvri' [The case of 17 November], in *Anti*, No. 282 (1985), p. 8.

[103] Angelopoulos, aged 79, a Greek steel magnate was shot and killed by a lone gunman in a central Athens street on his way to work on 8 April 1986.

[104] Four separate tax revenue offices around Athens were bombed on 5 October 1986.

[105] Angelopoulos attack communiqué, undated.

monograph than a communiqué, the group made an attempt to develop and give substance to the view that the deep polarizations, running from top to bottom of Greece's inequality-riven society, were the product of systemic economic causes. 17N added that unless these causes were addressed, a diminution of wealth and income inequalities could never be achieved. The group devoted several pages to explaining how the country's plutocrats, the LMAT or 'lumpen big bourgeois class', used their ailing companies to enrich themselves at the expense of working-class people. Although these companies, 17N argued, faced massive financial difficulties, their chairmen, like Angelopoulos, diverted enormous sums of state subsidies, intended for restructuring and modernization, into bank accounts abroad. It added that billions of drachma of state money which found their way into Swiss and Luxembourg banks were used on foreign investment and a luxurious lifestyle – all at the expense of working-class lives lost in industrial accidents.[106] 17N defined LMAT as '100 families attached onto the country's flesh like leeches, sucking its labour and preventing any autonomous development if that ran against their interests'.[107] Referring contemptuously to Papandreou as the 'champion of big capitalism', the group again repeated its claim that PASOK, having capitulated to the demands of big business and Western imperialism, 'betrayed the bloody struggles of three generations'.[108] Because of LMAT's relentless exploitation, the text concluded that the country was 'heading with mathematical precision towards economic bankruptcy and catastrophe'.[109] The assassination of Angelopoulos was undertaken to halt Greece's economic downward slide and prevent the crisis from becoming more acute. By attacking 'one of the main representatives of LMAT', 17N believed it attacked 'deceit, self-interest, scandalous privileges of tax exemptions, capitalist exploitation and corporate greed' which were the root causes for the country's economic decline, de-industrialization, total stagnation and miserable working-class living standards.[110]

---

[106] Ibid.
[107] Ibid.
[108] Ibid.
[109] Ibid.; on Greece's financial problems and runaway deficits (from $1.8 billion in 1984 to $2.8 billion in 1985 and to $3.2 at the end of 1986) see *Financial Times*, 20 March 1986 and *International Herald Tribune*, 13 May 1986.
[110] Angelopoulos communiqué.

Combating LMAT-led capitalist exploitation also motivated further bomb attacks against tax revenue offices. 17N described the country's taxation system as 'a mechanism of robbing the people's income'.[111] At the same time, the state itself was seen as the key agency for undermining the notion of public morality. Exploring the connections between the state, big business and the current malaise, endowed 17N with a strong sense of conviction in the correctness of its motives and intentions. The group charged that this depressing state of affairs should not surprise anyone given the fact that 'the swindler-state' used taxation to 'steal from the working people to give to the sharks of LMAT and international imperialism'.[112] Determined to talk directly to the working class, 17N used the bombings as a device to bring to wider attention what it saw as a blatant provocation. The group believed that Greek society should no longer tolerate tax evasion on the existing massive scale. To make the point clearer still, 17N said that more than '450 billion drachma in tax revenues flew abroad each year' and that was having a disastrous effect on the population's living standards as it undermined 'the provision of essential public services such as education, health, welfare, infrastructure, and national security'.[113]

National health care, in particular, was a 17N central concern and the group held that Greece's health system was a disgrace. Public expenditure on health was extremely low and the quality of services dismal. 17N described PASOK's ESY (National Health Service) as a serious disappointment. Despite all the rhetoric about fundamental health reform, the group argued, PASOK had failed to equalize the distribution of health care in Greek society. The Kapsalakis communiqué painted a picture of management ineptitude, collapsing hospitals, administrative chaos and dehumanization. The group contended that an extreme lack of public-spirited ethos and humanity in the medical profession bedevilled the ESY. According to 17N, health professionals and managers were primarily responsible for the poor quality of care and shambolic services. Instead of delivering decent health care to patients, 17N declared, doctors ruthlessly exploited them. Disinterested in

---

[111] Tax offices attack communiqué, dated 3 October 1986.
[112] Ibid.
[113] Ibid.

the public's health, it added, the medical profession in Greece sought only status and money. To further this point, 17N claimed that although national health service insurance covered virtually the entire population, a patient wanting to be cured and treated with respect in 'a dingy Greek hospital would still need up to ten brown envelopes to take care of the whole medical staff ranging from the surgeon, the consultant, the anaesthesiologist and their assistants to the nurses and the hospital porter'.[114] Under these circumstances, 17N concluded that the position of the economically insecure Greek breadwinner with a serious health problem was tragic:

He is a powerless and weak victim of a cruel blackmail done to him by the coalition of the swindler state and the big doctors, smugglers of people's health. He is forced to 'select' between 4 possibilities: one worse than the other: either to go to the public hospital with a brown envelope or take the risk of not being cured, or to face the spectre of his financial destruction by paying huge sums which surpass a million to the monopoly of big doctors, or to pay even more by going to a hospital abroad.[115]

Throughout, 17N believed the US was behind 'expansionist Turkish militarism'. The group used episodes such as the Sismik-I crisis[116] to substantiate its claim that Washington was, among other things, deliberately instigating Turkey's expansionist designs in the Aegean and in Cyprus in order to increase Greek reliance on US military protection. In the *'The Prime Terrorist of the People is US Imperialism – Americans are the Murderers of the People'*, the group linked US manipulation to the Cyprus conflict and the anti-colonialist struggles of the 1950s and showed how the United States encouraged and exploited the growth of ethnic tension between the island's Greeks and Turks.[117]

---

[114] Kapsalakis attack communiqué, dated 1 February 1987.

[115] Ibid.

[116] A clash of the two countries' warships was avoided when, after 48 hours of frantic NATO diplomatic mediation and the personal intervention of the NATO secretary-general Lord Carrington, the Turkish premier Özal declared that the research vessel, Sismik-I (involved in a similar crisis back in the summer of 1976) would operate only in Turkish territorial seas, in return for assurances from Greece that it had halted its own exploration in disputed waters. This long-running dispute revolves around more than 500 Greek islands in the Aegean near the Turkish coast, where part of the area is rich in oil and territorial claims overlap.

[117] In his updated book on the Cyprus conflict and the influence of the outside powers,

History teaches us that 'Divide and Conquer' is imperialism's permanent strategy ... This strategy has created the present tragic situation in Cyprus against the backdrop of the last three decades ... Having as its permanent goal not only the perpetuation of its military presence on the island, given Cyprus's geographical position, but also the island's subsequent transformation into the main advance outpost of its terrorist forces in the Middle East, imperialism successfully played the Turkish card. By allying itself closely with the Turkish fascist militarists and significant portions of the Greek upper bourgeois class ... it transformed what was in the 1950s a completely secondary problem, that is, a Turkish 18% interspersed proportionately among all the villages of the island and with no serious co-existence problems with the Greek community, into a major problem.[118]

By converting, the group further explained, 'a politically limited' anti-colonialist and anti-imperialist struggle into 'a supposedly eternal' Greco-Turkish conflict, in which the US had assumed ever since then 'the role of the purportedly neutral arbitrator', American imperialism managed to fulfil all the goals it set back in the 1950s, namely establishing military bases in Turkish-occupied northern Cyprus.[119] 'The same story', it added, 'is now being repeated in the Aegean'.[120] In the final section of '*The Prime Terrorist of the People is US Imperialism – Americans are the Murderers of the People*', 17N cited recent US military activity in Grenada, Nicaragua and Libya to attack the Greek media, asking why it came to regard the group as 'ruthless terrorists' when Americans in Tripoli bombed 'hospitals and houses ... killing and wounding old people, children and non-combatants'.[121] The text charged that such 'murderous, Nazi-type mass attacks against the innocent people of a sovereign state clearly and indisputably proves that the chief terrorist mass murderer of people is US imperialism' and stressed that the struggle against it was both in a Greek and

---

Hostage to History: Cyprus from the Ottomans to Kissinger (London: Verso, 1997), Christopher Hitchens gives more or less the same version. Although he does not deny that ethnic tensions between the Greek majority and the island's Turks existed, Hitchens shows how they were heightened and exploited, first, by the British and then the United States.

118 *The Prime Terrorist of the People is US Imperialism – Americans are the Murderers of the People* communiqué, backdated 9 April 1987.

119 Ibid.

120 Ibid.

121 Ibid.

international context, 'the most important issue and imperative of our day'.[122] 17N added that the struggle against US imperialism was also 'a struggle against military arms, nuclear weapons, SDI, and Third World hunger and exploitation'.[123]

Opposition to US imperialism and the impending Greek-American talks over the extension of the US military bases accord in Greece increased 17N attacks on US and Turkish targets.[124] The 17N leadership assumed that a consistent level of military activity against US targets could have a direct pressurizing effect on administrations in Washington and Athens. Declaring that Greek national sovereignty was non-negotiable 17N warned that it 'would not allow any Papandreou to sell it off'.[125] Until the Papandreou government closed all American bases, removed the 164 nuclear warheads and took the country out of NATO, 17N was determined to continue its battle at all costs against 'the murdering American imperialists' stationed on Greek soil.[126] 17N's single-minded determination was dramatically illustrated with the well-planned and masterfully executed[127] assassination of William Nordeen. In the 17N's leadership's view, Nordeen was 'a high-ranking official of US imperialism's military forces' in Greece and such individuals were 'principally responsible for the Turkish invasion in 1974 and the continuing occupation of Cypriot territory, as well as the escalation of Turkish claims against our country in the Aegean, our airspace, and the continental shelf'.[128] The attack on Nordeen, the fourth against a US target in the space of less than 14 months, was intended to outrage Washington and strain relations between Greece and America.[129]

122 Ibid.
123 Ibid.
124 24 April 1987: US military bus I; 10 August 1987: US military bus II ; 21 January 1988: failed assassination attempt against George Carros, head of DEA (Drug Enforcement Agency); 23 May 1988: Bombs were placed under four cars used by Turkish diplomats; and on 28 June 1988: a road-side bomb killed the US embassy attaché in Athens, Navy Captain William Nordeen.
125 US military bus I attack communiqué, dated 5 August 1987.
126 Attack communiqués on US military buses, dated 11 April and 5 August 1987 respectively.
127 On 17N's increasing operational sophistication see US State Department profile of the group, Office of the Secretary of State Coordinator for Counter-Terrorism, (July 6, 1989), p. 3.
128 Nordeen attack communiqué, dated 14 June 1988.
129 See Ch. 4.

At the same time, the Greek armed forces came under scathing criticism. Castigating the Greek army for 'no longer being a national army but a NATOite one instead', 17N urged the military establishment to do its duty and 'give a dynamic, violent' and long-overdue 'answer' to the Turkish foreign policy aggression.[130] Such a policy of dynamic action which successive political and army leaders had been reluctant to undertake for the past 14 years would include the shooting down of Turkish military aircraft violating Greek airspace, sabotage operations and commando warfare in the occupied part of northern Cyprus.[131] Although the group recognized that such hard tactics might lead to a small-scale clash between Greece and Turkey 'lasting maximum two to three days', it confidently asserted that the whole episode would benefit Greece for the following reasons:

- It would create insecurity in the Turkish sector of Cyprus and thus hinder Turkey's effort to consolidate its holding.
- It would keep the Cypriot issue in the limelight internationally.
- It would ease the negotiating position of the Greek-Cypriots.
- It would send a clear message to Turkish expansionism that there was going to be a dynamic answer from Greece to any Turkish aggression.[132]

Following 1988, corruption became the focus of attention for the group. The prosecution of Papandreou and four of his senior ministers on corruption charges related to the multi-billion drachma Bank of Crete embezzlement[133] and illegal phone-tapping only served to confirm the group's belief in deep flaws in Greek democracy. 17N called the Bank of Crete scandal yet 'another example of a corrupt political system that has wreaked havoc on the Greek economy'. Having declared that Greek politicians on all sides had cheating in their bloodstream, 17N also made plain that it particularly detested Papandreou's government for its corruption and misrule. A communiqué directly linked Papandreou and the Socialists with the fugitive banking tycoon, George Koskotas, who controlled the bank.

---

130 Nordeen communiqué, dated 14 June 1988.
131 Ibid.
132 Ibid.
133 35 billion drachma = £135m.

Koskotas, 17N explicitly argued, could never have committed fraud and malfeasance on such a massive scale without PASOK's political support.[134] The Bank of Crete scandal, 17N explained, was symptomatic of 'a society in a political, financial, cultural and moral crisis'.[135] The fact that the scandals implicated large chunks of the state structure in illegality and misuse of government power, meant that 'the rot went too deep for parliamentary manoeuvring to stop it' and thus 'catharsis was unlikely to come from inside the regime'.[136] Greece, 17N argued, was in desperate need of catharsis but 'effective catharsis and corruption-cleansing had to go hand-in-hand with the wholesale change of its political and judicial world'.[137] Denouncing the parliament, the political parties, the courts, the media and the judiciary, 17N reached the conclusion that there was no real alternative to this decaying mess other than revolution.

As a result, 17N targeted two state magistrates and two politicians of each main party for their alleged involvement in the scandal. The aim of 17N's intensive military activity was to keep popular attention focused on the underlying political causes of the crisis and unmask the key figures responsible for the looting of the Bank of Crete. 17N used the Bakoyiannis assassination, in particular, to further destabilize the state, dictate the course of events and send a clear signal to the 'corrupt and rotten establishment'.[138] Bakoyiannis was targeted by 17N because the group believed that

he was one of those who helped Koskotas to take his first steps. We therefore decided to execute the swindler and plunderer of the people's money. This man is guilty not only because he has stolen the first 60 million from the initial Grammi company funds, but also because he has stolen additional hundreds of millions in co-operation with Koskotas from the Bank of Crete in order to increase the capital of Grammi Company [a publishing firm owned by Koskotas and run by Bakoyiannis]. Bakoyiannis was the primary and basic collaborator of Koskotas, therefore, he was his accomplice in the first stages of his career which was crucial for his eventual rise to the summit of the banking and publishing establishment.[139]

---

[134] 17N communiqué-announcement on the Bank of Crete scandal, dated 11 November 1988.
[135] Ibid.
[136] Ibid.
[137] Ibid.
[138] Bakoyiannis communiqué, dated 18 September 1989.
[139] Ibid.

In the same mode, the communiqué attacked the Tzannetakis-led conservative-communist interim government formed to investigate the scandal and pursue the prosecution of Papandreou and his ex-ministers. 17N said that it was under no illusions about what the 'so-called Catharsis Tzannetakis government' stood for: 'a sham coalition conducting a sham investigation'.[140] More specifically, the group saw the Tzannetakis coalition government as a cynical attempt by ND and the communists to 'offer an emotional outlet to the people's wrath and indignation and proceed to elections with the PASOK leadership indicted for trial which will ensure a parliamentary majority for ND'.[141] The group was certain that during the elections 'charges will be dropped and not one of the accused will be punished'.[142] Since it saw the Tzannetakis coalition as a sham and thus incapable of national catharsis, the group sought to carry through its own process of political change and renewal. Entitled 'the Catharsis has now begun' and threatening in tone, the Bakoyiannis communiqué stressed that 'hitting Bakoyiannis alone does not mean that Papandreou, Koutsogiorgas, Petsos, Roumeliotis and Chalikias have now become less responsible for the Koskotas scandal – far from it'.[143]

Raids against an Athens police station, a military warehouse and the National War Museum expanded the group's arsenal considerably and suggested the lengths to which 17N was prepared to go in order to influence everyday political discourse. A solid mixture of ideological absolutism and militant vanguardism which soon degenerated into cold-blooded extremism led the group to assert that its armed struggle was crucial. 17N contended that its 15-year armed struggle 'was the only remaining legitimate and moral struggle against the homicidal and barbaric political regime'.[144] 17N also claimed that 'it had succeeded in putting a brake on the gradual and continual process of marginalisation, stagnation and insolvency which the regime inflicted upon the revolutionary project after 1974, making it again topical, credible ... the rallying point for all revolutionaries'.[145]

---

[140] Ibid.
[141] Ibid.
[142] Ibid.
[143] Ibid.; It must be emphasized that 17N allegations were not substantiated.
[144] 17N communiqué-commentary, dated 9 October 1989.
[145] Ibid.

In the same period, 17N's ideological antipathy towards the new government was fortified by Mitsotakis's near-dogmatic free-market approach. The premier's determination to privatize or close 40 heavily indebted industries under state control infuriated the group. Although these companies had been draining state resources for years,[146] 17N saw New Democracy's economic policy as a sustained assault against the labour force and the public sector. Soon after Mitsotakis's first draconian budget designed to reduce the massive 15 trillion drachma deficit and meet the 1992 European integration requirements, the group began to use its recently acquired military ammunition. After a rocket attack against the Athens offices of multinational Procter & Gamble in June 1990, the group said that it was Mitsotakis's privatization programme which enabled the Americans to make 'such a scandalous sale arrangement and buy up the Greek engineering Koupa company, valued at least 1.3 billion drachma, for a mere 454 million'.[147] The group cited its attack against Procter & Gamble as a warning to other potential buyers of Greek companies. From this point, 17N charged, 'any Greek or foreigner who buys a state company without paying its debts, will be automatically considered to be robbing the Greek people of the amount which is equal to the debts that were donated and, as a consequence, we shall strike without any warning. The Greek people are not going to let their social wealth be sold out'.[148] At the same time 17N said that Mitsotakis's privatization programme ensured that 'new scandals began to pile up and new ambitious Koskotas and Koutsogiorgas

---

[146] Over the past seven years, these unprofitable companies had cost Greek taxpayers about 510 billion drachma just to keep them going.

[147] 17N Procter & Gamble attack communiqué, dated 10 June 1990.

[148] Ibid.; The group makes the same point when discussing the selling of the Greek cement company Chalyps to the French company Ciments Français. Chalyps, the group explained, 'had a debt of 6 billion to the banks and 1.3 billion to DEI, the Greek power company. Of these debts, the French company pays today 1.4 billion to the banks plus 760 million to DEI. Parallel 2.4 billion will be paid in the following scandalous way which is an open mockery of the people. A three-year grace period and payment in seven instalments which are without interest. This unprecedented procedure is not a mockery, only because this capital of the market is being paid from the future profits of Chalyps and not from the French, but also because the sum of 2.4 billion is going to de-inflate with an average yearly inflation of 15 per cent which is equal to 940 million drachma today and not 2.4 billion'. (N.B. Quoted from the Procter & Gamble communiqué despite mathematical ambiguity).

types began to appear ... proceeding to a complete selling out of everything, without keeping even the appearance of honest dealing'.[149] In 17N's opinion, the selling of each nationalized industry was

> a separate scandal in itself. Not just because it is done without any openness, not just because the social property is offered at ridiculous and gratuitous prices to our new owners, but also because each one is accompanied by commissions of hundreds of millions that are collected in Switzerland by the various ministers and bank governors handling the affairs, without giving an account to anyone anywhere.[150]

At an ideological level, 17N believed that New Democracy's conservatism with its neo-liberal, integrationist policy, served the interests of foreign capital and multinationals and aided American global economic hegemony. Having reviewed New Democracy's economic policy stance, the group concluded that the main motivation behind the sale of state assets and industrial relations legislation, presented by the Mitsotakis government as part of a plan to revive and modernize the Greek economy, was an attempted structural rejuvenation of Greek capitalism.

17N held that 'the de-Hellenization and sell-out of the Greek economy', together with 'the generalized attack on working-class lives by LMAT [lumpen big bourgeois capitalists] and the resultant impact on social and political interests', were the central themes of the age.[151] The group insisted that a combination of unbridled capitalist restructuring, fiscal conservatism and continuing EC membership was economically exhausting the country. 17N's determination to sustain a high level of anxiety among the political and business élites culminated in violent attacks essentially designed to strike at the heart of Greece's LMAT. Dedicating a multi-rocket attack against Vardis Vardinoyiannis to the 'Unknown sailor', 17N characterized him as 'a gangster Mafia shipowner who endangered sailors' lives through his ready-to-sink old rotten ships ... and unsafe working conditions'.[152] In seeking to present a close-up business portrait of the family and its methods, the group explained that the Vardinoyiannis brothers,

---

[149] Procter & Gamble communiqué.
[150] Ibid.
[151] Vardinoyiannis attack communiqué, dated 13 November 1990.
[152] Ibid.

Vardis, George and Theodoros, had expanded their empire both in Greece and throughout the world to include transportation, banks, hotels, newspapers, radio stations, oil goods, refineries and football teams. 17N attributed the success of the Vardinoyiannis brothers to their ruthlessness and gangster tactics:

Following closely the brilliant traditional practices of other Greek gangster Mafia shipowners like Onassis, Niarchos, Andreadis and Latsis, the Vardinoyiannis Group amassed in a few years huge financial power, and consequently political power which allows them to influence and control the summits of the real political power in the country.[153]

The next international institution to be targeted was the EC. A double-rocket attack on the European Community offices in Athens in December 1990 allegedly hit the 'EC model of West European parliamentary fascism'.[154] According to 17N, this EC-induced regime 'has been operating for years now in all West European countries with the vanguard being Germany and Italy: two countries whereby classic representative bourgeois democracy had never sunk deep roots in society, unlike Fascism and Nazism which reigned – the former over a 20-year period, the latter for a decade – with broad social consensus and led to the barbarity of war and crimes against humanity'.[155] In Greece, the group said, the project of parliamentary fascism through post-dictatorship parliamentarism was completed in 1990 with the introduction of anti-strike and anti-terrorism bills by the Greek Parliament at the behest of the EC. Seeking to define and reveal 'the primary characteristics' of the parliamentary fascist regime, 17N offered three key examples:

- Systematic brainwashing and manipulation of the people through the mass communications media. Dozens of electronic and other media belonging to, or controlled by powerful financial groups of the ruling class, control and filter the news, manipulate it, shape it and dish it up in a way that serves their own interests and manipulates the masses. Lies, deception and distortion are the order of the day. Behind the pluralism of the media is hidden the most repulsive monolith that turns people

---

[153] Ibid.
[154] EEC offices attack communiqué, dated 17 December 1990.
[155] Ibid.

into cretins and sheep. The right to free information, without which no democracy can survive, was essentially done away with a long time ago.

- Systematic stifling control of the citizen through the police state and especially through the Orwellian-type mass computer dossier. Using computerized individual files, data is gathered on the individual's political, trade union, financial, professional, and personal activities, even his health problems. Unknown to the citizen, this information is stored in both public and private data banks to be used when needed. If a person clashes with the orders of the system or with powerful financial interests of the ruling class, whether it be in the political arena, in the trade union or in the media, this information is hauled out and used to blackmail him, to break his resistance.[156]

Using the new ND labour and anti-terrorism legislation as its final example, 17N declared that 'the outlawing of strike action and the abolition of individual rights and freedoms by the new law 509 was of crucial significance'[157] and had broader moral implications since

the preconditions for jailing a citizen and thus his state of freedom are no different from those under the last phase of the dictatorship in 1972–73. This is what defines a regime as parliamentary fascism rather than authoritarian democracy since any citizen can lose his freedom, can be arrested and imprisoned without any judicial guarantees and, without a lawyer, can be held for days in white cells in total isolation, tortured, subjected to modern psychodrugs, even convicted – practices no different from those of the Junta.[158]

17N declared that a decade of Greek EC membership amounted to nothing. Full commitment to Euro-integration 'did not bring about the much-touted economic convergence nor did EC membership rescue the country from its structural weaknesses'.[159] On the contrary, as the group explained, Greek governments became progressively more unable to exercise sovereignty in the economic sphere and other key policy areas and Greece became a

[156] Ibid.
[157] Ibid.
[158] Ibid.
[159] Ibid.

weaker country than it was before it entered the Community in 1981. The group said that the trajectory of the Greek economy had been downwards ever since. It argued that crude EC competition between the weak and fragile Greek economy and mainstream European member states had a disastrous effect on the country since it led to

- the increase of the trade deficit
- the rapid subjugation of our domestic markets by Community products, where we had a quintupling of community penetration into the primary processing sectors between 1980 and 1987
- a 10 per cent drop of exports in relation to the overall world processed goods exports
- a deterioration of the foreign balance of trade, resulting in continuous borrowing from western banks and the conversion of our country into a country that constantly borrows to pay off interest on the sinking funds, while the much-touted transfer of EC resources constitute nothing but a sugared pill, since they do not even come to 30 per cent of the trade deficit with the rest of the EC member states.[160]

17N also argued that the 2.2 billion ECU (£1.5bn) loan secured by ND gave the Brussels bureaucracy *carte blanche* to undermine national authority and run key state institutions as it pleased. Because of the harsh conditions set by Brussels,[161] 17N was alarmed that systematic surveillance of national economic performance would 'convert the EC into the supervisor of Greece and the Greek people'.[162]

17N opposition to EC financial arrangements and the American-led Operation Desert Storm in the Persian Gulf motivated a wave of attacks on 'European' and 'Atlanticist' targets. Strikes on British and American banks, British Petroleum offices and the

---

[160] Ibid.

[161] The EC agreed to extend the loan to Greece on condition that tough domestic austerity measures were swiftly introduced. To win the loan the Mitsotakis government had undertaken to reduce inflation (from 21.8 per cent to below 10 per cent by 1993) and to reduce drastically its current £10bn public expenditure deficit. Other conditions for the loan included an overhaul of the pension system, sweeping tax reforms and a 10 per cent cut in the civil service payroll. The three-year stabilization programme was intended, somewhat over-ambitiously, to prepare the drachma for entry to the exchange rate mechanism by the end of 1993.

[162] EEC offices attack communiqué.

French military attaché maintained an astonishing momentum and expressed the group's angry reaction against Western military intervention. Describing Operation Desert Storm 'a terrorist campaign', 17N declared that 'in the face of such barbarous Western aggression against a Third World country, not any fighter and revolutionary but also any simple human being has no choice but to be radically and wholeheartedly opposed and to do whatever is possible to express his opposition and abhorrence'.[163] At the same time, 17N ridiculed the Greek government's military involvement in the region charging sarcastically that 'since Greek governments are incapable of liberating Cyprus they might as well try now to liberate Kuwait'.[164] The group saw the Gulf War against Iraq as a classic case of military aggression by the American imperialist machine. The symbolic assassination of US Air Force Sgt Ronald Stewart in March 1991 confirmed this view. 17N used the attack on Stewart to underline the fact that the Kuwaiti crisis 'had nothing to do with respect of international law and everything to do with the imposition of an American-dominated "new world order" in the region ...'.[165] Following this line of argument, 17N added that the air assault on Iraq was 'a classic imperialist, neocolonial war where the rich, arrogant West, using the liberation of Kuwait as an excuse, has for a month devoted itself with particular zeal to the total destruction of the economy of a feeble Third World country and to the genocide of its people giving, at the same time, a lesson/warning to all countries of the South that might in the future not kowtow'.[166] The group cited its own attack on Stewart as a challenging response to US bullying and barbarity in the region. By attacking an American sergeant working at the Hellenikon air force base in Athens, 17N believed it attacked a representative of 'the criminal genocide machine called the US Armed Forces'.[167] On the closing page of

---

[163] 17N communiqué, entitled 'We react to the Savage Raid' claiming responsibility for the rocket attacks against the Athens branches of Barclays, Citibank and American Express, BP, the Inter-American Insurance Company and the offices of the French military attaché in protest against Operation Desert Storm, dated 29 January 1991 and published two days later in Athens daily *Eleftherotypia*.

[164] Ibid.

[165] 17N attack communiqué on R. Stewart, dated 12 March 1991.

[166] Ibid.

[167] Ibid.

the Stewart communiqué, entitled '*Yesterday Vietnam, Today Iraq, on to the Next Genocide!*' the group claimed that

the total destruction of a poor Third world country for decades and the genocide of 130,000 Iraqis, most of them civilians, constitute a crime against humanity committed by the governments of the West and headed by the United States. They also constitute a triumph of Western parliamentary Nazism. After Vietnam, where the US destroyed a poor country for 100 years – not least ecologically – and annihilated 1.4 million Vietnamese, and after Algeria where in five years 'democratic' France annihilated 1 million Algerians out of a total population of 10 million came Iraq, where in one month Western humanists annihilated 130,000 Iraqis and destroyed the country. Vietnam, Algeria and Iraq are the Auschwitzes and the Gulags of Western parliamentary totalitarianism, of parliamentary capitalism.[168]

After the war in the Persian Gulf, US president George Bush became a particular focus for denunciation by the group. America's ideological triumph in the Cold War and its emergence in the 1990s as the only superpower was greeted with deep disdain. The 1991 US presidential official visit to Athens aggravated 17N's resentment for 'Bush and American imperialism' and its 'self-serving' globalist vision of a new world order.[169] The group tried to use the Bush visit to force the 'Cyprus issue' to the forefront of national debate. After targeting three Turkish diplomats,[170] 17N declared that Bush had come to impose through 'the agent government of petty Mitsotakis',[171] 'a partition-confederation solution to the Cyprus issue, which does not include full withdrawal of the Turkish occupation troops and the return of all Greek Cypriot refugees to their homes'.[172] Comparing Saddam Hussein's attack on Kuwait to the Turkish invasion of northern Cyprus, 17N accused the Euro-Atlantic community of double standards in the application of international law. 17N's position was that in

---

[168] Ibid.

[169] See 17N communiqué, dated 29 January 1991.

[170] On the eve of Bush's arrival, on 16 July, 17N tried but failed to kill Turkish embassy chargé d'affaires, Deniz Bolukbasi and administrative counsellor, Nilgun Kececi, when a remote-controlled bomb exploded next to their car. Less than three months later, on 7 October, the group in a follow-up attack assassinated the embassy's 28-year-old press attaché, Cettin Gorgu.

[171] 17N attack communiqué on Gorgu, dated 7 October 1991.

[172] 17N attack communiqué against Bolukbasi and Kececi, dated 16 July 1991.

the case of Kuwait, 'the West refused any understanding with Saddam unless his troops withdrew'.[173] 'The rapist and invader of Kuwait', it added mockingly, 'not only was compelled by force of arms to withdraw, but, more than that, the "butcher" of Baghdad was punished in an exemplary manner'.[174] In Cyprus, by contrast, 'the West did not demand with the same persistence the withdrawal of the Turkish troops. Never was a decision made for an economic embargo on Turkey. Never was a military operation attempted against Turkey to force her to withdraw from Cyprus'.[175] As a consequence of this, 17N concluded, the

Ankara butchers, to use the West's terminology, can invade, destroy, and occupy one-third of Cyprus without intervention. They can commit crimes, create a de facto state, the current actual partition, and the future confederation with the blessings of the international community and particularly of the Anglo-Americans, who in this case did not sense any violation of legality.[176]

17N's attitude towards the practice of violence changed after 1991. The Paleokrassas attack signalled an apparent inability to impose control over the military instrument. Subsequent efforts by 17N to defend its action and transfer blame for the casualties on to the police authorities also revealed a growing detachment from reality. Attacked by the media for 'blind, indiscriminate terrorism',[177] 17N made a succession of statements describing the whole affair as 'a tragicomic, propagandist campaign launched by the regime against the group'.[178] 17N argued that the police authorities deliberately left the 20-year-old student to bleed to death in a crude attempt to use the incident against the group.[179] However, the kneecapping of an inconspicuous New Democracy backbencher, Eleftherios Papadimitriou, for endorsing his 'leader's policy of selling off public

---

[173] Ibid.

[174] Ibid.

[175] Ibid.

[176] Ibid.

[177] See *Eleftherotypia, Ta Nea, Apogevmatini, Kathimerini, Ethnos*, 15 July 1992 and *To Vima*, 19 July 1992.

[178] Because of continuing media attacks and public revulsion, 17N issued, in a damage-limitation exercise, a 'communiqué-condemnation' (dated 18 July 1992) arguing that the main responsibility for the death of the unfortunate university student Axarlian lay with the police.

[179] Ibid.

property' and his part in 'the corruption and depravity of the political world' offered additional evidence of the group's confused thinking and nihilistic ideological mindset.[180] In fact, the release of a document entitled *Manifesto 1992* on 17 November 1992 confirmed that the assaults against Paleokrassas and Papadimitriou were part of a radical shift in the group's attitude and focus.

A mixture of political analysis, social commentary and polemical hyperbole, *Manifesto 1992* represented a 17N attempt to display its revolutionary optimism and ideological continuity. At the same time, the 15-page text was organizationally ordered to explain and justify the group's continuing presence on the post–1974 political scene. Attacking parliamentarism, capitalist democracy and reformism, 17N re-affirmed its ambition to organize working-class resistance and sustain 'the popular movement' in its revolutionary mission. In discussing 'the on-going propagandist attack of the regime' against the group, 17N cited the Aldo Moro murder case. There was ample evidence, the group argued, to indicate that the Italian secret services had tried through rumours and sophisticated disinformation operations to exploit the Moro kidnapping and killing for their own political ends. After savaging circulating theories and newspaper stories about 17N infiltration by the Greek secret service agents as 'mythology', the group used several pages to demonstrate that the inculcation of such slander was a standard regime practice. Referring to the Moro case, 17N explained that a 'mythology' which accepted that 'the Red Brigades were infiltrated and manipulated into killing Moro by the Secret Services, or the P2 Masonic Lodge or Gladio etc.' served the regime's propaganda purposes in arguing that 'an authentic popular revolutionary struggle' was unreal and non-existent.[181] In Greece, the group asserted, the '17N-Secret Service links mythology' served a similar purpose. Despite the confident rhetoric of *Manifesto*

---

[180] 17N attack communiqué on New Democracy MP E. Papadimitriou, dated December 1992.

[181] In *Manifesto 1992*, 17N cited evidence from a recently published book on the Red Brigades: *To Phenomeno tis Tromokratias: I anodos kai i ptossi ton Erythron Taxiarchion* [*The Phenomenon of Terrorism: The rise and fall of the Red Brigades*, Athens: Livanis, 1992] by a Rome-based Greek journalist, Dimitri Delliolannis, to argue that 'without ignoring the existence of the Secret Service and P2 and Gladio and their ambitions to exploit the militant revolutionary struggle, there is plenty of evidence in the book which shows that the security services played absolutely no role in guiding the BR to the Moro operation'.

1992, 17N no longer seemed to have a coherent political strategy. The practical effect of 17N's 1993 intermittent low-level bombing campaign against tax offices and vehicles was to make its violence appear politically worthless.[182] The group's language, at the same time, was becoming insistently bombastic, repetitive and sententious in tone. Although the attack on Vranopoulos meant to symbolically serve as yet another warning to all individuals involved in 'specific' privatizations, 17N armed struggle was having less and less impact on the public consciousness, long inured to years of persistent 'revolutionary' violence.

17N pledges to sustain a consistent level of military activity failed to materialize as the rate of violence continued to decline. By 1995 the level of 17N attacks had fallen to one, down from a peak of 22 in 1991. At the same time, 17N motives became more difficult to decipher. The mortaring of MEGA TV studios in March 1995 during the station's main evening news confirmed the impression that 17N's attachment to unregulated violence had become the only way for the group to maintain its ideological identity and preserve its *raison d'être*. Claiming credit for the attack,[183] 17N tried to deflect criticism and vindicate its extremism by suggesting a CIA-FBI-Greek media conspiracy plot against the group. Pointing to the 'Machiavellian manipulation' and hypocrisy of the Greek media, 17N attacked both the MEGA TV ownership and the *Eleftherotypia* newspaper editor for deliberately ignoring the group's telephone warning in an attempt to make the strike seem 'a blind attack designed to provoke casualties'.[184] Rather than 'functioning independently', 17N added, 'the Greek media have accepted instead to follow blindly CIA-FBI orders aimed at creating a carnage that would overturn the public sympathy 17N currently enjoys'.[185] At the same time, 17N castigated *Eleftherotypia*, MEGA TV and the Athenian media establishment for disorienting the electorate and 'systematically hiding from the Greek public the continuing corruption and manifest bribe-taking' in political life.[186] The group argued

---

[182] See Ch. 4.

[183] MEGA channel television was in the middle of its main evening news bulletin when two 17N rockets smashed into the building in Peania, east of Athens, destroying a newsroom that luckily happened to be empty at the time.

[184] 17N attack communiqué against MEGA TV, dated 27 March 1995.

[185] Ibid.

[186] Ibid.

that unlike in Italy and France 'where former prime ministers and ministers indicted with corruption charges are put behind bars . . . in this country the last two premiers, Mitsotakis and Papandreou, both routinely and openly bribed, never felt the need to try conceal that fact'.[187] In such circumstances, 17N concluded, 'giving up' its struggle was 'out of the question'.[188]

After hitting Peratikos, 17N declared 'de-industrialization' to be one of the major problems facing the country's economy since *metapolitefsi*. The group argued that by blindly accepting directives from Brussels, successive Greek governments of both PASOK and New Democracy have led to the gradual dismantling and shrinking of the country's productive industrial infrastructure. According to 17N, industry's contribution to the GNP fell from 25 per cent in the 1970s to 12 per cent in 1996.[189] Pointing to the fact that Greece was the only country in the West to decrease its industrial production during the 1986–96 decade, 17N contended that one of the practices which contributed to this was privatization scandals like that of the Elefsis shipyards in 1992. To illustrate the point and demonstrate its argument, the group provided a detailed analysis of the sale.

It is a well established fact that in any buy-and-sell procedure of an economic good the buyer is the one who pays the price and the seller is the one who collects it. However, in the country of the jolly orange tree commonsense is not the norm, but exactly the opposite is common. The Peratikos shipping group may have bought the Elefsis shipyard from the state, but it is the latter that pays. Peratikos, not only did not pay a dime, but furthermore he collected, collects, and will collect from the state a huge amount that exceeds the price of the 'purchase'. This may sound surrealistic, but even a glance at the real facts of this privatization leads to the undisputed conclusion that we have before us one of the biggest politico-economic scandals in recent years, one of the biggest frauds at the expense of the country. According to the purchase contract signed by Peratikos under New Democracy's government in 1992, the final purchase price of the yard was set at 10.6 billion drachmas while according to repeated accusations by workers the yard's real value amounted to 25 billion. The payment of this amount would be made in four stages. Peratikos paid immediately in July 1992 cheques worth two

---

[187] Ibid.

[188] Ibid.

[189] 17N attack communiqué explaining its targeting for the assassination of Costas Peratikos, dated 7 April 1998 [sic] and reprinted in *Eleftherotypia*, 30 May 1997.

billion. In a second three-year grace period July '92–July '95 he paid nothing. In a third ten-year period he was to pay two semester instalments equalling 1/30 of the price until the year 2005. And finally, at the end of the summer of 2005 he would pay the remaining amount. As anybody can understand though, both the six-month instalments of the third period as well as the remaining amount for the year 2005 will not come from Peratikos' own capital, but from the profits of the Elefsis shipyard itself, since it will be operating for a period lasting from 3 to 13 years. Accordingly, the only capital presumably paid by Peratikos is the 2-billion-drachma cheques of 1992. Given that, at the same time, in 1992, he was given low-interest rate loans by the state banks amounting to 8.8 billion drachma, everyone also realizes that Peratikos not only did not pay even a dime out of pocket in order to buy the Elefsis shipyard, but also collected a net amount of 6.8 billion in bad risk loans. [190]

Throughout the communiqué 17N maintained that the country was run by thieves. Attacking politicians, shipowners, technocrats and judges for their collaboration in the general squandering of public property, the group made it clear that its aim was to challenge those who had turned the Greek polity into a kleptocracy. Greece, 17N declared, was not a banana republic. Its institutions, political world, justice system, mass media, 'might be those of a banana republic, but the Greek people are not going to allow the ship-owners to deceive and rob them repeatedly of billions of drachmas and go unpunished, while ordinary workers are thrown into jail for small debts of a few thousand drachmas to the State'. [191]

The Ocalan affair convinced the 17N leadership of the hypocrisy of a capitalist-dominated system of international law and order. For the group, Ocalan and the protests by the Kurdish people at his arrest became symbols of the EU's criminal disrespect for political and human rights. 17N claimed that the EU's decision to brand Ocalan as a terrorist 'without uttering a word about the ethnic cleansing and genocide of the Kurdish people by Turkey, or their right to self-determination' was 'the utmost disgrace for the EU and its socialist state-members', revealing at the same time 'the total renunciation of classic western political principles'. [192] The group's point was that

[190] Ibid.
[191] Ibid.
[192] 17N communiqué-commentary on the Ocalan affair, dated 8 March 1999.

the so-called human rights that constitute the foundation stone of western democracy and are mentioned in the introductions to all constitutions ... do not exist outside the nation-state as can be seen in the present tragic fate of Third-world nationals and non-Western immigrants.[193]

17N said that it was therefore difficult to avoid the conclusion that modern-day Western political democracy was a sham. The fact, it stressed, that nearly 200 years after the liberal triumph of the Enlightenment against the reactionary attempts of the Holy Alliance at preserving the *status quo*, the supposedly 'progressive' European Union was now fully in line with 'the Alliance's darkest positions' confirmed the EU's

sorry state and the present theoretical bankruptcy of human and national rights. A logical consequence of all this, is the current monstrous situation whereby the guilty person becomes the plaintiff. Instead of the 'civilized West', a supposed advocate of 'rights', condemning Turkey for carrying out ethnic cleansing and genocide against the Kurds and violating their right to self-determination, what we get is fascistic Turkey doing the condemning, openly making threats and imposing its demands on the EU and several other countries.[194]

The group even quoted from the *Déclaration des droits de l'homme,*[195] to argue that although individual rights and basic principles were recognized as early as 1789, the Kurdish people's fundamental right to self-determination, two centuries later, had yet to be secured.

After hitting Saunders, 17N justified its act as a response to 'a murderous imperialist war'.[196] NATO's military campaign in Yugoslavia, the group declared, was never a humanitarian mission in the region but an attack on a sovereign state in blatant violation of long-standing international agreements and conventions. Presenting the NATO leaders as a self-constituted posse of international vigilantes, 17N further argued that NATO's strategy towards the Balkans had been shaped by the United States' strategic interests and geo-political ambitions in Europe rather than the local needs for conflict resolution and peacekeeping. According to

---

[193] Ibid.
[194] Ibid.
[195] Declaration of the Rights of Man.
[196] 17N attack communiqué on Brigadier Stephen Saunders, dated March 2000.

the group, the West's failure to seek authorization from the UN security council for the 78-day campaign of bombing against targets in Kosovo and Serbia represented the spirit of the new globalized international conscience. Unapologetic about Saunders, 17N claimed that he was 'a professional murderer' who worked for a government which had been conducting 'Nazi-like crimes'.[197] As the British military attaché, the group contended, Saunders

took an active part in the planning of last year's barbarous air strikes against Yugoslavia and, therefore, he is one of those responsible for last year's Nazi crime, the murder of thousands of unarmed civilians and the destruction of the country's economy and infrastructure. We chose a senior British military officer not only because Britain participated actively in the bombings – as it does along with the US in the continuing, periodic bombing against Iraq – but because British policy as it was articulated by [British premier Tony] Blair, [Foreign Secretary, Robin] Cook and [then British Defence Secretary George] Robertson beyond the traditional British hypocrisy, has surpassed in provocation, cynicism and aggressiveness even the Americans.[198]

The group saw the application of violence as the most effective form of political pressure against a US-run 'world disorder'. By attacking Saunders, 17N thought it attacked the inbred arrogance of the Anglo-Saxon political and military establishment and its 'deeply-rooted belief that they are superior people and are therefore legalized to annihilate' through sanctions and bombardment 'pariah nations' bringing misery, disease and death upon innocent people (' ... Arabs, Palestinians, Libyans and Iraqis yesterday, Yugoslavs today, Chinese, Russians and others tomorrow').[199] Seeing its struggle as a part of a new global political struggle for sovereignty, national self-determination and human dignity, 17N hinted at further 'just, armed popular resistance' unless the behaviour of 'USA and Co.' altered.[200]

Throughout its campaign, 17N constantly adjusted political reality to suit its revolutionary ambitions. In spite of the fact that conditions in post-junta Greece were not remotely revolutionary, 17N analysed the Greek political situation in terms of popular insurrection and revolutionary conflict. Its obsessive

197 Ibid.
198 Ibid.
199 Ibid.
200 Ibid.

determination to stigmatize the 1974 *metapolitefsi* inhibited 17N from understanding its workings and constitutional centrality. Throughout, 17N never disguised the centrality of violence to its strategy and organizational system. Blindly confident of the ideological authenticity of its belief system, 17N saw itself as 'a significant revolutionary political force' on the Greek political scene.[201] As its campaign grew more fanatical, the group repeatedly endorsed the claim that class conflict was permanent and fundamental. Oblivious of the impotence of its struggle, the group even suggested, paraphrasing Ernesto Guevara's famous revolutionary urge, the creation of 'two, three, many 17Ns'.[202]

17N's ideology and political violence

The three phases of 17N's ideological development were 1975–83, 1984–90 and 1991–6. The group's motives, behaviour, arguments and use of violence varied in each chronological period. 17N raised issues that have dominated national politics ever since *metapolitefsi*: national sovereignty, anti-Americanism, Anglo-Saxon capitalism, Mediterranean socialism, European integration and international economic interdependence. The majority of these issues have critically divided both sides of the Greek political spectrum while others defined the parameters of the intellectual debate inside both the mainstream and extra-parliamentary left. Their presence in 17N's thematic agenda was part of the group's effort to attract attention and participate in public political debate.

17N aspired to be the ideological shaper and consciousness-raiser of the Greek working class which it believed to be voiceless and politically unselfconscious in the post-junta parliamentary process. Because of KKE indifference and trade-union inertia, the group argued that the working class did not possess an articulate revolutionary consciousness nor the desire to struggle on its own behalf. 17N therefore believed that, like AD in France, it was 'redeeming an error and violently reconstructing an authentic working-class struggle'.[203] Unable, at the same time, to grasp the complexities of post–1974 political life and unwilling to accept the return of Konstantinos Karamanlis in power, 17N despised *metapolitefsi*.

---

[201] *Manifesto 1992*, dated 17 November 1992.
[202] 17N attack communiqué against MEGA TV, dated 27 March 1995.
[203] Dartnell, *Action Directe*, p. 122.

Even after Papandreou's election as Prime Minister in October 1981, the group used an accusatory terminology of betrayal, compromise and corruption. Constantly questioning the authenticity of the country's conversion to liberal democracy, the group attacked the entire political class as a hypocritical and demagogic clique pursuing its own interests at the expense of both the people and the nation.

17N's ideology was an amalgam of revolutionary adventurism, militaristic nationalism and anti-establishment rhetoric. Marxism-Leninism provided the group with intellectual legitimacy and an arsenal of revolutionary catch-phrases. Far from seriously engaging with Marxist theory, 17N none the less identified principal lines of social division and proposed a revolutionary project which promised to force them back on to the political agenda and eradicate them. At the same time, it tried to revive the political language of the November 1973 period. The group saw the 1973 events as an important historical moment in Greece's revolutionary politics. In 17N's view, the *Polytechneio* revolt inaugurated a historical process whose dynamics and significance continued to illuminate contemporary political-cultural values.

17N's conception of the political environment was one of protest, resistance and violence. Between 1975 and 2000 the group's *modus operandi* incorporated high-profile assassinations, kneecappings, armed raids, bombings and rocket attacks. 17N saw the application of violence as the most effective way to crystallize public disaffection against the regime and embed itself in mainstream consciousness. In that sense, the Italian Red Brigades (BR), German Red Army Faction (RAF) and French Action Direct (AD) all influenced 17N in several different ways. Although it did not establish any operational relationship with them, 17N copied RAF's careful selection of symbolically significant and well-protected targets and like the BR, timed its attacks to coincide with important political developments.[204] In *Manifesto 1992*, 17N acknowledged that it would have never been able to survive and avoid capture, had the group not drawn lessons from the substance of the mid-1972 Red Brigades' experience when the Italian authorities discovered several hideouts, arresting

---

[204] See D. A. Pluchinsky, 'Germany's Red Army Faction: An Obituary', in *Studies in Conflict and Terrorism*, Vol. 16 (1993), pp. 135 and 144.

a number of *brigatisti* in the process.[205] Unlike BR, however, 17N never successfully moved beyond terrorism designed to embarrass the authorities and express resentment of the existing order. With no real support base upon which to expand, the group never progressed beyond the far fringes of mainstream Greek society.

---

[205] *Manifesto 1992*; on the BR arrests in mid-1972 see Robert C. Meade, Jr., *Red Brigades: The Story of Italian Terrorism* (London: Macmillan, 1990), pp. 48–51.

6

DEALING WITH TERRORISM

THE STATE'S RESPONSE

Greece is an interesting laboratory not only for studying terrorism but also anti-terrorism. After two-and-a-half decades of bombings, rocket attacks, assassinations, kneecappings and shootings in broad daylight, one might assume that Greece would have been able to resolve the problem as most other European countries have done. Yet any study of Greece's counter-terrorism effort quickly reveals it to be ramshackle. Indeed, governments in other countries have their shortcomings but the ineptitude of the Greek state has been unparalleled.

The main purpose of this chapter is to analyse the attitudes of Greek political élites towards the terrorist problem and examine the tactics and responses which they utilized to combat it. Focusing on the major political parties, it explores opinions and reactions to different manifestations of the problem of political violence. At the same time, it attempts to show that the evolution of Greek anti-terrorism policies was marred by inconsistency and a lack of unity of action. Although in principle each party stood against terrorism, the overall response of the Greek state has been lethargic, dilatory and unbalanced. Different political and operational approaches to combating terrorism and the absence of a consensus on the 'definition, history, theory and effects of terrorism'[1] impeded the development of both a coherent anti-terrorist strategy and an integrated counter-terrorism capability.

The chapter also focuses on the relationship between terrorism and the media, seeking to explore if and how 'the media influence

---

[1] Grant Wardlaw, *Political Terrorism: Theory, Tactics, and Counter-measures* (Cambridge: Cambridge University Press, 1990), p. xii.

our images of terrorism'.[2] Concentrating on the Greek experience, it shows that although there is no clear evidence that media coverage of terrorism encourages more terrorism, the media inevitably provide 'a medium for the terrorists' message, and coverage contributes to motivation for the individuals and groups'.[3] Publicity constitutes a vital component in the propaganda war of violent political organizations. In fact, terrorist groups 'wage physical and propaganda wars that are inseparable'.[4] The central aim of a terrorist attack is to gain publicity, which the media by definition provide, and thus to influence public opinion. Given the fact that terrorism provokes competition for allegiance – either to the terrorists or to the government – the news the media choose to place before the public (any bias or emphasis placed on that news and the timing of that news), influences the public perception of that information and the conclusions drawn from it. Experience in Italy has shown that without sufficient restraint on the coverage and dissemination of facts and opinion, the media can become an unwitting instrument in the terrorist cause.[5]

Students of terrorism,[6] politicians[7] and intelligence analysts have condemned media behaviour towards terrorism suggesting 'a symbiotic relationship' between terrorists and the modern mass media.[8] In addition, law enforcement agencies have maintained

---

[2] A.J. Jongman, 'Trends in International and Domestic Terrorism in Western Europe, 1968–1988', in *Terrorism and Political Violence*, Vol. 4, No. 4 (Winter 1992), p. 27.

[3] Bruce Allen Scharlau, *Left-Wing Terrorism in the Federal Republic of Germany*, (Unpublished PhD dissertation, University of St. Andrews, 1991), p. 258.

[4] Yonah Alexander & Richard Latter (eds), *Terrorism and the Media: Dilemmas for Governments, Journalists and the Public*, (McLean, VA: Brassey's, 1990), p. xi.

[5] See Giorgio Bocca, *Il terrorismo italiano 1970–1978* (Milan: Rizzoli, 1978).

[6] 'The media are the terrorists' best friends', Walter Laqueur quoted in A.P. Schmid, 'Terrorism and the Media: The Ethics of Publicity', in *Terrorism and Political Violence*, Vol. 1, No. 4 (October 1989), p. 539; Paul Wilkinson has criticised the media for having 'made the terrorists' task all too easy' in P. Wilkinson, 'Terrorism and Propaganda', in *Terrorism and the Media*, p. 30; and Richard Clutterbuck has called television 'the most powerful weapon in the terrorist's arsenal', in R. Clutterbuck, *The Media and Political Violence* (London: Macmillan, 1981), p. 162.

[7] Former British Prime Minister Margaret Thatcher has accused the media of having 'become the unwilling – and in some cases, willing, – amplifier of the terrorists' publicity campaign', Margaret Thatcher, quoted in *Washington Post*, 18 July 1985.

[8] Russell F. Farnen, 'Terrorism and the Mass Media: A Systemic Analysis of a Symbiotic Process', in *Terrorism: An International Journal*, Vol. 13, No. 2 (March–April 1990), pp. 111–15.

that in most Western industrialized societies 'reporting of terrorist violence is excessive, sensational, and sometimes unbalanced and that these factors produce a contagion effect'.[9] In Greece, as this chapter shows, 'the use of terrorists by the media became as crucial as the use of the media by the terrorists'.[10] An examination of media reporting of 17N terrorism suggests that a certain type of violence can determine the scale, intensity and visibility of the coverage. For example, ELA's extensive but low-level campaign of terrorism attracted considerably less media attention than the murderous 17N. In fact, 17N's campaign of rocket attacks and political assassinations received sustained nationwide media coverage because it made the Greek state appear naive, inept and politically powerless. At the same time, lack of arrests and the limited information available in connection with 17N also ensured that the group achieved mythical status in the national media and was eventually immortalized as the *organossi phantasma* (phantom organization).

In 1990, the conservative government of New Democracy under Constantine Mitsotakis introduced legislation that went to the heart of the relationship between terrorists and the media. Having denounced the print media, in particular, for playing the role of a megaphone to 17N terrorism, the Mitsotakis government passed an anti-terrorism bill which forbade the publication of terrorist communiqués/announcements in the press and the media.[11] Although the national media consistently sensationalized and over-dramatized terrorist events, this law had a dividing effect on Greek society. Government circles and some leading writers and academics hailed it as the first serious step in countering terrorism but it was labelled by the opposition and prominent legal circles as 'an abrogation of the fundamental provisions of the constitution' and 'the beginnings of a police state'. Overall, this analysis seeks to demonstrate that Greece's response to domestic and international terrorism reflected the country's uneven development and embodied historically defined notions of

---

[9] Wardlaw, p. 78.

[10] A.P. Schmid, 'Terrorism and the Media', p. 539.

[11] According to the widow of New Democracy MP Pavlos Bakoyiannis assassinated by 17N in 1989, from 1975 to 1995 'terrorist communiqués covered more than 1500 pages in the Greek press – the equivalent of 3 billion drachmas' worth of advertising'. See Dora Bakoyiannis, 'Terrorism in Greece', in *Mediterranean Quarterly*, Vol. 6, No. 2 (Spring 1995), p. 22.

political progress and reaction. Aggressive parliamentary and intellectual debate on terrorism dominated the political scene for more than a decade and showed that conflict in Greek politics and society had been overcome in a less profound way than was suggested by conventional wisdom.

The first response to terrorism: Law 774/1978

On 29 April 1975, eight cars belonging to US servicemen in the military base of Elefsina were firebombed. An unknown group calling itself *Epanastatikos Laikos Agonas* (ELA) claimed in a two-page diatribe against the United States credit for the attack and threatened further retaliations against 'American imperialism'. Eight months later, on 23 December, three 17N gunmen stalked Richard Welch, the CIA station chief in Athens, shooting him down at point-blank range in front of his wife and driver. The Karamanlis government refused to intervene. State authorities speculated that the Welch attack was a consequence of score-settling between foreign intelligence services.[12]

At the time of 17N's appearance, Greece was in a civil and moral state of flux. Despite the fall of the Colonels' fascist regime, a climate of amorality, individualism and disconnection was formed in Greek society. Although the institutions of a democratic polity were introduced, the legacy of decades of authoritarianism, together with the lack of civil expertise, marked the limits of *metapolitefsi* and soon a stasis settled over most areas of national life. As a result, national modernization began to take shape against a background of ideological excess and sharp political divisions. At the same time, Karamanlis's authoritarian style and contradictory responses to a series of governmental crises further polarized political stances and increased social tension. Disputes over values and priorities repeatedly led to upheaval and violence. Beyond that, urgently needed reforms in the country's internal political arrangements, in the restructuring of the state apparatus and in the direction of educational and foreign policy were not undertaken. *Metapolitefsi* increased Greece's constitutional legitimacy but at the same time exerted a profound influence on political behaviour by exacerbating conflictual interpretations of

---

[12] See Ch. 4.

democratization. These divisions had long-term effects on post-1974 political culture within which ultra-left terrorism developed.

The first attempt by the Greek state to deal with the problem of terrorism came in 1978. The continuing mystery surrounding the assassination of the CIA station chief in Athens together with the kidnapping of Aldo Moro and the rising number of terrorist episodes in neighbouring Italy alarmed the Greek authorities.[13] As a consequence, the Karamanlis government introduced special anti-terrorist legislation called 'Bill to combat terrorism and protect the democratic polity'. The law (774/1978), which came into force in April of that year, was mainly based on the Italian and German anti-terrorism bills.[14] More specifically, article 1, section 1, referred to one or more persons forming a terrorist group in order to attack the Greek state by using weapons, hand grenades, explosives and bomb-parcels. Such crimes carried up to a 20-year prison sentence. Furthermore, article 1, section 2, referred to one or more persons acting in concert to commit, attempt or otherwise aid in the commission of any of a list of serious felonies: homicide, kidnapping, hijacking, harming the security of an aircraft and hostage-taking. The person or persons committing such crimes faced either life imprisonment or the death sentence. In article 2, giving refuge to a terrorist was also regarded as a crime, incurring sentences of up to ten years. In article 4, the bill authorized financial incentives for police informers, 'whose contribution may lead the authorities to the arrest of terrorists', up to one million drachma. Unlike the 1978 West German anti-terrorist legislation and the 191 Anti-Terrorist Law of 1978 in Italy[15], the bill did not increase police powers in areas of search and seizures, mail opening, examination of bank records or detaining individuals without specific charges.

The central argument of the Karamanlis government in passing

[13] The number of left-wing terrorist episodes in Italy was 197 for 1977 and reached 240 in 1978. Sources: D. della Porta and M. Rossi, 'Il Terrorismi in Italia tra il 1969 e il 1982', in Gianfranco Pasquino (ed.), *Il sistema politico italiano* (Bari: La Terza, 1985), pp. 418–56; See also Robert H. Evans, 'Terrorism and Subversion of the State: Italian Legal Responses', in *Terrorism and Political Violence*, Vol. 1, No. 3 (July 1989), p. 326.
[14] See *Kathimerini*, 16 December 1990.
[15] Donatella Della Porta, 'Institutional Responses to Terrorism: The Italian Case', in *Terrorism and Political Violence*, Vol. 4, No. 2 (Winter 1992), pp. 156–8.

the anti-terrorist legislation was that the Greek state was obliged to take necessary measures to thwart terrorist attacks against Greece's still-fragile democracy and prevent events such as the kidnapping of Moro in Italy. The Minister of Justice and the bill's sponsor, George Stamatis, opened the parliamentary debate by arguing that the government could not 'remain indifferent after what happened in neighbouring Italy. What happened there could very easily happen here'. 'The kidnapping of Aldo Moro,' he added, 'amounted to a serious and urgent warning which we must not ignore'.[16] Stamatis also pointed out that the sporadic cases of political violence which had recently appeared in the country had created serious doubts about the effectiveness of the state's counter-terrorist mechanisms. Terrorism, he declared, was 'a fundamental attack on democracy, and the Government of New Democracy, feeling responsible towards the Greek public, had decided to combat this evil phenomenon before it escalated with dramatic consequences for the country'.[17]

Throughout the parliamentary debate it was emphatically stated by several New Democracy speakers that the existing criminal law system had no deterrent effect and when dealing with politically motivated violence would prove to be inadequate. New Democracy's main speaker, Aristeidis Katsaounis, argued that 'the Greek penal code was insufficient to cope with this new kind of crime and the introduction of special legislation was absolutely necessary and appropriate to the situation at hand'.[18] It was also argued that Law 774/1978 was intended to create a more effective framework of law to strengthen state security in the fight against terrorism and subversion. Having recognized the need for a concerted effort against terrorism, Katsaounis lamented the fact that the bill did not secure the support of the government's main parliamentary opponents.[19] The lack of cross-party consensus drove Katsaounis to the conclusion that PASOK and the communists had failed to acknowledge the seriousness of the problem and recognize the need for the terrorist danger to be warded off before it reached Italian and German proportions.[20]

---

[16] Parliamentary Discussion Papers – Greek Parliament, 12 April 1978, p. 2483.
[17] Ibid.
[18] Parliamentary Discussion Papers – Greek Parliament, 10 April 1978, p. 2401.
[19] Ibid., p. 2399.
[20] Ibid., p. 2402.

In response to claims that Law 774/1978 was not a bill that a serious democratic parliament should pass, New Democracy repeatedly stressed that it 'was the primary duty of every government to take every step possible to protect the lives and property of its citizens'.[21] One speaker made reference to several European states which had suffered protracted campaigns of terrorism, arguing that experience showed that the most effective strategy entailed anti-terrorist legislative initiatives. Greece, he asserted, was 'no less democratic than Italy and Germany which confronted the problem by enacting special anti-terrorist legislation'.[22] Following this line of argument, another speaker maintained that terrorism was not 'a phenomenon invented by the Minister of Justice or by the Government' but 'a disease of our time'.[23] 'The purpose of the present legislation', he added, 'was not to restrict people but to deter terrorists and prevent attacks of the kind of which Aldo Moro and others became victims'.[24]

Meanwhile, the definitional problem of terrorism polarized the discussion. The New Democracy's position was that the debate about the meaning and usage of terrorism had unnecessarily turned parliament into a battleground. Dealing briefly with the difficulties inherent in defining and operationalizing the concept, the Minister of the Interior, Kostis Stephanopoulos, took the view that the absence of a single definition was not an obstacle to the investigation of terrorist phenomena. 'The meaning of terrorism', he argued, 'is clear to everyone: it is clear to us inside the House and it is clear to those, outside, who use it as a technique to influence political developments'.[25] According to Stephanopoulos, there was no ambiguity about terrorism. Terrorism, he said, was as much about the threat of violence as the violent act itself.[26] Against those lawyers and civil liberty groups who claimed that the lack of a tight, comprehensive definition of terrorism and political violence made the legislation dangerous, the Minister of the Interior responded that 'New Democracy was a party fully dedicated to Democracy and as such, it intended to use the law not

---

21 Parliamentary Discussion Papers – Greek Parliament, 10 April 1978, p. 2407.
22 Ibid.
23 Ibid., 13 April 1978, p. 2574.
24 Ibid.
25 Ibid., 17 April 1978, p. 2675.
26 Ibid., 12 April 1978, p. 2494.

against student and worker opposition but against killers and bomb-carrying terrorists'.[27]

Throughout the discussion, New Democracy used the potential danger of terrorism to Greek democracy to attack the main opposition parties as demagogic, partisan and indifferent to the country's security interests. The suggestion was that there was collusion between PASOK and communist KKEs to manipulate the terrorist issue for party-political reasons. Allowing a climate 'of fantasies and exaggeration to develop inside parliament', New Democracy maintained, was a major mistake that only undermined the processes of interparty dialogue and collaboration.[28] Urging the leaders of both parties to elevate the nature of the political debate, New Democracy stressed the need for a new and responsible method of argument.[29] At the same time, New Democracy MPs took issue with the opposition's common hostility towards Karamanlis himself. While dismissing left-wing criticisms of his ruthlessness and authoritarian style of governance, several speakers consistently emphasized that Karamanlis was 'the one man' who gave Greece 'more democracy than the country had experienced ever since the 1940s'.[30] To reinforce the point, they argued that it begged the question of whether Karamanlis, the man systematically demonized by the mainstream left as antidemocratic and authoritarian, was 'the same man as the Karamanlis who in 1974 put Greece back on a constitutional footing and whose policies restored the country's credibility and independence of action'.[31]

Moving back to the main theme of the debate, New Democracy argued that terrorism was not only a national but also an international phenomenon and in many European states a clear connection existed between the two.[32] It also argued that a close co-ordination between European states was vital if the continuing threat posed by terrorism was to be effectively countered. The fact, Minister of Justice George Stamatis said, that talks between EC member states about the policy and operational aspects of combating terrorism had been held at

27 Ibid., 17 April 1978, p. 2675.
28 Ibid., 12 April 1978, p. 2495.
29 Ibid.
30 Ibid., 13 April 1978, p. 2548.
31 Ibid.
32 Ibid., 12 April 1978, p. 2492.

ministerial and civil servant levels with increasing frequency
reflected the gravity of the problem.[33] 'It was only last week in
Copenhagen,'[34] he added, 'that the Council of Europe stressed its
firm resolve to do everything to protect the rights of individuals and
the foundations of the democratic institutions, passing a resolution
to intensify joint efforts in the face of international terrorism'.[35] The
year before in Strasbourg, another speaker said, the Council of
Europe's European Convention on the Suppression of Terrorism
recognized the need for more effective co-operation between security forces and adopted a resolution on extradition. 'The 1977 Convention', he added, 'was signed by 15 countries – France, West
Germany, Great Britain, Portugal, Sweden, the Benelux countries
and Italy among them – with the highest quality of civic values and
democratic governance'.[36] New Democracy's concluding argument was that it was imperative that Greece followed the example
of most European states and, through the initiation of anti-terrorist
legislation and the implementation of internal security measures,
contained terrorism in an effective and meaningful manner.[37]
Referring to the RAF's April 1975 seizure of the German Embassy
in Stockholm,[38] the Minister of the Interior, Kostis Stephanopoulos, asked Parliament: 'Shall we wait for another Embassy, in
Greece perhaps, to be blown up before we react? Or, shall we
promptly take the necessary measures required to protect our
democracy against terrorists and extremists'.[39]

---

33 Ibid., p. 2486.
34 European Council meeting, 7–8 April 1978 in Copenhagen.
35 Parliamentary Discussion Papers – Greek Parliament, 12 April 1978, p. 2554.
36 Ibid., 10 April 1978, p. 2409.
37 Parliamentary Discussion Papers – Greek Parliament, 12 April 1978, p. 2492.
38 On 24 April 1975, six terrorists took over the West Germany embassy in Stockholm
    and seized twelve hostages. They demanded the release of 42 'political prisoners in the
    FRG' – almost all RAF members. During the 12-hour siege, the terrorists killed the
    military and economic attachés. The West German government refused to give in to
    the terrorists' demands. While attempting to escape from the embassy, the terrorists
    accidentally detonated the explosives (15 kilograms of TNT) they had placed inside
    the embassy. One of the terrorists was immediately killed, one was seriously injured
    and the other four were captured. Source: D. A. Pluchinsky', An Organizational and
    Operational Analysis of Germany's Red Army Faction Terrorist Group (1972–91)', in
    Yonah Alexander and Dennis A. Pluchinsky (eds), *European Terrorism: Today and
    Tomorrow* (McLean, VA: Brassey's US, 1992), pp. 59–60.
39 Parliamentary Discussion Papers – Greek Parliament, 12 April 1978, p. 2554.

However, the anti-terrorist legislative measures taken by the government did not receive a positive response from the Greek public. Concern over potential civil liberties infringements and restrictions generated considerable debate about the kind of counter-terrorist response acceptable to a liberal democratic society. During large public demonstrations in Athens, Larissa, Patras and Salonika, workers, intellectuals and civil rights groups questioned the government's political intentions insisting that the bill 'would result in the erosion of civil rights and liberties'.[40] Similarly, opposition parties and the liberal media maintained that the bill had the characteristics of an oppressive political regime. Temporarily united, PASOK and the communists denounced 774 and accused the government of introducing legislation which would suppress civil liberties, the constitution and democracy itself.

PASOK, the official opposition, characterized Law 774/1978 as the first step to a despotic, undemocratic and tyrannical rule of law. PASOK's main argument in opposing the law was that 'in Greece modern-day terrorism does not exist and could not exist simply because the preconditions did not exist'.[41] 'Terrorist actions', it was further argued, 'are committed by fascist and anarchical elements marginalized from society. In Greece, anarchists do not exist, and even if they did, the appropriate political climate is not conducive for them to act'.[42] At the same time, PASOK noted that 'if and when terrorism became a problem existing legislation was more than sufficient to deal with it'.[43] Andreas Papandreou's party went on to claim that the government of New Democracy used the events in Italy as a subterfuge in passing a law which violated individual freedoms and introduced a police state. The implication was that 'the government deliberately, on the pretext that it combats terrorism, enacts the policing of political life and the suppression of democratic freedom of those who oppose it'.[44]

PASOK's position was that Karamanlis and the government had decided to mobilize the law to control protest. The government's recent legislative assaults, it was argued, on labour

[40] *Eleftherotypia*, 8 April 1978 and *International Herald Tribune*, 14 April 1978.
[41] Parliamentary Discussion Papers – Greek Parliament, 12 April 1978, p. 2509.
[42] Ibid.
[43] Ibid, p. 2512.
[44] Ibid., 10 April 1978, p. 2411.

syndicalism were clear enough both in their intention and effect. PASOK speakers maintained that it came as no surprise that, after curbing strikes and trade-union power, New Democracy had speedily moved into passing another piece of legislation which restricted democratic pressures. At the same time, Papandreou held that the issue of terrorism served as a useful distraction from governmental failure to deal with major social and economic problems. The PASOK leader believed that 'the Government's heavy-handed tactics inside and outside Parliament were directly related to economic stagnation'.[45] Attacking Karamanlis's 'Europeanist policies' which were held responsible for the country's 'slide towards bankruptcy', Papandreou argued that it was the combination of 'inflation, unemployment and lack of investment which had produced the present wave of anxiety and discontent'.[46] 'To confront increasing popular resistance effectively', he explained, 'the government was setting up a framework of paraconstitutional measures of which Law 774 was the first to emerge'.[47]

Papandreou also raised the issue of direct foreign influence in national matters. Without hesitation he warned that in every circumstance, Greece should preserve its autonomy and freedom of choice to decide both its internal and external policies. Given the picture painted by numerous reports in the media, the opposition leader said that it seemed likely that Karamanlis committed himself to introducing anti-terrorist legislation, during his official visit to Germany in January.[48] The fact, Papandreou argued, that 'the government made no effort to deny these stories confirms this impression'.[49] In expounding his thesis, Papandreou also said that decisions affecting Greece should be made in Athens and not in Washington or Bonn. He also stressed that it was worth reminding the House that in 'present-day Germany a centralized, authoritarian police form of government is in the making, which hardly constitutes a model of democracy for a country which has just emerged from a seven-year dictatorship'.[50] In line with his

[45] *Eleftherotypia*, 20 April 1978.
[46] Ibid.
[47] Ibid.
[48] Parliamentary Discussion Papers – Greek Parliament, 10 April 1978, p. 2406.
[49] Ibid.
[50] Ibid., p. 2407.

leader's argument, another PASOK speaker, Vassilios Papadopoulos maintained that 774 was clearly inspired by 'a country
which likes to play the role of the policeman-supervisor and the
only state in Europe to introduce this type of legislation'.[51] 'The
bill under discussion', Papadopoulos insisted was not 'in any case
the product of domestic legislative process but rather an attempt
by a government, under foreign influence or even pressure, to
engage in extensive bilateral co-operation on matters of justice
and home affairs'.[52]

At the same time, considerable emphasis was placed upon the lack
of a legal definition of terrorism. PASOK's starting point was that
'since the government cannot provide a precise definition of what
constitutes terrorism and terrorist groups', the bill could not withstand proper parliamentary scrutiny.[53] Pointing to the slippery nature
of the concept and its selective use, the socialists repeatedly argued
that if there was to be a serious public discourse concerning the problem it was vital that the government defined terrorism in a precise
way. PASOK added that it was politically convenient for the government to suggest that there was a strong impetus to introduce new
legislation which would strengthen the arm of the state against terrorists but its robust reluctance to clarify the nature of the threat and
the meaning of the word 'terrorism', generated widespread insecurity and fear among the general public.[54] PASOK looked to history to
explain why 774 might be used for regressive political ends. Aside
from anything else, it asserted, 774 revived traumatic memories of
right-wing ideological bias, political discrimination and gross misap-
plication of the law. 'If the past has anything to teach us', one speaker
said, 'it is that everything in this country ranging from the political
centre to the left is persecuted and penalised'.[55]

Another criticism was that New Democracy planned to use the
security services for law enforcement as well as a public order
body. PASOK said that this became particularly evident in a
number of clauses where the role of the security services was
broadened to include supporting the police in the prevention and

---

[51] Ibid., p. 2430.
[52] Ibid.
[53] Ibid., p. 2431.
[54] Ibid., pp. 2404–5.
[55] Ibid., p. 2433.

detection of serious crime.[56] PASOK's emphasis on the fact that repressive control mechanisms survived *metapolitefsi* led the socialists to make a connection between the police and dictatorial remnants inside the security apparatus. It was argued that the absence of a systematic political purge after 1974 had left key branches of the bureaucracy, such as the judiciary, with enclaves of fascists. Papandreou contended that the failure to remove fascists and junta sympathizers from key administrative posts had seriously weakened the credibility of the new republic in the eyes of ordinary Greeks.[57] The essence of PASOK's argument was that in spite of all the governmental promises and rhetoric for fundamental reform, the ethos and *modus operandi* of the state apparatus remained unchanged. 'Instead of making an attempt to restore the police and judiciary in the people's conscience', one PASOK MP observed, 'the government's first instinct is to introduce a law that is dangerous and divisive and will undermine the country's political equilibrium'.[58]

PASOK established that the passing of anti-terrorist legislation by New Democracy carried an additional motive. Apart from using 774 as a device for gaining greater coercive powers over the Greek people, PASOK argued that the bill also served as a demonstrative gesture on the government's pro-Europe credentials with a view to an eventual accession of Greece to the European Community.[59] Quoting from an *Economist* article which 'suggested that European capital and multinationals anxious to avoid disruption of their operations by industrial conflict and political discontent had pressurised Karamanlis to control public order and guarantee tranquillity', one PASOK MP concluded that 774 was 'the smaller of the prices the Government had to pay for the panacea of EC membership'.[60] While castigating New Democracy's 'servility and subjugation', PASOK also admitted that 'once such legislation is introduced, the path to national discord and violence would be wide open'.[61] To justify the point, PASOK made reference to article 4 of the bill. PASOK saw parallels between

---

[56] Ibid., 18 April 1978, p. 2728.
[57] Ibid., 12 April 1978, p. 2495.
[58] Ibid., p. 2512.
[59] Ibid., pp. 2515–16.
[60] Ibid., 13 April 1978, p. 2563.
[61] Ibid., 12 April 1978, pp. 2515–16.

article 4 and the anti-communist Laws 375 and 509 of the civil-war period.[62] Discussing New Democracy's decree on financial incentives for informers in close detail, PASOK claimed that article 4 legitimized *hafiethismos* (stool pigeon practice). According to one speaker, article 4 gave anyone tempted by the astronomical rewards offered by the government the right to appear before the authorities and, by producing false evidence, accuse innocent people of terrorism.[63] One MP remarked that it 'rewarded betrayal and the fabrication of charges'.[64] Another PASOK speaker insisted that article 4 had to be 'completely removed from the bill because it takes the country back to the years of the dictatorship'.[65] *Hafiethismos*, he pointedly remarked, 'constituted the junta's most fundamental and effective law enforcement instrument'.[66] He added that during 'the Papadopoulos terrorist dictatorship, the police had made use of more than 300,000 informants in Athens alone'.[67]

During the debate, PASOK repeatedly emphasized that 'if the government's proposals were passed into law, then a bill supposedly designed to counter terrorism and promote security will soon turn into a bill that counters Democracy itself'.[68] Papandreou several times lamented that the Act 'will herald a return to and will fully legitimise state-sponsored terrorism against the polity'.[69] Drawing attention to the vagueness of articles 1 and 4 in particular, another PASOK speaker concluded that the legislation's '*Occasio Legis* was not the prevention of terrorism but instead the intimidation of individuals'.[70] At the same time, PASOK linked the framework and scope of anti-terrorist measures across Europe and other parts of the industrialized world to the 'deepening crisis of the capitalist system'.[71] Papandreou held that the emergence of Eurocommunism and national liberation movements posed a serious challenge to the existing structures of state power and

---

[62] Ibid., p. 2487.
[63] Ibid., 13 April 1978, p. 2573.
[64] Ibid., 10 April 1978, p. 2409.
[65] Ibid., 18 April 1978, p. 2728.
[66] Ibid., p. 2725.
[67] Ibid.
[68] Ibid., 12 April 1978, p. 2490.
[69] Ibid.
[70] Ibid., 17 April 1978, p. 2665.
[71] Ibid., 12 April 1978, p. 2491.

bourgeois democracy in the contemporary world.[72] The development of an international model of counter-terrorism, it was argued, went beyond an efficient European response to criminality. It provided capitalist stabilization and ensured the long-term interests of the financial and economic oligarchy.[73] For Papandreou and his party it was 'doubtless that the government of New Democracy designed, at the command of Western Europe, the EC and the American mechanisms of NATO, a bill to crush the popular movement, if that chose to go too far'.[74] PASOK saw a correlation between domestic and foreign power centres 'attempting through legislative action to drag the country backwards'.[75] PASOK's main conclusion was that Law 774/1978 was 'clearly not about terrorists but aimed instead at putting in place the ideological and political conditions to terrorize the Greek populace'.[76] Sensitive to modern Greek history, PASOK insisted that New Democracy discourse in this period reflected an inability to break with the authoritarian thinking of the 1960s.[77] It also added that 'by introducing these far-reaching provisions into law, New Democracy came to confirm the view that "capitalist democracy, minus civil liberties, equals fascism" '.[78] PASOK predicted that 774 would be short-lived and pledged to abolish the law as soon as it became government.[79]

The Communist Party's (KKE)[80] reaction to Law 774/1978 was on the same lines. KKE declared that the anti-terrorism bill was unconstitutional and posed a grave threat to individual liberties. At the same time, it described the bill as a 'nasty, useless and provocative piece of legislation with no connection to the present Greek reality'.[81] KKE's main focus of hostility was the survival of what it termed a political regime whose authority depended on a climate of fear and denunciation. 'After seven years of dictatorship', KKE explained, 'and having restored a semblance of

---

[72] Ibid.
[73] Ibid.
[74] Ibid., 17 April 1978, p. 2649.
[75] Ibid., 12 April 1978, p. 2518.
[76] Ibid., 13 April 1978, p. 2588.
[77] Ibid., 17 April 1978, p. 2667.
[78] Ibid., 13 April 1978, p. 2559.
[79] Ibid., 17 April 1978, p. 2666.
[80] KKE = Kommunistiko Komma Ellados
[81] Parliamentary Discussion Papers – Greek Parliament, 13 April 1978, p. 2581.

democracy, the Greek people are faced once more by a reactionary and coercive state'.[82] Like PASOK, KKE subscribed to the view that the increased international attention to 'the threat of terrorism' was part of a Euro-Atlantic offensive to neutralize protest and the contradictions created by the American domination of Europe. In Greece's case, KKE believed that 774 was part of 'a wider NATO-American-inspired plan that would ultimately force the country to accept unconditional terms on all important national issues'.[83] As KKE explained, that would mean 'immediate reintegration to NATO's military wing, partition of Cyprus, retention of the US bases and accession to the EC of multinationals'.[84] Throughout the discussion, KKE's comments on the conduct of the government were scathing. KKE's general-secretary, Harilaos Florakis, attacked the Karamanlis administration for 'following directives from abroad'.[85] Discussing briefly the Karamanlis visit to Bonn, Florakis declared without hesitation that 'this bill was imposed by the West German chancellor, Schmidt'.[86] Another important part of KKE's main argument was its proposition that 'for there to be emergency legislation, there must also be an emergency – and, in Greece, that is not the case'.[87] 'The Government's rush to introduce emergency measures', it sardonically observed, 'shows that apart from having submitted to every international pressure, New Democracy even committed itself to legislate within a given chronological deadline'.[88] Criticizing the measures taken by the government, KKE insisted that 774 was never designed 'to meet the threat from terrorism and protect the constitutional state but intended instead to curb the freedom and rights of the individual citizen and popular groupings'.[89] The Communists, in fact, saw the new law as the phantom of a new fascism. Thus, KKE made it clear that the scars left by the civil war and the junta were in imminent danger of reopening. 'The Greek people', one KKE MP remarked, 'have a

[82] Ibid.
[83] Ibid., 13 April 1978, p. 2580.
[84] Ibid.
[85] Ibid., 12 April 1978, p. 2484.
[86] Ibid.
[87] Ibid., 10 April 1978, p. 2419.
[88] Ibid.
[89] Ibid., 10 April 1978, p. 2420.

bitter experience from emergency and special legislation. Espionage Law 375, for example, was primarily enforced against KKE political activity. Anti-communist Law 509, on many occasions, was even applied to fanatical anti-communists'.[90] KKE warned that it was the compact of 'emergency legislation and parastate violence' used to preserve a politically autocratic system which effectively brought about 'political anomaly and, ultimately, seven years of military dictatorship'.[91] Concluding that 774/1978 was 'a law far worse than 509' and that 'it will become in the hands of the state a tool of violence and oppression', KKE announced a walkout from the House before the bill's individual clauses were subjected to scrutiny.[92]

Centre-left EDIK (*Enossis Dimokratikou Kentrou*) approached the bill from a different angle than PASOK and the communists. EDIK agreed with the government's view that there was a significant increase in political violence both at home and abroad. According to EDIK, 'recent acts of political violence like the kidnapping of Moro in Italy and the bomb attacks against cinemas and bookstores in central Athens provided evidence for the assertion that various extremist organisations are at work'.[93] EDIK also recognized that it was necessary for Greece to 'fall in line with other European democracies in developing effective response models for dealing with terrorism'.[94] At the same time, however, EDIK pointed out that 'any anti-terrorist measures have to combine effectiveness with democratic acceptability'.[95] The key question, it added, about anti-terrorist legislation, whether at the international or the domestic level, was how security can be achieved without sacrificing democracy, the fundamental principles of the rule of law and the basic rights and freedoms of the individual.[96] While insisting on the importance of anti-terrorist legislation, EDIK argued that 'anti-terrorist laws should be exclusively aimed at the terrorists and not at the government's innocent subjects'.[97] In taking legislative action,

---

[90] Ibid.
[91] Ibid.
[92] Ibid., 17 April 1978, p. 2640.
[93] Ibid., 10 April 1978, p. 2417.
[94] Ibid., p. 2418.
[95] Ibid.
[96] Ibid., p. 2417.
[97] Ibid., p. 2414.

EDIK believed that the government had done little to balance the extent of the response with the seriousness of the problem and the rights of the citizens. To drive the point home, EDIK's leader, Yiannis Zigdis, remarked: '774/1978, the Government claims, is designed to suppress terrorist activity. What this law will suppress, if anything, is the constitutional rights and basic liberties of the Greek citizen'.[98] Discussing the lack of consensus inside parliament with regard to terrorism, the EDIK leader pointed to the conflictual nature of the political process in Greece and concluded that while 'on the one hand, the Government, using the fear of terrorism as a device to introduce emergency legislation that will take civil liberties away; on the other, precisely because of the threat, which is credible, to democratic freedoms that special anti-terrorist legislation poses, the Opposition except EDIK, refuses to see both the terrorist danger and the need for that danger to be contained'.[99]

However, Law 774 had no deterrent effect. By the end of decade, 222 incidents of terrorism had occurred.[100] Although the majority of these incidents, primarily arson attacks and low-level bombings, were carried out by indigenous groups, a considerable increase in international terrorist incidents suggested that Greece was gradually becoming a theatre of operations for Middle Eastern terrorism. As the 1980s progressed Greece together with France, Italy, Cyprus and the UK became the main battlefields for radical Arab-Palestinian terrorist factions such as the Abu Nidal Organization, Islamic revolutionary groups such as the Islamic Jihad and Middle Eastern rogue states like Syria and Libya.[101]

The abolition of Law 774/1978

In May 1983, 19 months after coming into office, PASOK abolished New Democracy's anti-terrorist legislation. With a majority of 57, PASOK made no modifications to its original argument that 774 was 'dangerous, unconstitutional and 100 per cent

---

[98] Parliamentary Discussion Papers – Greek Parliament, 13 April 1978, p. 2556.

[99] Ibid., p. 2543.

[100] Statistics provided by the PASOK Minister of Public Order, Andonis Drossoyiannis, during a parliamentary debate. Parliamentary Disussion Papers – Greek Parliament, 16 February 1987, p. 3620.

[101] Dennis A. Pluchinsky, 'Middle Eastern Terrorist Activity in Western Europe in the 1980s: A Decade of Violence', in *European Terrorism: Today & Tomorrow*, pp. 4–7.

unnecessary' and should therefore be abolished completely without replacement.[102] Insisting that special laws like 774/1978 were the concrete expressions of a tyrannical government, several PASOK MPs maintained that 'the provisions of the criminal law were adequate in protecting the democratic polity against acts of extremism and terrorism'.[103] At the same time, PASOK's Minister of Justice, Georgios-Alexandros Mangakis, claimed that 'in Greece terrorism is non-existent'.[104] Referring to a series of recent bomb attacks in Athens against foreign diplomats, Mangakis argued that it did not follow from these incidents that Greece was afflicted by terrorism. 'Whatever interpretation is given to these events', he said, 'firm evidence suggesting that Greece is experiencing the same phenomena of violence which occurred in Germany and Italy, is nowhere to be found'.[105] 'What we have in this country', Mangakis added, 'is not terrorism but isolated episodes of terrorism like the ones experienced by nearly all nations, even the most peaceful, non-violent such as Austria and Switzerland. For it is nowadays no longer possible for a country not to have endured some form of political violence'.[106] Mangakis also touched upon the issue of foreign interference in domestic legislation, suggesting that New Democracy's mistake was 'that it drafted 774 under pressure from abroad'.[107] Once the government had succumbed to external pressures, he suggested further, it became a mere mouthpiece for authoritarian practices, leaving no scope for genuine national debate. PASOK concluded that since Law 774/1978 'constituted a major threat to basic freedoms and a fundamental erosion of civil liberties', it was 'imperative' that it was abolished.[108] It quickly added that 774's abolition 'takes nothing away from the country's legislative armoury which was already adequate for dealing effectively with isolated criminal acts as they sporadically occurred'.[109]

Unsurprisingly, New Democracy saw things differently. It did not accept the position that terrorism in Greece was non-existent and

---

[102] Parliamentary Discussion Papers – Greek Parliament, 18 May 1983, p. 6542.
[103] Ibid., 16 May 1983, p. 6417.
[104] Ibid., p. 6429.
[105] Ibid., 18 May 1983, p. 6542.
[106] Ibid.
[107] Ibid., 16 May 1983, p. 6428.
[108] Ibid., 18 May 1983, p. 6542.
[109] Ibid.

castigated the socialists for not seriously addressing such an 'important and genuine problem'.[110] New Democracy's main focus of criticism was that 'the Government's arguments for abolishing anti-terrorist Law 774 were legally and generally untenable'.[111] In their view, political terrorism had become 'a big issue',[112] and 'the abolition of anti-terrorist legislation should only follow the disappearance of the phenomenon itself'.[113] The notion, New Democracy argued, that terrorism was virtually absent in Greece was nonsensical. 'Terrorism today', several conservative MPs insisted, 'is not extinct but escalating'.[114] The opposition was equally sceptical of PASOK's contention that '774 had to go because it was used in the past by the New Democracy government for purposes outside of its intended ambit, notably to criminalize and discredit its political opponents'.[115] After castigating the socialists for misleading the House, New Democracy's former Minister of Justice and sponsor of 774, George Stamatis, went on to make the claim that 'ever since the Act first came into force in 1978, there is no real evidence that the any of its provisions have been used by the then New Democracy Government wrongly'.[116] Anti-terrorist Law 774, according to Stamatis, proved effective because governmental policy responses to terrorism were pre-emptive/preventive rather than ad hoc.[117] At the same time, he declared that the 1978 law 'did not damage the country's democratic structure, did not curtail civil liberties, did not restrict freedom of thought and did not violate any constitutional rights'.[118]

Throughout the discussion, the picture New Democracy attempted to paint of PASOK was that of a government reluctant to recognize the growing terrorist threat and lacking interest in protecting its citizens against the extremists. New Democracy's parliamentary spokesman, Konstantinos Mitsotakis, asserted that the capacity to protect its citizens against terrorism and subversion was a necessary attribute of any modern state. PASOK's decision,

---

[110] Ibid., 16 May 1983, p. 6411.
[111] Ibid.
[112] Ibid., 18 May 1983, p. 6545.
[113] Ibid., 16 May 1983, p. 6411.
[114] Ibid.
[115] Ibid.
[116] Ibid., 18 May 1983, p. 6555.
[117] Ibid., p. 6558.
[118] Ibid., p. 6556.

Mitsotakis said, to ask Parliament to abolish 774 when at the very same time bombs explode against foreign diplomats[119] was 'an act of utter madness'.[120] At the same time, the New Democracy spokesman urged Parliament and PASOK in particular to avoid becoming bogged down in arguments about different definitions of terrorism. Asking Mangakis 'to approach the problem of terrorism not as the University Professor of Law that he previously was but rather as the country's Minister of Justice', Mitsotakis said that 'in such circumstances a national strategy to combat all terrorist activity was required'.[121] The government, he emphatically added, 'has the majority, and thus the responsibility not to allow Greece to become a launching pad for either domestic or international terrorism'.[122]

Near the end of the debate, New Democracy suggested that the governmental failure to recognize the shifts in terrorist tendencies and adjust its strategy accordingly, 'raised question-marks about PASOK's stand on the issue of politically motivated violence'.[123] Citing intelligence and media sources, New Democracy MPs wondered whether there was some truth in allegations of direct links between terrorist groups and high officials in the Papandreou administration.[124] New Democracy argued that governments, through omissions and misjudgements, could create situations which might encourage more terrorism. It added that PASOK's main responsibility was to take the evidence seriously and do whatever was necessary to present a credible response to the terrorist threat. New Democracy's primary conclusion was that the 1978 anti-terrorism law had 'proved its indispensable value as part of the state's armoury against terrorism and it is vital that its powers are continued by this House'.[125] Its abolition, New Democracy concluded, was 'ill-advised, dangerous'[126] and would 'lead to even more terrorism and bloodshed'.[127]

---

[119] New Democracy's parliamentary spokesman was making reference to two bomb attacks against foreign diplomats in Psychiko which coincided with the beginning of the debate for the abolition of Law 774/1978.

[120] Parliamentary Discussion Papers – Greek Parliament, 18 May 1983, p. 6537.

[121] Ibid., p. 6545.

[122] Ibid.

[123] Ibid., 23 May 1983, p. 6713.

[124] Ibid., p. 6714.

[125] Ibid., p. 6727.

[126] Ibid., 18 May 1983, p. 6556.

Anti-terrorist Law 1916/1990

On 26 September 1989, in its most brazen attack to date, 17N in broad daylight shot and fatally wounded Pavlos Bakoyiannis, New Democracy's parliamentary spokesman and son-in-law of party leader and premier Konstantinos Mitsotakis.[128] The entire nation was shocked. It was the first time a member of the Greek Parliament had been targeted by a terrorist group. Taking on her husband's seat with the promise of strong action against terrorism, Dora Bakoyiannis declared that 'a significant part of Greek society has yet failed to fully realize the seriousness of political terrorism and the threats that it poses'.[129] Focusing on the attitudes of Greek governing élites towards the problem and the lack of national consensus, Bakoyiannis said that 'democracy can be defended only by the determination of all political and social forces to isolate and eliminate its enemies'.[130] 'After every terrorist strike', she asserted, 'expressions of anger and indignation are being monotonously reiterated on all sides, but the actions taken and the decisions made by the political leaders do not show the emergence of a cross-party consensus to break with undue tolerance and compromise and to isolate terrorists in public opinion'.[131] At the same time, Bakoyiannis argued that Greece was 'the only country in Europe which has not only failed to arrest any terrorists but where publicity is given to their views'.[132] Although she acknowledged that terrorism and the media over most of the world were bound together in an inherently symbiotic relationship, Bakoyiannis argued that in Greece terrorists had 'even reached the point of imposing their communiqués and their terms with respect to publicity'.[133] Convinced that communiqués provided the terrorists with free publicity and a recognized political role and that their prohibition would be a crucial step in eradicating terrorism, Bakoyiannis mounted a campaign to prevent the Greek media from publishing them.

[127] Ibid., 23 May 1983, p. 6727.
[128] See Ch. 4.
[129] *Ecomomicos Tachydromos*, 29 November 1990.
[130] Parliamentary Discussion Papers – Greek Parliament, 25 January 1990, p. 514.
[131] *Economicos Tachydromos*, 29 November 1990.
[132] Parliamentary Discussion Papers – Greek Parliament, 25 January 1990, p. 513.
[133] Dora Bakoyiannis, 'Allages sta Valkania: Messa Mazikis Enimerossis kai Tromokratia' [Changes in the Balkans: Terrorism and the Media] in Yiorgos Voukelatos (ed.) *Tromokratia kai Messa Mazikis Enimerossis* [Terrorism and the Media] (Athens: Elliniki Euroekdotiki, 1993), p. 22.

As a consequence, on 28 December 1990, the Greek Parliament passed a tough and controversial anti-terrorism bill entitled 'Bill for the Protection of the Society against Organized Crime' (1916/1990). In essence, the bill embodied all the provisions of Law 774/1978 with the exception of the death sentence. Officially, the new bill was an organized crime law and did not use the word 'terrorism'. However, the majority of the articles were counter-measures against forms of political terrorism. In fact, the bill referred to 'organized crime' (article 1, section 1) as 'two or more persons acting in concert to commit, attempt, finance or otherwise aid in the commission of any of a list of serious felonies: kidnapping, homicide, causing injury with weapons or explosives, hijacking, harming the security of an aircraft, hostage-taking, arson, attacks on police and military personnel and installations, and dealing in illegal drugs or biological warfare agents'. The new law (articles 11, 12) also increased police powers in the areas of wiretaps, search and seizure, mail opening, examination of bank records, and freezing and confiscating bank accounts. Moreover, it gave police the right (article 14) to detain individuals for fifteen days without specific charges and without evidence if disclosures might harm an investigation. Article 8 made provision for the special protection of judges (and their families) conducting investigations and interrogations associated with organized crime. Article 16 of the bill authorized financial rewards of at least 25 million drachma as an incentive for police informers. Article 17 made provisions for the reduction of sentences of those people associated with criminal acts in exchange for information leading the authorities to the dislocation of terrorist groups. However, the most contentious issue in the bill was article 6, which forbade 'publicizing in the press or the mass media, announcements, proclamations and all forms of declarations by organizations or groups' as defined in article 1, section 1. The prohibition was to take effect only when the chief prosecutor of the Supreme Court announced a ban on publishing a particular document. Violators were subject to three months' minimum imprisonment and up to 50 million drachma in fines.

From the viewpoint of New Democracy it was imperative that the government took the necessary measures to eradicate terrorism. During the three-day parliamentary debate, it was repeatedly stated by New Democracy speakers that 'the legislative arsenal at the Government's disposal was not adequate for cracking down on terrorism'.[134] Dora Bakoyiannis, deputy minister to the Prime Minister, used 17N's most recent multi-rocket attack against shipping magnate V. Vardinoyiannis to argue that the escalation of terrorist tactics and the increasing sophistication in terrorist weaponry made the threat to public security greater than ever before.[135] As terrorists became technologically more adept and their targets widened, 'this Government', Bakoyiannis argued, 'has the moral and political obligation to do all in its power to defend the lives of its citizens'.[136] Minister of Justice, Thanassis Kanellopoulos, argued that a number of drastic legislative changes were needed if the government was to reassert control over 'an obviously deteriorating situation'.[137] In similar vein, New Democracy's parliamentary spokeswoman, Virginia Tsouderou, made the argument that it was 'absolutely urgent that counter-measures are swiftly taken because terrorism does not merely strike at innocent individuals but at society as a whole'.[138] 'Society', she added, 'has to be seen as terrorism's greatest victim'.[139] On the impact of terrorism, another speaker observed that it was 'important to recognize that organized crime apart from undermining the constitution, parliamentarism and the security of the people, also damages the country's economic growth and development'.[140]

New Democracy looked back at the past to draw implications for the present. Historical evidence, it was argued, 'shows clearly that Greek people for many years have been striving for the efficient functioning of the country's democratic institutions'.[141] As ND explained, it was these institutions that 'are being targeted by organized crime and it is therefore imperative for the Greek state to take effective action'.[142] At the same time, New Democracy made extensive use of European Council and United Nations conventions concerning political violence to show the scale of the problem and demonstrate that 'there is no country in the civilised

134 Parliamentary Discussion Papers – Greek Parliament, 10 December 1990, p. 4568.
135 Ibid., 12 December 1990, p. 4670.
136 Ibid.
137 Ibid. 10 December 1990, p. 4550.
138 Ibid., p. 4549.
139 Ibid.
140 Ibid., p. 4552.
141 Ibid., p. 4553.
142 Ibid.

world that has not taken counter-measures against organised crime'.[143] Governing party speakers made particular reference to the April 1978 Council of Europe meeting when 15 member states – France, Germany, Italy, Belgium, Portugal, the United Kingdom among them – declaring their deep distress at the kidnapping of Aldo Moro agreed to take counter-measures against organized crime.[144] 'These countries', the argument continued, 'not only introduced special legislation but they also implemented it in a consistent and unambiguous fashion'.[145] Coming further up to date, Minister of Public Order, Yiannis Vassiliadis, spoke of the international agreements reached in the seventh congress of the United Nations in November 1985. He specifically referred to resolution number 1 of the UN which made provisions for strengthening legislative measures against organized crime and resolution 23 on combating international terrorism.[146] From New Democracy's point of view, Vassiliadis said, the Greek state had no alternative but 'to follow the experience of most Western liberal democracies and ensure that rules are framed and implemented so as to produce results'.[147] Meanwhile, the Minister of Public Order damned the opposition for not putting party politics and partisan calculations aside when dealing with terrorism. Vassiliadis was scornful of the idea that terrorism had a dividing rather than a unifying effect on Greek politics. By any standards, he complained, it was extraordinary that the main political parties displayed such intractable differences on how to approach the terrorist problem.[148]

During the discussion, New Democracy did not overlook the fact that Greece had been plagued by terrorism for the past 15 years and that the state had remained virtually apathetic towards the phenomenon. For the government, the main issue at question was 'whether the Greek state will continue a passive spectator or strongly react against this social plague that is called terrorism'.[149] Similarly, another speaker said the question to be asked was: 'Shall we take heed from past mistakes or shall we remain a society of

143 Ibid., p. 4553.
144 Ibid., p. 4554.
145 Ibid.
146 Ibid., p. 4568.
147 Ibid., pp. 4568–9.
148 Ibid., p. 4569.
149 Ibid., p. 4561.

intimidated citizens?'[150] Mitsotakis's party constantly stressed that the problem of terrorism could not be resolved with aphorisms and incoherent theorizing but required collective will and awareness from all sectors of the public.[151] Recognizing at the same time that the roots of the opposition's intransigence were essentially historical, New Democracy maintained that the law was not introduced for its own sake but to correct the impression that the government could not provide basic security. New Democracy also noted that it was deeply unfortunate that the parties of the left in general, and the communists in particular, were 'still living in the post-civil war decade of the 1950s'.[152] Attacking the opposition's aphoristic style and emotional tendency to debate largely on the basis of its political memories, Bakoyiannis argued that the left 'seemed incapable of realizing that its pursuit of phantoms from an earlier era meant that the real issue of how to deal with terrorism went unexamined'.[153] Following this line of argument another speaker pointedly remarked that 'the decade of the 1950s has irrevocably gone', and suggested that 'it would be considered beneficial for the Parliament and the country as a whole if you contributed on how to eradicate terrorism instead of ceaselessly discussing the 1950s'.[154] The Minister of Public Order was similarly scathing in discussing PASOK's overall law-and-order approach to terrorism. Vassiliadis's fiercest criticism was reserved for his predecessor at the ministry whom he held responsible for 'doing everything at your disposal to divide and demoralise the security forces'.[155] In Vassiliadis's view, 'PASOK was running both the country and the police force for eight years but did absolutely nothing to confront the problem. Eight years marked by indifference and incompetence'.[156]

However, it was Dora Bakoyiannis and the former president of the Association of Athens Newspaper Editors, MP Vassilios Korahais who, in the parliamentary discussion, numerous press conferences and interviews, attempted to defend the bill's most controversial aspect – article 6 which enabled the district attorney to issue an

[150] Ibid.
[151] Ibid., 13 December 1990, p. 4710.
[152] Ibid., 10 December 1990, p. 4562.
[153] Ibid., 12 December 1990, p. 4670.
[154] Ibid., 10 December 1990, p. 4562.
[155] Ibid., p. 4567.
[156] Ibid.

Europe's Last Red Terrorists

injuction forbidding the publication of terrorist communiqués after an assassination. Bakoyiannis's starting-point was that 15 years of terrorist experience which continued to grow in intensity, daring and sophistication made the introduction of special legislation imperative.[157] Bakoyiannis pointed out that 'the legislative strengthening of both judicial and security authorities will greatly contribute to tracking and neutralizing terrorist organizations'.[158] 'With an organized, systematic and patient effort by the security agencies', she explained, 'combined with an appropriate legislative arsenal, the Government believes that organized crime can be successfully tackled'.[159] At the same time, Bakoyiannis referred to other European countries (Italy, Spain, Germany) which like Greece had past fascist experience, but where 'the main party political opponents, having fully realised the threat that terrorism posed to Democracy, agreed unanimously in passing anti-terrorist legislation'.[160] Pleading with the opposition not to reject the bill on the basis of temperament, prejudice and habit, Bakoyiannis declared that 'the state response to terrorism must have no ideological colours'.[161] In Italy, she insisted, 'it took the co-operation of all parties, the Communists included, to deal successfully with the Red Brigades'.[162]

As article 6 became the epicentre of the debate, Vassilios Korahais said that the government's decision to take such measures was in the interests of more effective democracy. Against the charge that article 6 was unconstitutional, Korahais argued that it was 'not the article itself that abrogated the freedom of the press, but a band of paranoid dropouts setting themselves up as judge, jury and executioners on those whom they classify as their enemies, while at the same time poisoning and polarizing society with their lying and distorted proclamations'.[163] Focusing on the controversy surrounding article 6, Korahais made a strong argument about the opposition's efforts in resisting the prohibition of the publication of terrorist communiqués. 'Why should', he asked, 'the communiqués written by anonymous terrorists be publicized?'[164] 'In any period', he added,

[157] Ibid., 12 December 1990, p. 4670.
[158] Ibid.
[159] Ibid.
[160] Ibid., p. 4672.
[161] Ibid., p. 4682.
[162] Ibid., p. 4670.
[163] Ibid., 10 December 1990, p. 4574.

'no newspaper, no editor would publicize an anonymous text. It is the most fundamental principle of journalistic ethics. Why, therefore, so much sensitivity about anonymous assassins?'[165] Korahais quoted a passage from *La Republica* commentator Giorgio Bocca on the Red Brigades to make the point that Greek journalists like their counterparts in Italy had become 17N's messengers.[166]

Recognizing the fact that 'modern terrorism provided first-class material' and was 'a circulation booster that cannot be ignored in the competitive world of media', Bakoyiannis said that past experience had shown that 'the marriage of convenience between terrorists and the media was appallingly useful only to the terrorists'.[167] Bakoyiannis was insistent that the Greek media 'acted as a sounding board for terrorists'.[168] Because of the fact that they 'almost always appear on the front pages of newspapers and dominate radio and television on prime time, their views acquire tremendous topicality, publicity and circulation'.[169] Terrorist organizations, she added 'use the printed press and television as a second-degree means to its end, after a first-degree act of terrorism'.[170] The best solution to the problem, Dora Bakoyiannis observed, would be for the Greek press to commit itself not to publicize the terrorists' communiqués, as was the case with the rest of the European press. 'Regrettably here', Bakoyiannis said, 'the main reason behind the publication of such texts by the press lies exclusively with the fact that they are written by assassins'.[171] Bakoyiannis maintained that the Greek media 'could have made a greater contribution to making public opinion more sensitive and to creating a social conscience that could isolate terrorist action both ideologically and politically'.[172] Instead, she argued, 'we experience the revolting phenomenon of some newspapers advertising the exclusivity of the communiqués'.[173] The deputy minister to the premier expanded her argument by arguing that since the press

[164] Ibid.
[165] Ibid.
[166] Ibid.; see Giorgio Bocca, *Il Terrorismo Italiano 1979–1980*.
[167] Dora Bakoyiannis, 'Terrorism in Greece', in *Mediterranean Quarterly*, p. 22.
[168] Ibid.
[169] Dora Bakoyiannis, 'Allages sta Valkania', p. 22.
[170] Bakoyiannis, 'Terrorism in Greece', p. 22.
[171] *Economicos Tachydromos*, 29 November 1990.
[172] Bakoyiannis, 'Terrorism in Greece', p. 22.
[173] *Economicos Tachydromos*, 29 November 1990.

conveyed the terrorist propaganda it essentially functioned as a multiplier of terror. 'In the name of freedom of the press', Bakoyiannis asserted, 'the media unwittingly contributes to the creation of a pedestal over which terrorism can freely develop'.[174] To illustrate her point, Bakoyiannis made reference to the Vyronas police station raid by 17N commandos in August 1988. 'The raid on the police station took place because the terrorists wanted to impress the public and ridicule the state'.[175] Attempting to gain maximum publicity, Bakoyiannis said, the terrorists demanded that the newspaper recipient of their communiqué published it in full or suffered the consequences which were to send the text to a rival newspaper. To substantiate this claim, Bakoyiannis quoted the cover letter of the Vyronas attack communiqué sent to an Athens daily editor stating: 'We are sending the following text together with three photos only to your newspaper, without sending it elsewhere. If you are unable to publish as it is, that is without cuts and captions contrary to its contents, we shall then send it elsewhere'.[176] 'Does this freedom of the press', Bakoyiannis asked, 'entitle journalists to yield to demands dictated by terrorists in order to secure the exclusivity of a pamphlet that would have no interest if it were not spilled with blood?'[177] 'This is the grossest abuse of the freedom of the press', she told Parliament.[178] Lamenting the fact that in Greece 'political parties, newspapers, journalists and other social factors could not yet come to a morally binding agreement on the media's role in dealing with this menace ... ', Bakoyiannis concluded that the government of New Democracy had no time to waste in creating an effective framework to protect the life, property and well-being of all its citizens and defeat terrorism.[179]

However, PASOK saw the anti-terrorist bill in a different light. Andreas Papandreou described 1916 inside and outside parliament as another deplorable mistake committed by the government which reinforced his party's impressions of the degeneration of the country's democratic institutions.[180] While condemning every form

---

[174] Ibid.
[175] Parliamentary Discussion Papers – Greek Parliament, 12 December 1990, p. 4671.
[176] Ibid.
[177] Ibid.
[178] Ibid.
[179] Bakoyiannis, 'Terrorism in Greece', p. 24.
[180] Papandreou statement to Athens daily *Eleftherotypia*, 11 December 1990.

of terrorism and violence 'which constituted the worst type of fascism and had no place in a democracy',[181] the Socialists protested that the bill under discussion was 'particularly dangerous and profoundly threatening to civil liberties'.[182] PASOK's central thesis was that 'the Government, on the pretext that it combats terrorism and contrary to constitutional principles, enacts the curtailment of democratic rights and fundamental freedoms of the citizens'.[183] Its essential argument in opposing 1916 was that the party's sensitivity and respect towards the victims of terrorism was absolute but that respect was extended to the preservation of the basic rights of the individual.[184] PASOK also argued that the speed with which legislation with such serious human rights and civil liberties implications was being rushed through meant that 'the Government aimed at gagging both Parliament and the parliamentarians'.[185] Similarly, PASOK speakers drew attention to the fact that although the bill had attracted widespread hostility from lawyers and the judiciary as well as from academics and the media, the government decided, without public opinion behind it, to move ahead in complete isolation.[186] PASOK insisted that it was time for New Democracy to 'change their attitude and revise their unacceptable methods to fit the altered circumstances of the 1990s'.[187] At the same time, PASOK criticized the government for utilizing legislation introduced in other European countries in an effort to convince parliament that counter-terrorist measures were necessary. The government, in PASOK's point of view, had failed 'to appreciate that certain traumatic experiences in Greece's modern political history are incompatible with those of any other country in Europe'.[188] For the socialists, 'parallels with other European states like Italy and France could not be elaborated simply because there is a distinctive difference in both historical conditions and ideological trends'.[189] According to PASOK's argument, the terrorist problem in Greece

---

[181] Parliamentary Discussion Papers – Greek Parliament, 25 January 1990, p. 515.
[182] Ibid., 12 December 1990, p. 4675.
[183] Ibid., p. 4669.
[184] Ibid., 10 December 1990, p. 4556.
[185] Ibid., 12 December 1990, p. 4669.
[186] Ibid., 10 December 1990, p. 4563.
[187] Ibid., 12 December 1990, p. 4676.
[188] Ibid., 12 December 1990, p. 4661.
[189] Ibid., 10 December 1990, p. 4566.

was 'radically different from the one Italy, Germany and other states endured. Different roots, different characteristics and different evolution'.[190] Citing statistical data, one socialist speaker made the point that 'in France for one year alone there were 21 deaths and 191 injuries and in Italy 300 to 350 deaths'.[191] PASOK was equally emphatic in claiming that 'Greece's problem was nothing more than the activity of a small terrorist gang of 10–15 with low operational capabilities and incoherent political goals'.[192] PASOK asserted that in stark contrast to the Red Brigades in Italy, 17N 'have never pursued numerical or geographical expansion and never attempted to integrate their objectives with those of the masses'.[193]

Throughout the debate, the socialists made it plain that the abolition of 1916 was to be PASOK's top priority once they returned to office. Characterizing 1916 'as an even more dangerous law than its predecessor 778/1978', PASOK sought to distinguish between a recalcitrant, conservative government and a reformist, progressive opposition by stating that the former denied the effective functioning of democracy.[194] The question PASOK raised most frequently during the debate was 'to what extent does New Democracy believe that, in order to meet the threat from terrorists, basic freedoms and liberal precepts on which the constitutional state was founded have to be curbed and challenged?'[195] PASOK saw every reason why parliament should not vote for 'the gagging of the press, the wiretapping and mail opening, the fabrication of suspects and the legitimization of *hafiethismos* (stool pigeon practice)'.[196] The government was severely criticized for article 14 in the bill which made provision for the extended detention and exclusion of individuals without specific charge and evidence for the maximum period of 15 days. Attacking the government for copying the German practice of 'white cells', PASOK speakers argued that the suspect's constitutional rights could not be satisfactorily safeguarded.[197] As they

190   Ibid., 12 December 1990, p. 4665.
191   Ibid., 10 December 1990, p. 4566.
192   Ibid., p. 4665.
193   Ibid., 12 December 1990, p. 4676.
194   Ibid., 10 December 1990, pp. 4565 and 4570.
195   Ibid., 12 December 1990, p. 4676.
196   Ibid.
197   Ibid., 10 December 1990, p. 4557.

explained, 'there are many different degrading ways apart from torture and ill-treatment that can have damaging psychological effects on a person who is kept isolated for days in a basement cell at a police-station jail'.[198] Another clause that came under PASOK's harsh criticism was article 10 which gave police powers to trespass on and enter a person's property to undertake searches in relation to individuals suspected of terrorist acts or complicity in or defence of such acts. PASOK's viewpoint was that article 10 evoked bitter junta memories when the regime's security services on a daily basis raided houses and arrested people on charges of terrorism.[199] PASOK concluded that article 10 was 'intended by New Democracy to terrorize its political opponents'.[200]

The inefficiency of the Greek security forces was another critical aspect of the debate. PASOK argued that the fight against terrorism had been unsuccessful not because of the lack of appropriate legislation but primarily because of the incompetence of the country's law enforcement agencies.[201] According to PASOK, the solution to the problem of terrorism lay with 'the potentiation, modernization, and democratization of the security forces'.[202] One PASOK MP, Sifis Valirakis, accused the government of 'doing everything in their power to hamper the counter-terrorist effort and undermine the morale of the anti-terrorist force'.[203] Valirakis attacked the New Democracy government for sacking intelligence and security force personnel involved in counter-terrorist operations for party-political reasons. To support his case, Valirakis produced evidence from administrative files which he claimed 'proves that in the department of intelligence-gathering and information-analysis alone, New Democracy reduced the number of personnel from 100 to 17'.[204] 'How could the security forces possibly confront the terrorists under such conditions?', Vallirakis asked the House.[205]

---

[198] Ibid.
[199] On the Greek junta's law enforcement tactics see George Mangakis, 'Letter to Europeans', in *An Embarrassment of Tyrannies: Twenty-five years of Index on Censorship* (London: Gollancz, 1997), pp. 25–38.
[200] Parliamentary Discussion Papers – Greek Parliament, 10 December 1990, p. 4565.
[201] Ibid.
[202] Ibid.
[203] Ibid., 12 December 1990, p. 4666.
[204] Ibid.
[205] Ibid.

The financial incentives for police informers were another area
of dispute and PASOK suggested that the government clearly
encouraged the practice of *hafiethismos*. Article 16, according to
PASOK, brought back the authoritarian decades of extensive surveillance practices which had formally ended with the fall of the
military junta.[206] PASOK also maintained that 'the financial
rewards will lead to a massive gathering of plausible or false information which in the end will undermine the security services'
efforts by making the collection and processing of valuable information an impossible task'.[207] Further, PASOK attacked article 6
which forbade 'publicizing in the press or the mass media
announcements, proclamations and all forms of declarations by
organizations or groups'. PASOK reiterated their position that
article 6 violated fundamental constitutional rights and further
abrogated the freedom of the press and the right of people to
information.[208] At the same time, the socialists wondered how
would 'media prohibitions, 5-year prison terms for publishers and
journalists and maximum individual fines of up to 100 million
drachma prevent 17 November from killing and maiming'.[209]
Paraphrasing Edmund Burke's dictum: 'bad laws are the worst
type of tyranny', PASOK condemned the government for 'driving
the country into deep political, social and institutional crisis'.[210]
Papandreou said that his party would not stay to vote for such an
appalling piece of legislation and proposed instead a referendum
'whereby the Greek people will speak for themselves'.[211] The bill
for the Protection of the Society Against Organized Crime,
PASOK concluded, was an inclination to injustice and 'terrorism's greatest victory against Greek democracy'.[212]

Greece's communist coalition's (Synaspismos) central argument in opposing 1916 was that the bill did not offer any solutions
to the problem of terrorism. Synaspismos was adamant that 1916
was in many respects pernicious, particularly because of the way it
flouted basic principles such as fairness, equality and human

[206] Ibid., p. 4669.
[207] Ibid.
[208] Ibid., p. 4675.
[209] Ibid., p. 4683.
[210] Ibid., p. 4672.
[211] Ibid., 10 December 1990, p. 4566.
[212] Ibid., 12 December 1990, p. 4666.

dignity. In their view, Law 1916 produced disequilibrium between taking counter-measures against terrorism and the maintenance of political rights and civil liberties.[213] The party's parliamentary spokesman, Fotis Kouvelis, criticized the government for introducing legislation that 'violates fundamental civil liberties, defies international declarations on the protection of human rights and clashes with basic principles of the penal code/law'.[214] At the same time, Kouvelis made the point that 'if stern legislation with emergency powers and draconian forms of punishment like the abolished 774 failed to prevent terrorism why and how could the new one bring about positive results?'[215] Like PASOK before, Synaspismos launched an attack on the government for 'hypocritically' using the problem of terrorism as 'a convenient political alibi to introduce authoritarian control mechanisms and police state practices'.[216]

Synaspismos attached great importance to discord and conflict in parliamentary political life. They believed that an operative liberal democratic state 'must avoid the errors of panic and over-reaction and be able to absorb marginal socio-political ills such as terrorism and provide solutions without putting basic civil liberties and democracy at risk'.[217] The government of New Democracy and its security advisers, Kouvelis argued further, 'have failed to realize that heavy-handed over-reaction by the state is what terrorist groups deliberately seek to provoke'.[218] Over-reaction, he asserted, was the worst policy because it clearly played into terrorists' hands. Of equal importance for Synaspismos were the practical policies and measures devised by the state to strengthen the law enforcement agencies in countering terrorism. Insisting that the legislative framework for tackling terrorist crimes was adequate, Synaspismos stressed that the main reason behind the state's failure to contain terrorist activities was the lack of modernization and expertise of the Greek security agencies.[219] Synaspismos was equally emphatic that attempts at police reform after *metapolitefsi* were never seriously tried and showed that the methods, tactics and ethos of the security apparatus had remained the same.[220]

---

[213] Ibid., 10 December 1990, p. 4560.
[214] Ibid., p. 4559.
[215] Ibid.
[216] Ibid., p. 4573.
[217] Ibid., p. 4560.
[218] Ibid.
[219] Ibid., p. 4559.

Synaspismos repeatedly argued that the bill was unacceptable and warned of the 'dismal implications its implementation would have for the country's political and social life'.[221] The communists maintained that several clauses of 1916 introduced an element of fear and social distrust which would seriously affect the democratic norms of political behaviour.[222] More specifically, the government came under harsh criticism for the clause in the law which authorized financial incentives for police informers. Article 16, Synaspismos argued, institutionalized *hafiethismos* and opened the path for false testimonies, fake witnesses and fabricated information.[223] At the same time, Synaspismos maintained that articles 11 and 12, which contained measures in areas of wiretaps, search and seizures and mail opening, would enable the police to use their powers against individuals with no restrictions. Article 6 also came under Synaspismos's harsh criticism. Declaring that article 6 curtailed the freedom of the press, Kouvelis argued that 'media prohibitions and concealment of facts would lead to misinformation with the country becoming an inferno of constant rumours, innuendo and myth-making'.[224] Synaspismos also ridiculed the government's attempt to relate the Italian terrorist phenomenon to the Greek experience. The government's argument, Synaspismos's leader, Maria Damanakis, said, 'deliberately misled by making comparison between different types of political factions with different aims and different forms of action'.[225] 'Whereas in Greece we have a bunch of hotheads', Damanakis said, 'in Italy, left-wing terrorism had a strong societal emphasis, a sophisticated organizational structure and vast recruitment base'.[226] She added that in the 1978–80 period, commonly referred to as 'the years of lead', there were 6,394 attacks from which 184 died and 391 were injured. Throughout the debate, however, Synaspismos did not dispute New Democracy's claim that terrorism was a threat to civilized society and the rule of law but castigated the government for deducing that it could simply be legislated out of existence. 'What the Mitsotakis Government has failed to realize', Synaspismos

[220] Ibid., 12 December 1990, p. 4684.
[221] Ibid., 13 December 1990, p. 4730.
[222] Ibid., p. 4723.
[223] Ibid., p. 4728.
[224] Ibid., 10 December 1990, p. 4560.
[225] Ibid., 12 December 1990, p. 4658.
[226] Ibid.

concluded, was that 'the critical social and political problems are not resolved by laws. They are primarily resolved by political and social consensus'.[227]

Government vs. the media

Law 1916 was passed on 28 December 1990 and created a furore within the media community which until 1990 had enjoyed an absolute degree of freedom. With regard to terrorism, the press was free to publish and speculate on everything. Group communiqués – 17N's in particular – were always published in full. As a result, the Greek press began a confrontational campaign against the law denouncing the restrictions on their freedom of opinion and expression. Declaring that 1916 smacked of the 1967–74 military junta period, newspapers maintained that the law conflicted with Article 14, paragraph 2 of the Greek constitution.[228] Six months later, on 6 June 1991, the prohibition came into effect. Following a 17N attack on a Turkish diplomat, the chief prosecutor of the Supreme Court announced a ban on publicizing the attack communiqué. Having received the 17N communiqué, the Greek daily *Eleftherotypia*, went ahead in total defiance of the governmental ban and published the whole text. At the same time, six other newspapers in protest against the law printed the same proclamation.[229] Explaining why he decided to break the ban, the *Eleftherotypia* editor, Seraphim Fyntanidis, maintained that

Besides the slogans coated in the usual waffle, the statement contained information that was of public interest. At the time, the air was thick with rumours that the attack against the diplomat had been the work of the Greek secret services – or even of a Turkish agent provocateur. Following editorial discussion, I decided to publish the statement, adding comment condemning actions of the terrorists. I made it clear that since their proclamation had useful information for the readers, I had no right to suppress it.[230]

---

227 Ibid., p. 4684.
228 According to the Greek constitution: 'The press is free. Censorship in any form . . . or prior restraint, is prohibited'; see also I. Manoledakis, 'I andisyndagmatikotita tou ar.6 tou n. 1916/1990' [The unconstitutionality of article 6 of Law 1916/1990], in *Yperaspissi*, No.5 (Sept–Oct 1991), pp. 997–1002.
229 Costas Beis, 'To dikaioma tis pliroforissis kai o n.1916/1990' [Law 1916/1990 and the right of information], in *Yperaspissi*, No.5 (Sept–Oct 1991), pp. 87–96.
230 Interview with Seraphim Fyntanidis, 15 September 1995, Athens.

The morning after, Fyntanidis, together with the editors of the other six dailies, was arrested on charges relating to the anti-terrorist law. The rift between the Mitsotakis government and the media was complete. A widespread public and international outcry followed. An open-air concert outside the Korydallos prison attracted 10,000 people who gathered to demonstrate their support and demand the release of the journalists. Aidan White of the International Federation of Journalists and Sandra Colliver of Article 19 International Centre against Censorship together with representatives from PEN International and Reporters Without Frontiers arrived in Athens to exert pressure on the Mitsotakis administration. When the case came to court, three months later, the seven editors were given prison sentences of several months. After serving 12 days, the case was finally closed when the Athens Union of Newspaper Publishers paid a fine in lieu of the remainder of the sentence.

Without doubt, 'the greatest defence of democracy lies in a free press'.[231] Freedom of the press is essential to the healthy functioning of democracy and is 'basic to our protection from arbitrary private or state power'.[232] Moreover, it allows the media to 'act as conduit and forum for critical public debate and ensures that the role of radio, television and press will never be reduced to, or exploited as, a passive transmission belt for government indoctrination'.[233] Journalism's fundamental purpose is to satisfy the desire for information and 'describe a situation with honesty, exactness and clarity'.[234] The public is entitled to know of terrorist events which occur and coverage and analysis of issues that affect collective interest are justified. At a deeper level, the media can provide a 'forum for informed discussion concerning the social and political implications of terrorism and the development of adequate policies and counter-measures'.[235] However, the media in Greece has presented terrorism with a baffling lack of responsibility and sophistication.[236] During the early 1980s, newspaper

---

[231] Jon Snow, 'Bylines, spy lines and a bidden agenda', *The Guardian*, 30 December 1994.

[232] Andrew Marr, 'Invasion of the prying press', *The Independent*, 7 June 1996.

[233] Peter Chalk, *West European Terrorism and Counter-Terrorism: The Evolving Dynamic*, (London: Macmillan, 1996), p.111.

[234] Christian Tyler, 'Where lies the truth?', *Financial Times*, 25 July 1998.

[235] Paul Wilkinson, 'The Media and Terrorism: A Reassessment', in *Terrorism and Political Violence*, Vol.9, No.2 (Summer 1997), p.60.

editors and proprietors began to recognize that 17N's name and
five-pointed star on the front page always sold thousands of extra
copies. As a result, a tendency to publish rumour and suspend editorial judgement developed. Unsubstantiated claims and theories
about the group were manipulated, over-dramatized, even
invented, in an attempt to maximize readership from a public
which can choose from 22 dailies and another 17 Sunday papers in
Athens alone. Throughout the 1980s and mid-1990s, 17N attacks
provided the raw material for countless pages of journalistic speculation presented as fact.[237] At the same time, the insatiable public

---

[236] George Kassimeris, 'Greece: Twenty Years of Political Terrorism', in *Terrorism and
Political Violence*, Vol.7, No.2 (Summer 1995), pp.86–8.

[237] A few examples of the terrorist coverage by the Greek press over the years adequately
illustrate the point: 'The hit-men of the terrorist organization 17 November must be
foreigners. This is the view of many officials dealing with the investigation of the
assassination of *Apogevmatini* publisher N. Momferatos[21 Feb. 1985]. In fact, there
are some police analysts who seriously doubt the existence of an organization because
they see indications that behind the name 17 November is the "Terrorist
International" or secret services of some foreign country, very likely the Soviet
Union', Source: *Acropolis tis Kyriakis*, 24 February 1985; – 'Police currently
investigating a case involving the discovery of weapons and ammunition in two Athens
apartments thought to be terrorist hideouts, believe they have established a link
between two people held in custody after last week's shoot-out in Galatsi and the
shadowy 17 November organization … Reports said yesterday that police found two
car keys in the hideouts where the weapons were discovered and these keys belonged
to getaway cars used after the December 1975 killing of CIA station chief Richard
Welch and of police officers Pantelis Petrou and Sotiris Stamoulis in January 1980 … '
Source: *Athens News*, 7 October 1987; – 'Most of the questions which are posed after
the latest action [failed attempt to assassinate DEA special agent, George Carros, 22
Jan. 1988] of 17N are certainly not new. But, nevertheless they create a different
picture from that which has been developed up until now about this phantom-
organization that strikes its targets like Zorro and vanishes without trace. Examination
of the facts that emerge from last Thursday's attempt reinforces the certainty that 17N
has lost this asset and demonstrates that at one level is vulnerable; to what extent, time
will tell … Furthermore, the style of the communiqués, the author's poor vocabulary,
and above all the absence of Marxist-Leninist terms, reinforce the impression that
inside the organization there have been rearrangements and a change in relationships
… In conclusion, we can report that the new and substantial fact given by last
Thursday's attempt in Filothei is that "something is happening" inside 17 November.
How serious this "something" is will become clear in due course. For the present what
is clear is that "the rank and file" of the current organization must feel deeply
disillusioned, as must the organization's sympathizers, and perhaps the leaders will
understand (just as happens with great prima donnas) that curtain-time brings
suffering with it. The red, five-pointed star of 17N seems to have started to set course

demand for 17N stories meant that the media consumed in pursuing terror 'spectaculars' became unable to cover terrorism intelligently.[238] Like its Italian counterparts during the *anni di piombo* (the years of the bullet), the Greek media has preferred 'the melodramatic to the analytical approach, emphasizing emotion, violence and speculation rather than a balanced explanation of facts'.[239] However, article 6 in the 1916/1990 Law, which prohibited the publication of communiqués by terrorist groups after an assassination, was a departure from traditional, covert forms of governmental pressure on the media. Exasperated with 17N and convinced that media attention to terrorism encouraged more of the same, the Mitsotakis government tried, without a sense of perspective, to limit the amount and type of publicity terrorists received. Although New Democracy defended the ban on the grounds that to beat your enemy in a war you have to suspend

for its own decline' Source: *To Vima*, 31 January 1988; – 'Today *Anti* reveals important proof about the identity of the 17N terrorist organization and its international links. The proof in question is a report to the Moroccan intelligence agency by its agent in Greece, Bassir Bayi who operated here under cover as a journalist. His report, which was prepared on 6 May 1987 and of which we publish below the original and a translation, reveals the following: 17 November maintains close relations and co-operates or forms part of another wider organization to which Libyans belong. In fact, Bayi refers to 17N as "le groupe grec de l'organisation du 17 Novembre", which translates as "the Greek section of the 17 November organization" ... At some point prior to 4 May 1987 there was a meeting between 17N and Libyans and others who probably belonged to the Abu Nidal group. Among those Libyans at the meeting was terrorist Abdelhamid Qubaidi, the personal agent of Colonel Gaddafi and probable perpetrator of many hitherto "unsolved" crimes against other Arabs in Greece ... Bayi's report shows clearly that the 17 November-Arab meeting came at a time when Libyan terrorism was attempting to reorganize after the blow Gaddafi's prestige suffered in the Gulf of Sidra attack ... ', Source: *Anti*, 23–29 March 1990; In April 1990, the right-wing *Eleftheros Typos* newspaper also 'identified several persons who either are 17N members or "protect" the organization: Kostas Tsimas, PASOK EuroMP, Sifis Valirakis, former PASOK Minister, Yiannis Kapsis, former PASOK Minister, Kostas Kakioussis, third secretary of the Greek embassy in Helsinki, Syrian diplomats serving in Athens: Muhamed El Said and Kasem Esber, a criminal held in prison who – from inside – had predicted that 17N would try to assassinate two judges and two politicians, and an unnamed official at the Ministry of National Defence' (Source: JPRS-TOT–90-01-L, 22 May 1990).

238 *Epopteia*, No. 169 (July-August 1991), pp. 5–8; see also *Economicos Tachydromos* editorials, 11 November 1993 and 17 February 1994.

239 See Alison Jamieson, 'The Italian Experience', in H. H. Tucker (ed.), *Combating the Terrorists: Democratic Responses to Political Violence* (New York: Facts on File, 1988), p. 152.

your civil liberties for a time,[240] the ban was an anomalous measure which polarized Greek society and did nothing to reduce the increase and seriousness of terrorist incidents.[241] Between 1990 and 1993 – when the law was abolished[242] by the newly installed PASOK government – Greece suffered 31 terrorist assaults at the hands of 17N alone.[243]

The state's strategy against terrorism

Walter Laqueur has argued that terrorism 'is an attempt to destabilize democratic societies and to show that their Governments are impotent'.[244] In Greece, 17N almost certainly accomplished the latter. One important reason for the state's astonishing failure to rise to the terrorist challenge was the inability of the political élites to agree on a common definition of political violence. The absence of a consensus on the nature of terrorism polarized the political environment and created negative administrative and operational impacts on the mechanisms responsible for dealing with the problem. At the same time, 17N's campaign of violence exposed several of the deficiencies of the political system and state structure: irresolute administrations, unreliable intelligence services, inadequate police forces and a cumbersome judicial system.

---

240 Parliamentary Discussion Papers – Greek Parliament, 10 December 1990, p. 4583.

241 Writing in 1995 for the American academic journal *Mediterranean Quarterly*, Dora Bakoyiannis accepted that 'today, with the ability to judge from a distance, we can say that the New Democracy Government committed a basic error... The mistake was in making publication a penal, rather than a civil offence. One result was that journalists, in the climate of conflict that prevailed, were sent to prison. This was an error that did not help the fight against terrorism. I voted for Article 6 in parliament, but it is now clear that it went a step beyond what Greek society would accept. A code of conduct, an agreement containing principles of self-restraint by the mass media, like the one achieved in Italy, may have been a more suitable solution. Perhaps the New Democracy Government should have been more persistent in seeking the consent and sense of duty of the mass media, which could have led to closer co-operation and better results for the protection of democracy'. Dora Bakoyiannis, 'Terrorism in Greece', in *Mediterranean Quarterly*, Vol. 6, No. 2 (Spring 1995), pp. 24–25.

242 See 'Law 1916/1990 as revised by Article 4 of Law 2145/1993', in *Governmental Gazette-Greek Parliament*, Vol. 1 (28 May 1993).

243 George Kassimeris, 'Bombers and bunglers', in *The Times Higher Educational Supplement*, 15 December 1995.

244 Walter Laqueur, 'Reflections on Terrorism', in *Foreign Affairs*, Vol. 65, No. 1 (Fall, 1986), p. 87.

Since its inception, Greek terrorism might have been more easily contained had the governing élites and the security authorities acted decisively against the extremists. However, their slow and indecisive response, their deliberate manipulation of left-wing violence to their own political advantage and, above all, their outright failure to grasp the nature and dynamics of terrorism – all these factors can be seen to have contributed significantly to the growth and consolidation of serious revolutionary violence in Greece. Terrorism is a political and social phenomenon which must be understood within context. When a terrorist war begins, there is a reason for every bombing and each shooting. In Greece, at first, there was a failure to recognize what 17N and ELA were, what they wanted and how dangerous they could become. During the mid-1970s, a remarkably broad range of mainstream politicians, academics and newspaper analysts preferred to advance barely substantiated conspiratorial explanations and theories which continued to flourish well into the 1990s.[245] They sought to explain Greek terrorism as a 'foreign plan' aimed at destabilizing the nation's fragile new democracy, thus ignoring the general climate of popular dissatisfaction with the chronic immobility of the political system. Another reason for the state's repeated failure to gather intelligence on the movements of 17N terrorists lies in the nature of the Greek police and intelligence services. For nearly five decades until 1974, their main aim was to stop the country from becoming communist rather than to prevent and investigate crime. Given that the conflict of 1946–9

continued through other means until the fall of the military dictatorship in 1974 ... insitutionalised anticommunism coincided with permanent internal security policy – affecting the lives of thousands, but also ... the perceptions about 'crime' and 'punishment', and the political attitude of the entire police apparatus.[246]

---

[245] One government official to advance oversimplified conspiratorial theories about 17N in public was the Greek mininster for public order, Stelios Papathemelis, who, in 1994, argued in a interview with the *The Guardian* newspaper that 17N and ELA terrorism was orchestrated by elements of foreign services! Mr. Papathemelis said that 'our impression is that they [17N and ELA] no longer have the same financial resources that they once had even though I believe – and I say this without full evidence – that both are still controlled by foreign agents who have certain interests to strike in Greece', Source: The *Guardian*, 30 September 1994; For a survey on the most 'popular' conspiracy theories in relation to 17N see *To Vima*, 10 July 1994.

[246] See A. Th. Symeonidis, 'Greek Internal Security Policy', Paper delivered at a Europe

Although reforms were made in the first years of *metapolitefsi* by the Karamanlis government, the poor quality of the security forces did not improve and their methods, tactics and ethos remained virtually unchanged.[247] Ignorant of who the terrorists were, Greek intelligence and law enforcement agencies continued – without hard evidence – to arrest, interrogate and detain 'usual suspects' from familiar opposition movements which they considered as 'subversive'.[248]

Although terrorism in the mid-1970s and early 1980s could probably not have been prevented altogether, Greek democracy should have defended itself and the lives of its citizens better. The state and its internal security organizations should have had enough indications at the end of 1983 when George Tsantes was murdered to reorganize their security systems and introduce organizational measures and operational procedures to counter the terrorism which was to follow.[249] Until the mid-1980s, domestic incidents of terrorism[250] were regarded as casual events perpetrated by isolated anarchic agitators rather than a sustained campaign of violence directed at the Greek government.[251] At the same time, the authorities' security services also appeared to have difficulties in understanding what the terrorists wrote in their communiqués and commentaries.[252] This inability on the part of

2000 conference on *Organized Crime and Terrorism in the New Europe*, 26–28 November 1991, pp. 52–3.

[247] See *Meleti yia tin Organossi kai Leitourgeia ton Ypiression tis Elliniki Astynomias* (A study for the Organization and Operation of the Greek Police forces), Minstry of Public Order, Research Department, Athens: December 1993; see also *To Vima*, 5 July 1987 and *Ta Nea* leader, 9 May 1994.

[248] See *Eleftherotypia* 12 November 1977, 11 November 1978 and 10 February 1979.

[249] According to a 1985 confidential report, offers from western governments of help in training anti-terrorist police and updating their equipment after a spate of terrorist attacks [the assassination of publisher Nicos Momferatos, the bombing of a seasisde bar full of US servicemen in Glyfada and the abortive bomb attack against the West German embassy in Athens] were turned down 'for reasons of economy'. 'Terrorism in Greece' in *Foreign Report* (The Economist Publications), 7 March 1985.

[250] From 1974 to 1985, 262 terrorist incidents occurred. Source: Mary Bossis, *Ellada kai Tromokratia: Ethnikes & Diethneis Diastasseis* [Greece & Terrorism: National and International Dimensions] (Athens: Sakkoulas, 1996).

[251] According to a 1995 confidential memo by the newly-installed think-tank to the Minister of Public Order, police investigations for years were 'exclusively focused on the "usual suspects" ' thus blocking other avenues of investigation and analysis. *Enimerotiko Simeioma*, dated 4 April 1995.

[252] Ibid.

the Greek intelligence community to read into the texts the mean-
ings of 17N offensive plans and to assess the nature and potential of
the threat gave terrorists invaluable time to organize themselves.

An early development of an intelligence infrastructure and
proper co-ordination between government, the police and the
judiciary might have enabled the terrorist organizations to be
identified and eliminated before their violent tactics could be
firmly established. However, due to a continued diffusion of
authority and responsibility, intelligence remained ineffectively
integrated – particularly in its dissemination and actual operational use.[253] At the same time, corruption within the security services limited even further the extent to which intelligence was
collected. As in most security policy matters, personal integrity in
counter-terrorism is as vital as organizational and administrative
ability. Although astronomical amounts of money have changed
hands over the years between the police/intelligence services and a
variety of informers/agents/operatives, their lack of success reinforced the view that 'information and informers are being manu-
factured for the absorption of state financial rewards'.[254] It might
have been better to dissolve the security services and to set up a
totally new organization rather than periodically reorganizing
them in an attempt to change attitudes in the force and remove
corruption but 'Governments, both left and right, generally
agreed that it was much safer to keep the secret services faction-
riven, inefficient and dependent on political control and
patronage than to modernise them into a powerful intelligence
apparatus'.[255]

---

[253] Until autumn 1991, Greece lacked the computerized data bank that would have
greatly helped with intelligence collection. Source: *Time* magazine article on 17N,
reprinted by *Pontiki*, 17 May 1991.

[254] Although the parliament is informed how much of the national budget goes to the
security services, it has, apart from the transparent costs of wages etc., no knowledge or
control over how the money is spent. According to the well-informed in security
matters *Ependytis* newspaper, the Ministry of Public Order, during the Mitsotakis
government of 1990–1993, allocated more than 700 million drachma for what was
supposedly 'correct and highly reliable information'. See *Ependytis*, 11–12 March 1995;
see also 'Money from terrorism fund goes missing' in *Athens News*, 21 March 1995 and
'700m for informers' in *Ependytis*, 14–15 December 1996.

[255] Interview with Mary Bossis (director of the anti-terrorism think-tank, 1994–6), 3
October 1995, Athens; see also 'War inside EYP' in *To Vima*, 8 May 1994 and 'Secret
squabbling' in *Ta Nea*, 4 June 1994.

Additionally, problems arose from bureaucratic jealousies and vendettas between and within different state agencies, especially YAAEV (Sub-Directorate for Special Crime of Violence) and EYP; from lack of meritocracy in the Greek police and the low educational level of recruits;[256] from outdated structures and training and from duplications of functions.[257] Despite claims to the contrary, government security forces were – and continue to be – structurally weak.[258] For most of the past 25 years, anti-terrorist strategy has been carried out by an under-resourced, under-trained and ill-equipped police force which lacks the motivation, discipline, dedication and expertise to wage an effective war against the professionalism and sophistication of 17N.[259] Dealing with experienced and heavily armed terrorists such as members of 17N, requires a combination of discipline, alertness and operational proficiency on the part of the security force. The Greek experience clearly illustrates that the terrorists have been able to act more cohesively than either the police or the intelligence services.[260] Critical mistakes in planning and execution of surveillance operations against 17N allowed the terrorists to escape on several occasions. The Sepolia and Riankour debacles, in 1991 and 1992 respectively, demonstrated that the Greek police force was neither prepared nor competent enough to deal with 17N.[261] 17N terrorists may not be invincible but they are committed and have learned from experience precisely how to exploit the serious weaknesses of the state's security operations.

[256] See article entitled 'Lack of Meritocracy' by Attica Police Officers' Union leader, Dimos Gogolos in *Ta Nea*, 15 February 1994.

[257] See *To Vima*, 20 January 1991 and 16 August 1992; see also *Ta Nea*, 15 February 1994 and *Athens News*, 29 April 1995.

[258] A 1995 confidential report to the Minister of Public Order on the state of YAEEV centred on 1) absence of an anti-terrorist policy and strategy; 2) fragmentary organizational arrangements within YAEEV; 3) the overall deficiency in the machinery available to do strategic long-term assessments of threats to Greece's security interests. It went on to talk about no systematic research and analysis of terrorist groups; difficulties in the collation and distribution of reports and absence of technological infrastructure.

[259] See article by criminologist Sophia Vidalis, member of the short-lived anti-terrorist think-tank, in *Ta Nea* newspaper, 16 July 1994.

[260] See *Eleftherotypia* special on 20 years of terrorism in Greece, 20–21 December 1995.

[261] On the unpreparedness and amateurism of the Greek police see 'How the Police got away from 17 November', *To Vima*, 24 November 1991; *Kathimerini*, 24 November 1991; *Eleftherotypia*, 5 May 1992 and *Kyriakatiki Eleftherotypia*, 10 May 1992.

At the same time, tensions and bureaucratic friction between various departments and agencies thwarted the development of an integrated counter-terrorism capability.[262] The counter-terrorist effort against 17N was always conducted against the background of rivalry and squabbling within the security apparatus.[263] The formulation of effective anti-terrorism policies was further complicated by the lack of agreement on the nature of the threat or how to deal with it. The establishment in 1994 of an anti-terrorism think-tank, the Scientific Committee for the Analysis, Investigation and Planning against Organized Crime,[264] aggravated tensions with regard to the development of policies and responses within the appropriate concerned agencies. Set up as 'a response to the 20-year failure of the security forces partly resulting from a total lack of scientific research and a total lack of political approach',[265] the think-tank aimed to provide, via research and information analysis, guidance on what policies the Greek intelligence and law enforcement agencies should consider in meeting the terrorist threat. The experiment proved short-lived[266] and the overall result was 'confused logistical planning', 'lapses in communication', 'animosity between the academic specialists and the law enforcement officers' and 'a total absence of a unified strategic plan'.[267]

Moreover, frequent changes in the leadership of Greece's law enforcement departments and agencies (eight anti-terrorist branch chiefs between 1989–98) and constant shifts of policy and structure (no newly installed government ever retained the counter-terrorism structure of its predecessor) impeded the implementation of a cohesive and common approach to all terrorist activity.[268] In the summer of 1994, when the US Diplomatic Security

262 See *To Vima*, 8 May 1994; *Ta Nea*, 9 May and 4 June 1994.
263 *Enimerotiko Simeioma*.
264 In Greek, *Epistimoniko Symvoulio Analyssis, Erevnon kai Programmatismou yia tin antimetopissi tou Organomenou Egklimatos*; the think-tank was established and chaired by the Minister of Public Order, Stelios Papathemelis who said in a magazine interview a month before he was replaced that the establishment of the think-tank was an indication of 'a radical change in philosophy with regard to 20 years of anti-terrorism failure'. Source: *Ekonomikos Tachydromos*, 16 February 1995.
265 Special report to the minister, dated March 1994.
266 The think-tank was dissolved in September 1996.
267 Interview with Mary Bossis, 7 December 1996, Athens.
268 See *Patterns of Global Terrorism: 1995*, US State Department, Release date, April 1996.

Service's Anti-terrorism Assistance Office (ATA)[269] began a series
of consultations in Greece to facilitate the development and operation of a Greek-American Task Force against 17N activity, the
American analyst and primary contact with the Ministry of Public
Order in Athens summed up the main reasons for the Greek
state's repeated failure to rise to the terrorist challenge. In a confidential memo to the minister, he wrote that the

task force strategy has been extremely successful for the FBI when used
correctly and staffed by the correct personnel. We believe that it can be
successfully applied in Greece against the criminal organization 17
November … In order for a task force to succeed, it will require an
ongoing commitment on the part of the Greek Police as well as hard
work and commitment by each individual on this task force. The
commitment of the Greek police must include the following: 1. Resources
and money for the unit to function; 2. Protection of the unit from
outside political influences. The unit must *not* be politically influenced
or motivated; 3. There must be *no* independent 17N criminal
investigations being conducted outside the unit. All information
received or developed by the Greek police pertinent to the investigation
of 17N must be channelled to the unit to ensure all information may be
analyzed, compared with other information and acted upon; 4. The team
must be given authority to function without any bureaucratic
interference from outside the Task Force. The chain of command for
this unit must be streamlined as much as possible; 5. The selection of
personnel is the *most* important and overriding factor in order for this
task force to be successful. Even the most carefully organized task force
with the best plan will fail 100% of the time if the proper personnel are
not chosen to make up this unit. The personnel must be hard-working,
intelligent, non-political, close-mouthed and must have no other
allegiances or duties except to the team; 6. All of the above must be
committed for a potentially lengthy period of time in order to achieve
the stated goals. For example, all selected officers must expect an
assignment for a minimum two year period due to the needs of Task
Force or request of the officer. [270]

[269] 'The Antiterrorism Training Assistance program sponsors training for civilian security
personnel from friendly governments in antiterrorism skills such as bomb detection,
hostage negotiations, airport and building security, maritime protection and VIP
protection. Each course is tailored to the requesting country's specific requirements.
ATA assesses the training needs, develops the curriculum and provides the resources
for the training'. Source: Regional Security Office, American Embassy in Athens,
undated.
[270] Ibid.

198 Europe's Last Red Terrorists

There can be little doubt that the capacity to protect its citizens against terrorism and subversion is a necessary attribute of any modern state. Whenever faced with a severe test of that capacity, the Greek state has failed to pass it. The histories of the BR in Italy, RAF in Germany and AD in France suggest that while liberal democracies are initially uncertain in their handling of domestic violent political organizations, they overcome them in time. Over the past twenty-five years, successive Greek governments have deployed a variety of measures to meet the violence of both 17N and ELA but have failed to demonstrate a firm grasp of the essentials, a clear sense of strategic priorities and a coherent approach achieving them. Greece's anti-terrorist policy and planning has been characterized by incrementalism, fragmentation and occasionally sheer ineptitude which are primary characteristics of Greek public policy. Far from sending an early and clear signal that violence would not be tolerated by taking a clear-cut stand and effective measures to confront the problem, state authorities and political parties allowed terrorism to grow so uncontrollably that it finally became a routine element of Greek contemporary life.

7

CONCLUSIONS

> The terrorist's success is almost always the result of mis-
> understandings or misconceptions of the terrorist strategy.[1]

As this study of 17N shows, the growth of democratic political
freedoms provides violent conspiratorial organizations with
much greater opportunities to conduct their campaigns of violence and challenge the values and processes of open liberal
democracies. Ultra-left terrorism in Greece emerged and developed not against an unresponsive, non-democratic socio-political
system but under a comparatively successful process of democratic transition and consolidation. The coexistence of growing
democratization alongside persistent terrorist violence has been a
major theme of this book. Terrorism, at the same time, remains a
profoundly disturbing phenomenon and one of the most difficult
and dangerous areas of contemporary life. Although not a syn-
onym for violence and insurgency in general, terrorism was, is
and will continue to be, a technique used by rogue states and
aggrieved groups which cannot see, or refuse to see, any other way
of influencing political developments.

The experience of Western democratic states in the twentieth century suggests that terrorists usually fail to pose a realistic threat to
domestic political and economic structures, yet 17N's case shows
that revolutionary violent organizations can still emerge and develop
in certain circumstances. Terrorist organizations are, in fact, more
likely to appear in open liberal democratic societies where political

---

[1] David Fromkin, 'The Strategy of Terrorism', in *Foreign Affairs*, Vol. 53, No. 4 (July
1975), p. 687.

and civil rights are well protected rather than in countries ruled by authoritarian governments. Focusing explicitly on one case, this work has sought to explain how a violent revolutionary organization emerged in a fragile democratic setting and to analyse the impact terrorism can have on 'power configurations, institutions and public policies'.[2] 17N tried to 'reconnect the broken links between society and its own past and future ... through a discourse of rupture and totality'.[3] Connecting past historical events to present experiences enabled 17N to construct a 'language' with which to publicize its existence, claim legitimacy, create impetus, and vindicate its actions. 17N narratives reinterpreted confrontational events of high ideologicopolitical symbolism (the Greek civil war, November 1973) as instructional paradigms for future references. Narrating its discourse through attack communiqués, strategic texts and special manifestos, 17N elaborated the presentation of political events and expanded the dimensions of their violent context in an attempt to dramatize the anomalies of the existing system, deny its legitimacy and to propound alternative models. From the beginning, and during its lengthy trajectory, 17N developed a inversionary discourse whose symbolic and ideological aspects were sustained by the use of extreme violence as a response to a crisis. The group was influenced by the BR view that military actions 'are intended as "armed propaganda"', and used violence to both 'illustrate new possibilities of political action and secure some form of political recognition'.[4] However, its revolutionary campaign underestimated the regime, its level of public acceptance, and the stabilizing effects of European influences. 17N's refusal to take account of the changing circumstances of post-1974 Greece meant that its deadly terrorist campaign juxtaposed a growing social consensus. As the group strove to realize its inversionary aspirations, a progressive fixation with the employment of physical force undermined the effectiveness of the military option and emphasized the doctrinal inflexibility and nihilistic character of the organization.

---

[2] Martha Crenshaw, 'Introduction: Reflections on the Effects of Terrorism', in M. Crenshaw (ed.), *Terrorism, Legitimacy and Power: The Consequences of Political Violence* (Middletown, CT: Wesleyan University Press, 1983), p. 14.

[3] Elisabeth Picard, 'The Lebanese Shi'a and Political Violence in Lebanon', in David E. Apter (ed.), *The Legitimization of Violence* (London: Macmillan, 1997), p. 216.

[4] David Moss, 'Analyzing Italian Political Violence as a Sequence of Communicative Acts: The Red Brigades, 1970–1982', in *Social Analysis*, No. 3 (May 1983), p. 85.

17N constitutes an example of militant revolutionary terrorism at its most peculiar. The group attacked its host system with increasing violence to generate a revolutionary situation but 'operated with the philosophy of a party that is obliged to maintain a permanent presence in the domestic political arena'.[5] Acting more out of necessity and survival instinct than conviction, 17N's longevity was directly proportional to its localism, negativism and modesty of aim.[6] In the Greek case, resort to violent direct action did not constitute a serious political threat to the proper functioning of a liberal-democratic society as in Italy in the 1970s and early 1980s; but 17N's recapitulation of macro-political cleavages and historical discontinuities lends some support to the proposition that 'terrorism, although inexcusable, sometimes reflects legitimate national grievances'.[7] 17N's political vision of Greece was both anachronistic and unrealistic but its motives were originally governed by rational calculation.

West European societies and their national institutions may have proved resilient and able to cope with various levels of terrorist activity without serious consequences but the political implications of such violent campaigns are not immaterial. Evidence abounds that terrorism is a form of warfare deeply implanted in late twentieth-century culture which can be contained but not eradicated. Given the right circumstances, secretive extremist organizations might always deploy physical force to frustrate government initiatives and dislocate liberal democratic societies. Although the intensity of violence varies according to the type of society and its impact on critical national decisions has been minimal at best, terrorism in many political systems escalates in times of reconstruction, modernization and reform. Given the inherently clandestine nature of terrorist organizations, dealing with terrorism is a highly complex and demanding task which requires a clear, coherent and integrated response strategy. One essential reason why both 17N and ELA were able to maintain their terror tactics for so long has been the failure of successive Greek governments to make a correct diagnosis of the problem. To counter

---

[5] '17N's Strategy and Ideology' in *Anti*, 1 March 1985, pp. 8–9.

[6] See 17N's *Manifesto 1992*, dated 17 November 1992.

[7] Richard E. Rubenstein, *Alchemists of Revolution: Terrorism in the Modern World* (New York: Basic Books Inc., 1987), p. 230.

terrorism effectively, governments need to understand the terrorists' strategy fully in both political and operational terms in order
to defeat it. At the same time, counter-terrorist efforts need a
broad consensus of support and co-operation from diverse sections of the community. While it is incumbent upon governments
to protect society and to bring the perpetrators of violence to justice, their action needs to be measured in terms of its effectiveness
in tackling terrorism without undermining the support of the
wider population for law and order and without putting basic liberties at risk. Any liberal response to terrorism has to reflect 'the
democratic, moral and legal principles inherent in democratic and
constitutional ideals and adherence to the rule of law'.[8]

West European experience of national responses to the challenge
of terrorism has shown that governmental attempts at striking the
right balance between effectiveness and acceptability can be particularly problematic.[9] Regrettably, Greece stands as an excellent
example of how 'responses to terrorism can be more dangerous for
a democratic society than terrorism itself'.[10] The draconian anti-terrorist legislation hastily passed by the Greek Parliament in 1990 had
two fundamental effects. Rather than facilitating the creation of a
peaceful society wedded to the rule of law, 1916/1990 undermined
respect for the rule of law and exposed the Greek state's inability 'to
make a sound balanced judgement between the need to act and the
need to ensure against over- or under- reaction'.[11] Insensitively
used, the law (article 6 in particular) polarized community relations, jeopardized national cohesion and did nothing to reduce the
level of terrorist activity or increase the rate of convictions for terrorist offences. A central lesson to emerge from the Greek anti-terrorism experience suggests that an effective response strategy
requires 'a concerted, multi-pronged approach, carefully calibrated
to the level required to deal with the scale of terrorism employed,
and combining the most valuable elements of political, legal, police

---

[8] G. Davidson Smith, *Combating Terrorism* (London: Routledge, 1990), p. 258.

[9] See, for instance, Kurt Groenewold, 'The German Federal Republic's Response and
Civil Liberties', in Alex P. Schmid and Roland D. Crelinsten (eds), *Western Responses to
Terrorism* (London: Frank Cass, 1993), pp. 136–50.

[10] Donatella della Porta, 'Institutional Responses to Terrorism: The Italian Case' in
Western Responses to Terrorism, p. 153.

[11] Peter Chalk, *West European Terrorism and Counter-Terrorism* (London: Macmillan,
1996), p. 99.

and socio-economic measures'.[12] As evidenced by the Greek case, an unfocused, disorganized, underfunded, and socially insensitive and politically patronizing governmental policy response to terrorism can only result in complete failure.[13] Another lesson is that statutory regulation of the media's coverage of terrorism is neither feasible nor desirable. Media self-restraint and self-regulation are the best policy options for an open democratic society regarding the media's response to terrorism. Finally, liberal-democratic states dealing with terrorism, however serious the threat may be, must not be lured into opting for quick-fix solutions which can create more problems than they solve or, ultimately, traumatize the very liberty and democracy which terrorism seeks to destroy.

Conclusions relating to Greek politics

17N's ideology was shaped within a Western universalist political culture. Posing as representative of the entire community, the group did not attack this universalism, only modernizing reformism which eventually set the scene for extreme violence. 17N repeatedly cited past national experiences like the wartime resistance movement, the civil war, the Colonels' dictatorship and the 1973 *Polytechneio* as guides for present action. Having significantly diverged from mainstream-left interpretations of post-1974 political realities, 17N's basic project was to show that *metapolitefsi* was a laundering operation and give a voice to the disenchanted of the transition. 17N was avowedly left-wing in character but its concept of politics was very different from that of the mainstream left. Politics for 17N leaders meant that armed struggle and terrorism were seen as the only strategy which would sidestep capitalist civilization. Having adopted a Blanquist stand in supporting a revolutionary struggle which was to be waged by a revolutionary avantgarde élite, the group refused to modify its political objectives to the needs of contemporary Greek society. 17N appeared at a historical moment when old left-right polarities declined significantly and a new political vocabulary based on *ekdimokratismos,*[14] *ananeossis*[15]

---

[12] See Paul Wilkinson, 'How to combat the reign of terror', in *New Statesman*, 2 August 1996.
[13] See Ch. 6.
[14] Democratization.
[15] Renewal.

and *allaghi*[16] emerged. During the period after 1974, the ideological themes and symbols that were previously used to divide Greek society and polarize parliamentary life no longer provided an adequate basis for open political conflict. In their place, themes such as European integration, health, poverty, environmental pollution, national security and the international situation in the southeast Mediterranean dominated political discourse. 17N was among the first political organizations to seize on these issues, but its bombastic leftism and refusal to forsake violent revolutionary direct action alienated Greek society and consigned the group to the political margins. By the end of the 1970s, intellectual opinion had shifted away from revolutionary politics. Evidence of this shift became salient when numerous extreme-left organizations renounced extra-parliamentary opposition and sought to integrate change into existing political structures via parliamentary methods. 17N's failure to grasp the implications of this development and its subsequent hostility to such organizations manifested its isolation from the overall evolution of the established extreme-left political culture.

In addition, 17N was appalled by the conditions surrounding Karamanlis's return.[17] Denouncing every stage of *metapolitefsi,* 17N believed that 'a democracy which does not confront the misdeeds and miscreants of the past is perpetually flawed'.[18] *Metapolitefsi* was essentially a transitional epoch and although it failed to produce a fully democratic model of society where conflict is exclusively resolved by discussion and compromise, it catered to a democratic ethos and institutionalized a competitive party system. Papandreou's election as Greece's first socialist Prime Minister in October 1981 seemed to have weakened any ideological rationale for extreme-left violent political action. The transfer of power from right to left in 1981 legitimized *metapolitefsi* in two important ways. First, it proved that the regime could withstand democratic alteration in power. Second, the 1981 legislative elections confirmed the stability of the multi-party system and

---

[16] Change.

[17] See George Kassimeris, Book Review: 'Modern Greece: A civilization on the periphery by Keith R. Legg and John M. Roberts' in the *Times Literary Supplement*, 20 March 1998.

[18] David Lehman, 'Order punctuated by explosions: Chile's legacy of distrust and the problem of Pinochet's return', in the *Times Literary Supplement*, 18 December 1998.

demonstrated a high level of political participation. In spite of the fact that a marginal fraction of the mainstream extra-parliamentary left remained uncompromisingly hostile to the government, the rest of the Greek left was willing to recognize the magnitude of PASOK and its impact on national politics. However, 17N execrated Papandreou's Panhellenic Socialist Movement (PASOK) for violating its pre-election platform and abandoning socialism. The group considered Papandreou an opportunistic demagogue and believed that his PASOK government was a social-democratic pro-American sell-out which presented a serious threat to traditional Greek left-wing values. 17N's 1983 condemnation of PASOK's embrace of European integration, commitment to the Atlantic Alliance, and the administration's refusal to terminate its defence agreement with the US expressed a classical leftist radical discourse.[19] The group contended that the use of 'popular revolutionary violence' against a pseudo-socialist administration whose governmental behaviour and programme of social and economic change which 'differs only in details from that of the New Democracy' was entirely justified.[20] Consistent with this stance, the group undertook actions designed to polarize the country's political attention and make a practical reality of revolution in Greece. Ultimately, 17N's confidence proved misplaced and its revolutionary alternative vision of modernizing reformism unrealizable.

The nature of the Revolutionary Organization 17 November

17N violence stemmed from an anachronistic interpretation of Greek communist traditions. The group believed that Greek left-wing behaviour justified extreme response. It also believed that PASOK's social reformism and economic rationalism had contaminated Greek socialism. In point of fact, the group thought that PASOK was mortally dangerous to the possibility of an authentic socialist political system. However, 17N's terrorist campaign subsequently centred on infusing revolutionary ideals into national discourse rather than on actually seizing power. Unlike the Red Brigades in Italy which took on 'the capitalist state

---

[19] See Ch. 4.
[20] 17N attack communiqué on US Navy Capt. George Tsantes, dated October 1983.

and its agents',[21] 17N hoped to create an insurrectionary mood which would empower people into revolutionary political action without promoting a generalized sense of chaos within Greek society. As such, 17N's violence was an audacious protest which aimed to discredit and humiliate the Greek *katestimeno* (establishment) and the US government, but it never moved beyond terrorism to reach the stage of revolutionary guerrilla warfare. This attitude contradicted 17N's symbolic construction of revolution and diluted the group's supposed existential experience. The targets that the group chose reflected its ideology which was anticapitalist, anti-imperialist, anti-statist and anti-totaliatarian. It attacked targets with maximum symbolic value seeking to demonstrate the state's lack of unity and legitimacy.[22] Like the French *Action Directe*, 17N's assassinations were motivated by 'its conviction that individual symbolic murders would vindicate errors and alter history'.[23]

National political life was the most significant base for 17N extremism. The group focused on domestic issues and referred its acts to international developments only insofar as they related to national events. 17N's repeated references to financial scandals, political ineptitude and abuse of power revealed its intense hostility to and mistrust of the Third Republic's parliamentary and economic élites. The group invented concepts such as *lmat* (lumpen big bourgeois class) to highlight capitalist exploitation and identify existing political divisions that could arouse popular protest. 17N's search for a new vocabulary to 'accelerate' events was also connected to the group's efforts to justify its revolutionary transformative goals and create an impression of power and

---

21 See Richard Drake, *The Aldo Moro Murder Case* (London: Harvard University Press, 1995), pp. 45–8.

22 T.P. Thornton writes in his 'Terror as a Weapon of Political Agitation' that 'If the terrorist comprehends that he is seeking a demonstration effect, he will attack targets with maximum symbolic value. The symbols of the state are particularly important, but perhaps even more so are those referring to the normative structures and relationships that constitute the supporting framework of the society. By showing the weakness of this framework, the insurgents demonstrate not only their own strength and the weakness of the incumbents, but also the inability of the society to provide support for its members in a time of crisis', quoted from Harry Eckstein (ed.), *Internal War: Problems and Approaches* (New York: The Free Press of Glencoe, 1964), p. 77.

23 See Michael Y. Dartnell, *Action Directe, Ultra-Left Terrorism in France, 1979–1987* (London: Frank Cass, 1995), p. 141.

organization. The group's penchant for violence went hand in hand with its rejection of instrumental politics and concept of active political struggle. 17N embraced AD's view of terrorist violence as a legitimate and logical

form of expression for those humiliated and ridiculed by the mechanisms of the capitalist mode of production; not a desperate reaction born from misery [but] a hopeful action which aims to surpass exploitation and domination through revolutionary practice.[24]

After 1983, 17N violence increased and its scope widened. Combining ideological rigidity, missionary zeal and tactical flexibility, the group conducted a systematic and very sophisticated terror campaign. Like all organizations which resort to terror, 17N claimed that its cause justified extremism. Appendixes 7.1 to 7.4 (pages 240–43) distinguish 17N's violence according to type and categorize it by quarry, intensity and cadence. Bombings are considered to be a more severe form of violence than rocket attacks but less intense than deliberate murders. 17N's political assassinations and assassination attempts were products of calculated collective efforts aimed at a specific audience. Persistent terrorist violence may 'polarize the political attitudes of citizens regardless of personal threat',[25] but 17N's impact on Greek public discourse was politically ineffective and statistically negligible.

Appendix 7.1 shows that 17N attacks expanded in four separate chronological periods: 1975–80, 1983–6, 1988–94 and 1997–9.[26] From 1975 to 1980, 17N sought to gain national recognition and resurrect extreme-left militancy. 17N's early revenge attacks served to publicize the group's ethno-patriotic credentials and to question the legitimacy of *metapolitefsi*.[27] Between 1983 and 1986, 17N's extremism escalated in intensity and the group became more provocative and militaristic. 17N resented PASOK and sought to undermine its system of government. The group ritually denounced PASOK's ideological retreat and continually analysed the implications of Papandreou's foreign policy for Greek

---

[24] '*Pour un projet communiste*' [For a communist project], *Action Directe*, theoretical text, dated March 1982.

[25] Crenshaw, *Terrorism, Legitimacy and Power*, pp. 14–15.

[26] See Appendix 7.1, Number of Attacks by *Revolutionary Organization 17 November*.

[27] See Ch. 4.

national security. Appendix 7.2 focuses on bomb attacks.[28] Bombs were not used during 17N's less radical and organizationally formative phase in 1975–80 but their use increased as 17N radicalized. In fact, the group inaugurated its bombing campaign soon after PASOK was voted back to power for a second term in 1985. 'Ideologicopolitical' targets like government tax offices, MAT riot police buses and US military buses were bombed more often than were, for example, foreign embassies and business facilities. Bomb attacks increased in 1986 when the group sought to exploit unrest over unpopular PASOK austerity measures. Appendix 7.3, which focuses on rocket attacks, can be similarly interpreted.[29] When New Democracy returned to power in 1990, 17N grew even more extreme and the number of bomb and rocket attacks rose dramatically. From 1990 to 1993, the group carried out 31 operations. 17N apparently increased the frequency of attacks to provoke the Mitsotakis administration and to defy its anti-terrorist legislation. Appendix 7.4 focuses on murders, which are used to evaluate the political threat of violence to the stability of Greek society.[30] Although 17N's murders are simply not comparable to groups like BR or the IRA since the number is small, the group did present a real danger to specific individuals. Although 17N's early attacks were sporadic and uneven, they immediately began to make a bloody mark. 17N found high-profile assassinations attractive. After 1980, 17N decided that political murder was an effective instrument of armed propaganda and it became a regular feature of group military activities.

Overall, 17N political terrorism was more threatening when it radicalized. Assassinations and assassination attempts, for example, rose and dropped according to political events. Given its conception of extra-parliamentary activism, 17N's ideological evolution was always certain to culminate into a full-scale terrorist campaign. However, 17N was never an 'armed people's revolutionary movement' which created a situation of crisis for the Greek establishment, only a fringe violent organization which ignored the fact that violence 'should not take the place of the

---

[28] See Appendix 7.2, Number of bomb attacks by *Revolutionary Organization 17 November*.
[29] See Appendix 7.3, Number of rocket attacks by *Revolutionary Organization 17 November*.
[30] See Appendix 7.4, Number of murders by *Revolutionary Organization 17 November*.

political purpose, nor obliterate it'.[31] Convinced that authentic socialist change could never result from reformist tactics, the group physically menaced officials in governmental and international organizations and in business, but failed to affect political order and remained a marginal phenomenon. As with other European violent political organizations, 17N was motivated by political revolution, egalitarian communism, contempt for parliamentary democracy, and opposition to imperialism and monopoly capitalism. However, what distinguished 17N from other groups, was that 17N's revolutionary intransigence grew as its political prospects shrank. Undaunted by its fringe status and obsessed with proving that its ideas were neither anachronistic nor irrelevant, 17N 'embraced "revolution" as an article of faith'[32] and tried to force events to conform with its vision.

[31] Peter Paret, 'Clausewitz', in P. Paret (ed.), *Makers of Modern Strategy* (Oxford: Oxford University Press, 1986), p. 200.
[32] Dartnell, p. 91.

APPENDIX 1

CHRONOLOGY OF EVENTS

1974

15 July – Archbishop Makarios deposed as president of Cyprus in a coup backed by the military junta in Athens.
24 July – Turkey invades northern part of Cyprus. Collapse of the Colonels' regime and replacement by civilian government headed by Konstantinos Karamanlis.
17 November – Karamanlis's New Democracy party secures 220 out of 300 seats in Greek Parliament.
8 December – referendum records 70 per cent vote for abolition of monarchy.

1975

13 February – Turkish Cypriot leader Rauf Denktash declares Northern Cyprus independent.
9 June – official promulgation of new Greek constitution, reinforcing the powers of the president.
12 June – Greece officially applies for membership of the EC.
24 August – Death sentences on Greek dictator George Papadopoulos and other 1967 coup leaders are commuted to life.
23 December – 17N assassination of CIA Athens station chief, Richard Welch, outside his house in Psychico.

1976

17 April – Karamanlis proposes a non-aggression pact with Turkey.
9 May – Ulrike Meinhof is found dead in her cell in Stuttgart after apparently committing suicide.

14 December – 17N assassination of Evangelos Mallios, police torturer during the 1967–74 military dictatorship.

1977

20 November – Karamanlis holds elections a year in advance of the normal term and wins a comfortable majority (171 seats, 21.9 per cent of the vote). Andreas Papandreou's Panhellenic Socialist Movement (PASOK) becomes the main opposition party.

1978

18 March – The Red Brigades release a photo of Aldo Moro, the former Italian premier, kidnapped two days earlier.
9 May – The body of Aldo Moro is found in central Rome.

1979

28 May – Karamanlis signs treaty of accession to the European Community.

1980

16 January – 17N assassination of Pantelis Petrou – deputy commander of the Athens Riot Squad (MAT) and former intelligence officer during the Greek military junta – and his driver, police officer, Sotiris Stamoulis.
10 May – Karamanlis elected president of the Greek Republic and George Rallis becomes Prime Minister.
19 December – Minion and Katrantzos superstores firebombed by RO-October '80.

1981

1 January – Greece enters the European Community as its tenth member.
12 February – Ex-king Constantine returns to Athens for the first time in 14 years for the funeral of his mother, Queen Frederica.
18 October – Papandreou's PASOK forms Greece's first socialist government.

1983

6 November – Turgut Özal wins general elections in Turkey.

15 November – Turkish Cypriot assembly unilaterally declares an independent Turkish Republic of Northern Cyprus, recognized only by Turkey.

15 November – 17N assassination of US Navy Capt. George Tsantes and his Greek driver, Nikolaos Veloutsos.

1984

28 March – British diplomat Kenneth Witty is shot dead in Athens.

3 April – US Army Sgt. Robert Judd shot and wounded by 17N commandos.

1 September – Konstantinos Mitsotakis becomes leader of the New Democracy party.

1985

21 February – Newspaper publisher Nikos Momferatos and his driver, Panayiotis Roussetis, are shot and killed by two 17N gunmen.

10–29 March – Constitutional crisis leads to the resignation of Karamanlis as president and election of Christos Sartzetakis.

2 June – PASOK re-elected for a second term.

14 June – Gunmen hijack a TWA airliner after taking off from Athens and demand the release of over 700 prisoners in Israel.

18 June – US State Department travel advisory on Athens airport.

7 October – PLO terrorists hijack the Italian cruise liner, *Achile Lauro*, in the Mediterranean Sea.

26 November – 17N car bomb explosion against a riot police (MAT) bus kills one and injures 14 officers.

1986

2 April – Bomb explodes in mid-air on board a TWA flight from Rome to Athens.

8 April – 17N assassination of Dimitris Angelopoulos, chairman of Halivourgiki steel company and personal friend of Prime Minister Papandreou.

5 October – 17N bombing of four tax revenue offices around Athens.

1987

4 February – Kneecapping of neurosurgeon Zacharias Kapsalakis by two 17N commandos.

26–27 March – Crisis between Greece and Turkey over oil rights and territorial limits in the Aegean.

24 April – A Greek military bus transporting US and Greek military personnel is hit by a roadside bomb planted by 17N. The explosion injures 16 US servicemen and the Greek driver.

10 August – 17N remote-controlled car bomb against US military bus injures 11.

1988

22 January – 17N assassination attempt on George Carros, head of DEA agency in Athens.

30 January – Meeting between Prime Ministers Papandreou and Özal in Davos, Switzerland, produces Greek-Turkish *rapprochement*.

1 March – 17N assassinates Greek industrialist, Alexandros Athanassiadis-Bodossakis.

23 May – Explosions under Turkish embassy cars. 17N claims responsibility.

18 June – Turkish premier Turgut Özal visits Athens for a three-day summit with Papandreou.

28 June – US Navy Captain William Nordeen killed by a car bomb planted by 17N.

11 July – Nine people die and 78 are injured when Arab terrorists open fire on Greek ferry, *City of Poros*.

15 August – Six 17N commandos raid Vyronas police station.

1989

10 January – 17N kneecaps public prosecutor, Kostas Androulidakis.

18 January – 17N kneecaps public prosecutor, Panayiotis Tarasouleas.

22 February – Two villas and one apartment belonging to Greek businessmen are bombed by 17N.

8 May – 17N assassination attempt on former Minister of Public Order, George Petsos.

18 June – A deadlocked election leads to temporary conservative/communist coalition government under ND deputy Tzannis Tzannetakis.

20 September – Greek Parliament officially charges ex-premier Papandreou with illegal wiretapping.

26 September – Pavlos Bakoyiannis, New Democracy chief parliamentary spokesman, is shot and fatally wounded by three 17N gunmen.

23 November – Inconclusive election leads to formation of all-party 'ecumenical' government under Xenophon Zolotas.

24 December – 17N commandos entered a military warehouse near Larissa, stealing 60 rockets, grenades, bullets and other explosives.

1990

5 February – Four 17N commandos raid the National War Museum, making off with two bazooka-type anti-tank weapons.

8 April – Konstantinos Mitsotakis's New Democracy secures 150 out of 300 seats in parliament and forms government.

3 May – Karamanlis becomes president of the Republic for a second time.

16 May – 17N detonates 28 bombs in Ekali, causing no injuries and minimal property damage.

10 June – 17N fires its first rocket against the offices of multinational Procter & Gamble.

20 November – Despite a 17N multi-rocket attack, Greek shipping tycoon, Vardis Vardinoyiannis escapes death.

13 December – Greek Parliament passes new anti-terrorism legislation.

16 December – 17N fires two rockets against European Community offices.

1991

16 January – Operation 'Desert Storm' to liberate Kuwait begins.

24 January – Explosions at the offices of the French military attaché, Barclays and Citibank by 17N, in protest against Operation Desert Storm.

28 January – 17N bomb attack on Inter-American Insurance Company and American Express offices.

29 January – 17N fires a rocket against the main BP office.

11 March – A series of pre-dawn explosions by 17N damages five tourist buses.

12 March – 17N detonates a remote-controlled bomb that kills US Air Force Sgt. Ronald Stewart.

31 March – 17N fires a rocket at Pentelikon Hotel.

25 April – 17N sinks the tugboat *Karapiperis 6* at Perama.

2 May – 17N fires rockets at the offices of DEI (Public Power Company).

7 May – 17N fires rockets at the offices of Siemens.

16 May – 17N fires rockets at the Halyps cement plant.

31 May – 17N fires rockets at the Löwenbräu brewery in Atalanti.

5 June – *Eleftherotypia* editor, Seraphim Fyntanidis, is arrested for publishing a 17N communiqué.

16 July – 17N assassination attempt on Turkish embassy officials.

7 October – Turkish embassy press attaché, Cettin Gorgu, is shot dead by 17N.

2 November – 17N double-rocket attack against police bus. One dead and seven injured.

18 November – Shoot-out between Greek police and 17N in Sepolia.

1992

23 March – 17N eludes police ambush in Louisa Riankour Street.

14 July – 17N fails to assassinate Finance Minister, Yiannis Paleokrasas, but kills a passer-by, university student Thanos Axarlian.

31 November – 17N rocket attack on Nea Philadelphia tax office.

3 December – Bomb attack by 17N on Maroussi tax office.

21 December – Kneecapping of New Democracy MP, Eleftherios Papadimitriou by 17N.

1993

11 February – Bomb attack by 17N on Moschato tax office.

23 February – Bomb attack by 17N on Chaidari tax office.

3 March – Bomb attack by 17N on Peristeri tax office.

9 March – 17N rocket attack on tax office in Kaminia.

11 March – 17N bomb attack on Petroupoli tax office.

26 March – 17N firebombs vehicles belonging to tax officials in Illisia, Pangrati, Patissia, Aghia Paraskevi and Galatsi.

10 October – Papandreou's PASOK wins 47 percent of the vote and forms government.

1994

24 January – 17N assassination of the former National Bank of Greece governor, Michalis Vranopoulos.
11 April – 17N rocket attacks against the Athens branches of Alico and Nationale Nederlanden.
11 April – Abortive missile attack against the British aircraft carrier *Ark Royal* in Piraeus port.
21 April – 17N bombs Mille offices in Psychiko.
18 May – A 17N rocket damages the offices of IBM in central Athens.
4 July – Turkish diplomat, Omer Haluk Sipahioglou, is shot dead in a 17N ambush.

1995

17 January – Turkish Cypriot leader Rauf Denktash warns that his side will oppose Cyprus's proposed EU membership until a peace settlement is reached.
8 March – The PASOK-controlled parliament elects Kostis Stephanopoulos as the new president of the Republic.
15 March – 17N fires rockets at the Mega Channel TV station.
13 September – Greece and FYROM sign in New York an 'interim agreement' that paves the way to Greek recognition of the former Yugoslav republic in exchange for clarification in the latter's constitution and change of flag.
19 September – ELA detonates a remote-controlled device in front of a police bus.
20 September – The Papandreou government announces a 6.5 billion drachma counter-terrorism package.
16 October – Greece formally ends its 18-month embargo against FYROM.
20 November – Prime Minister Andreas Papandreou, 76, is rushed to hospital with pneumonia.

1996

15 January – Andreas Papandreou resigns as premier.
19 January – Costas Simitis is elected PASOK leader and takes over as premier.

1 February – Greece and Turkey come to the brink of war over islet of Imia.

15 February – 17N rocket fired at American embassy.

23 June – Andreas Papandreou dies.

22 September – Simitis wins snap general election he called on 20 August. PASOK wins 41.5 per cent of the vote and 161 seats against 38.1 per cent and 108 seats for New Democracy.

1997

28 May – 17N ambushes and kills shipowner Costas Peraticos in Piraeus.

1998

8 April – 17N rocket attack at Citibank.

4 October – 17N bombs three General Motors dealerships and two McDonald's fast-food outlets in central Athens.

18 August – The Simitis government proposes a postponement of the deployment of Russian missiles in Cyprus in return for dialogue on demilitarization.

29 December – Cypriot president Glafkos Clerides announces his government's decision to cancel the deployment of S-300 missiles on the island.

1999

16 February – PKK leader, Abdullah Ocalan, is abducted by Turkish agents in Nairobi.

1 April – 17N mortars PASOK party headquarters in downtown Athens.

5 May – 17N rocket attacks at Chase Manhattan, Midland and Banque National de Paris.

8 May – 17N detonates bomb outside the Dutch Embassy.

17 May- 17N mortars the German ambassador's residence in Athens.

2000

9 April – Costas Simitis wins second term.

8 June – 17N ambushes and kills Britain's military attaché in Athens, Brigadier Stephen Saunders.

19–20 June – EU leaders at Oporto summit grant Greece approval of EMU membership.

APPENDIX 2

RO-17N COMMUNIQUÉS/ANNOUNCEMENTS AND LETTERS TO THE MEDIA

1975

December- communiqué claiming credit for the assassination of the CIA station chief, Richard Welch.
26 December – *'Anakoinossi pros ton Typo'* [announcement to the press].

1976

undated – communiqué claiming credit for the assassination of former police captain, Evangelos Mallios.

1977

April – *'Apantissi sta Kommata kai tis Organosseis'* [a response to parties and organizations].

1980

undated – attack communiqué against MAT deputy commander, Pantelis Petrou, and his driver, Sotiris Stamoulis.

1981

undated – *'Yia tin anaptyxi tou epanastatikou kai laikou kinimatos'* [for the development of the revolutionary and popular movement].

1983

October – communiqué taking credit for the attack on US Navy Capt. George Tsantes and his Greek driver, Nikolaos Veloutsos.

1984

April 1984 – communiqué on the failed assassination attempt against US Army M. Sergeant and JUSMAGG officer, Robert Judd.
29 May – letter to the satirical weekly *To Pontiki*.

1985

undated – attack communiqué against *Apogevmatini* publisher, Nikos Momferatos and his driver, Panayiotis Roussetis.
26 November – communiqué taking credit for the attack on a police bus.
4 December – '*Anakoinossi*' [Announcement] sent to *Eleftherotypia* newspaper.

1986

undated – attack communiqué on Halivourgiki chairman, Dimitrios Angelopoulos.
3 October – communiqué claiming credit for the bombing of four separate tax revenue offices in Athens.
14 October – letter-reply to *Pontiki* for article the weekly published on 17N's assassination attack on D. Angelopoulos.

1987

1 February – communiqué on the kneecapping of Greek neurosurgeon, Zacharias Kapsalakis.
9 April – communiqué released following the bomb attack against a military bus transporting US and Greek military personnel.
5 August – communiqué taking responsibility for the bomb attack against a second US military bus.
11 October – communiqué-announcement attacking Greek police authorities for disinformation.
14 October – communiqué-reply to the Minister of Public Order, Antonis Drosoyiannis, mocking the Minister's public statements about having evidence leading to 17N.

1988

15 January – communiqué on the assassination attempt against DEA agent, George Carros.
22 January – communiqué explaining the reasons behind the failure of the Carros operation.

22 February – communiqué claiming credit for the assassination of Greek industrialist, Athanassiadis-Bodossakis.

12 March – letter-reply to open letter by the *Eleftherotypia* political commentator, Yiorgos Votsis, to 17N on 7 March.

20 May – communiqué taking credit for bombs placed under four cars belonging to Turkish diplomats.

14 June – communiqué claiming responsibility for assassination of US defence attaché, William Nordeen.

16 August – communiqué- announcement on the Vyronas police station raid.

11 November – communiqué-commentary on the Bank of Crete scandal.

1989

17 January – communiqué taking responsibility for the kneecapping attacks on prosecutors Costas Androulidakis and Panayiotis Tarasouleas.

2 February – communiqué-commentary on press disinformation.

22 February – communiqué following the bombing of three unoccupied residences owned by Greek businessmen.

25 April – communiqué claiming responsibility for the attack on former PASOK public order minister, George Petsos.

17 May – communiqué-response to *Ethnos* newspaper article (11 May) by academic Vassilis Filias on 17N and the failed Petsos attack.

30 May – communiqué-response to second article by Filias (*Ethnos*, 22 May).

3 July – communiqué-commentary on the New Democracy – Synaspismos coalition government.

18 September – communiqué taking credit for the assassination of New Democracy parliamentary spokesman, Pavlos Bakoyiannis.

9 October – communiqué-response to media criticism regarding the attack on Bakoyiannis.

16 November – communiqué-election commentary.

1990

4 February – communiqué claiming responsibility for stealing weapons from a military warehouse near Larissa (24/25 December 1989) and for the raid on the National War Museum in Athens.

14 May – communiqué taking credit for numerous bomb explosions in Ekali.

10 June – communiqué following a rocket attack against the offices of Procter & Gamble.

14 September – letter to *Epikairotita* newspaper on the alleged connection of 17N-Michalis 'Pablo' Raptis.

13 November – communiqué claiming responsibility for the multi-rocket attack against Greek shipping magnate, Vardis Vardinoyiannis.

17 December – communiqué following a rocket attack on the EC offices in Athens.

1991

29 January – communiqué taking credit for the rocket attacks against the Athens branches of Barclays, Citibank, American Express, BP, the Inter-American Insurance Company and the offices of the French military attaché.

12 March – attack communiqué on US Air Force Sgt. Ronald Stewart.

16 July – attack communiqué against Turkish diplomats Deniz Bolukbasi and Nilgun Kececi.

7 October – communiqué on the assassination of Turkish press attaché, Cettin Gorgu.

27 October – letter-reply to article by Michalis 'Pablo' Raptis on 17N in *To Vima* (20 Oct.).

1992

8 May – communiqué on the Louisa Riankour Street incident.

14 July – communiqué following a rocket attack against the Minister of Finance, Yiannis Paleokrassas.

18 July – communiqué-condemnation regarding the death of passer-by Thanos Axarlian.

17 November – Manifesto 1992.

December – communiqué claiming responsibility for the knee-capping of New Democracy MP, Eleftherios Papadimitriou.

1993

June – communiqué taking credit for the assassination of the former Bank of Greece governor, Michalis Vranopoulos and for several bomb attacks against tax offices and vehicles belonging to tax officials throughout the year.

1994

4 July – communiqué following the assassination of senior Turkish diplomat, Omer Haluk Sipahioglou.

1995

27 March – communiqué claiming responsibility for the rocket attack on MEGA TV studios.

1997

7 April – 17N attack communiqué explaining its targeting of Costas Peratikos.

1998

8 April – communiqué claiming the responsibility for the attacks against McDonald's, General Motors and Citibank.

1999

8 March – 17N communiqué-commentary on the Ocalan affair.

2000

March – 17N communiqué claiming responsibility for the assassination of Brigadier Stephen Saunders and taking credit for the 1999 attacks against the Dutch Embassy and the German ambassador's residence.

APPENDIX 3

RO-17N COMMUNIQUÉ ON THE KNEECAPPING OF NEUROSURGEON ZACHARIAS KAPSALAKIS IN ATHENS ON 4 FEBRUARY 1987

Excerpts of 17N text, dated 1 February, found at the site of the shooting

The richest and most famous doctors and the state-impostor are responsible for the downgraded health services and hateful exploitation of the insured Greek patient.

In our last proclamation, in which we explained why we had bombed the hateful tax-offices, we claimed that in our country the capitalist state-impostor, while receiving the obligatory heavy taxes and kinds of wage deductions from the working people, currently does not offer even the most elementary health services of prevention and treatment for which it supposedly receives money. [passage omitted]

The leading faction of PASOK shamelessly mocks the people in the health sector, just as in all others. It knows very well that there can be no improvement, no national health system without a great increase in public expenditures. However, such expenditures are precluded because of the policy of austerity. Consequently, with unbridled talk the faction is trying to hide the inevitability of perpetuating the previous tragic situation, if not letting it get totally out of hand. They are trying to hide the fact that they have glossed things over with the circuit of rich, well-known doctors.

However, the policy of austerity is not a necessary policy for the stabilization of the economy. It is a fixed option aimed at reducing payment for work, thus dropping the working people's standard of living. It stems from the position the international imperialist system has given our country in the division of labour, the position of 'subjugated hotel' of the imperialist metropolis. It is an option that has been created by the Western banks, Brussels, and Washington, whose last concern is the health of the Greek people.

It is this option that the leading faction of PASOK has slavishly undertaken to carry out. However, so that it might conceal its true social content, it relates a fairytale about national defence. If the working people are currently tightening their belts, if they continue to have a medieval health system, it is because they are being sacrificed for the necessary national defence *vis-a-vis* Turkey and not because the great Western capitalists say so. It is not they who are making our country, with its huge economic weaknesses, kneel by imposing on it the highest military expenditures of all NATO countries. While 7.1% of its GNP goes for defence, the affluent Germany only spends 3.2%. It is not they who are forcing it to bleed constantly, making it incapable of rising to its feet so that Western banks, and the monopoly manufacturers of arms systems, Phantom [fighter planes], and so forth, can be paid. These are weapons that Greece is forced to buy, although they are quite useless as long as there is a fifth column, the US bases, and as long as the structure of the Armed Forces remain unchanged. They are useless because the Nea Makri base alone can neutralize them electronically, can misguide and immobilize them as it did in 1974 during the Cyprus tragedy. It kept planes from flying to Cyprus, thus revealing how the Greek people are mocked with the story of an alleged national defence. Finally, they are useless because the entire senior officer corps currently in control of the Armed Forces, precisely like during the era of the junta and Karamanlis, are agents of the interests of either foreign Western secret services or Western manufacturing firms. And they do not even attempt to hide this. As soon as they retire at the age of 45, they become their high-salaried employees.

Therefore, as long as a 7.1-percent expenditure is imposed on us for various useless arms and for lazy people who are called the Army, not only shall we have no defence but we shall also not emerge from our austerity programme, and finally, shall have no health. [passage omitted]

Consequently, we decided to act by shooting at the legs of one of the big-doctors-merchants of the people's health, neurosurgeon Zacharias Kapsalakis. As such, he is jointly responsible, together with all big doctors and political personnel, whether of

New Democracy or of PASOK, for the people's plight and tragic health situation.

Our act is a protest in practice, an act of dynamic resistance against the hateful, inhuman exploitation by the coalition of the state and the circuit of the big doctors.

This is a warning to all doctors, especially those who receive bribes in public hospitals or astronomical sums in private clinics. The latter work under conditions of monopolistic supply that force patients to go to them.

Finally, it is a warning to all senior state employees who manage the various state insurance institutions, like the Institute for Social Insurance [IKA] and others. They mock and exploit patients through months of harassment when the insured people want to be refunded for treatment, and then the patients are not even reimbursed for a tenth of their true expenses.

The struggle will continue for equal health benefits for all people; for clean, modern, and comfortable hospitals; for all expenses to be covered by insurance funds; and for popular power and socialism.

Athens, 1 February 1987
Revolutionary Organization 17 November

APPENDIX 4

RO-17N COMMUNIQUÉ ON THE ASSASSINATION OF US DEFENCE ATTACHÉ NAVY CAPT. WILLIAM NORDEEN IN ATHENS ON 28 JUNE 1988

Excerpts of 17N text, dated 14 June, sent to Ethnos newspaper on 28 June

US IMPERIALISM IS RESPONSIBLE FOR THE TURKISH OCCUPATION OF CYPRUS.

US IMPERIALISM IS BEHIND THE CLAIMS OF TURKISH EXPANSIONISM.

JUNTA, NEW DEMOCRACY, PASOK, ARMED FORCES SOLD OUT CYPRUS.

Our anti-imperialist action today constitutes the second phase of the 23 May action in which we bombed four cars belonging to diplomats of the Turkish dictatorial and racist regime.

At that time we said that, first of all, Davos constitutes a demand by US imperialism since Papandreou is its prey and there is not a Greek Army but only a NATOite army. We also said that US imperialism is behind the Turkish claims and that it is also the one that organized the 1974 conspiracy in Greece, Turkey and Cyprus which led to the Turkish invasion and occupation of Cypriot territory. The expansionist Turkish militarism is functioning today as the gendarme of US imperialism in the region.

However, in addition to US imperialism's obvious and self-evident responsibility for the Cyprus tragedy and Turkish claims, responsibility also lies with certain sectors inside our country. Therefore, we have said that the responsibility of the junta, the New Democracy and PASOK lies at the political level, while responsibility at the military level lies with the Armed Forces from the dictatorship to the present. [passage omitted]

However, the responsibility of the leaders of the political world and the army was not limited only to the period of August 1974 when Attila II operation took place. There is a third period of responsibility which extends from that time until today.

The Greek government under New Democracy at the beginning and PASOK later on, as well as the Army leadership, already were faced with the fait accompli of Turkish occupation of an independent state which followed a violent military invasion. At the same time, they also were faced with a series of escalating claims by Turkish expansionism at the expense of Greece. Over the past 14 years, in the face of all these aggressive actions, the various Greek governments and Army not only should have but were also obliged to give a dynamic, violent answer whose form and timing they themselves should choose. This would not mean a general war, which was and is ruled out for a number of reasons, but, in the worst case scenario, a clash limited in both area and time, lasting a maximum of 2 to 3 days. The option of dynamic action was not included in the discussions among the established forces, who used as a pretext their myth of a generalized war in order to shake off their responsibilities. However, such an option should be included in a series of strong, dynamic responses. The mildest of such responses would be, for example, the downing of a Turkish military aircraft found violating our airspace and escalating to more serious dynamic actions. The duty of Greek governments and Army leaders was and is to choose the dynamic answer which would be most favourable for the Greek forces in terms of area and timing. Such action should be followed by a proposal to hold talks, which the Greek side would attend from an enhanced negotiating position.

Because there is another myth that any dynamic military action was and still is impossible, we will at this point, give an example of such action. This, however, does not mean we propose such actions should be carried out but they are possible and feasible strictly from a military aspect.

Through all these years, it should have been possible to work out and implement a plan which, under the possible prerequisite of secrecy, would have militarily strengthened the defence capabilities of the Greek Cypriots. Such a plan would also be based on sending secret and small commando teams to carry out sabotage actions in the occupied territories. Such an action is possible, does not demand mobilization or supermodern and heavy weapons but on the contrary a few trained and élite forces such as parachutists, commandos and so forth for unorthodox warfare. Such an action would certainly be joined later by Greek-Cypriot refugees. Even if it were uncovered, as a result of possible arrests or injuries, that these forces were Greek, international public opinion could not condemn such an action against the Turkish conqueror. Such a course might not result in the recapture of territories, but would secure the following:

- Create some insecurity in the Turkish sector which, in turn, would prevent the consolidation of the occupation and the present de facto situation;
- Maintain the Cyprus issue as a current issue in the international arena which would serve as a reminder of occupation and the just cause of the Greek Cypriots;
- Make Greek Cypriot's negotiating position easier; and most importantly
- Give a clear message to Turkish expansionism that, in the event of any aggressive action, Greece would give a dynamic response, which would have the most serious repercussions on all of Turkey's current claims.

Such a policy of dynamic response was and is the duty and obligation of any politically independent Greek government which had and has no other possible option. If such policy has not been implemented in the past, it is because both New Democracy and PASOK governments have placed their own political interests of remaining in power above the country's national interests since such a policy clashes with the interests of US imperialism.

In other words, they have functioned as governments with low national stature and not as governments of a virtually independent country. This is why the responsibilities for the third period are concealed. They have shed a dazzling light on the nature of the current parliamentary system. They very clearly show that both the New Democracy and PASOK leaderships are preys of US imperialism. Consequently, the current political parliamentary system, which is based on bipartisanship, is one of low national stature.

However, the Armed Forces and basically their leaders are equally responsible for what has happened since 1974. The Greek Army constitutes one of the biggest scandals in Greek society about which nobody dares to talk, even today when we have a parliamentary regime. If we take a quick glance at the Army's task in the post-war period while overlooking the fact that it is a state within a state governed by fascist internal regulations as proven by the dozens of suicides committed by privates, we will notice that it has waged a civil war, attempted a coup d'état in 1951, organized and actively participated in the violent and rigged elections of 1961, carried out the Colonels' coup in 1967 and established the dictatorship. The only time it was necessary for the Army to go into action as a national army to counter the Turkish invasion of Cyprus in the summer of 1974 and the period which followed, when it distinguished itself by its absence.

This state of affairs becomes an open mockery and deception when we consider that, after the United States, the Greek people are burdened with the highest military expenditures in terms of the percentage of their gross national product. These expenditures total almost 7 per cent while the medium imperialist powers, such as France and England, which maintain extremely strong armed forces and nuclear weapons, spend about half of this, that is 3.5 to 4 per cent.

Therefore, the prerequisites for a policy of national independence are the assumption by the working class (we do not mean the KKE) and its allies, as well as the implementation of a series of measures to break the link of imperial dependency. The minimum prerequisites at the political level are the immediate closure of the US bases and the country's withdrawal from NATO. In the economic field, the prerequisites are the nationalization of vital economic sectors and the administration of economic units by councils comprised of those who work in these units and who would be elected from the grass roots at a general assembly of the working people.

Imperialism is not interested in the people's national civilizational identity, nor in their local culture. Its firm policy has been to destroy this identity in the Third World by all possible means, including violent ones. So, the petty generals of the US Pentagon, the champions of Machiavellian adventurism, who determine the policy of NATO and US imperialism, are completely indifferent today as to whether the ratio of Greeks living in Cyprus is 80 per cent and whether they have had a long history, rich local traditions and culture, and a strong national identity.

They are also indifferent to the fact that Turks comprised 18 per cent of the population and that they lived harmoniously with the Greeks as a minority, as also is the case in almost all countries, which spread throughout the villages with their own way of life and culture. They do not care about the fact that the Aegean and its islands have always been Greek. They are exclusively interested in the defence of NATO and the establishment of a gendarme against the national liberation movements in the Middle East. From this point of view – the geographic and military points which they only care about – the best gendarme in Cyprus, the Aegean and the airspace is Turkish fascist militarism since the Turkish mainland is adjacent to these areas. This explains the Turkish invasion in 1974 and the continuing occupation of Cypriot territory, as well as the escalating Turkish claims against our country in the Aegean, our airspace and the continental shelf.

On the basis of the foregoing, we decided to execute a senior official of US imperialism's military forces in our country while he was travelling in an armoured car with Greek plates YAM1727.

US imperialism is mainly responsible for the Cypriot tragedy, the continuing Turkish occupation of Cypriot territory, and the escalating Turkish claims at the expense of our country's sovereign rights.

Besides, even the Americans themselves do not hide the fact that they organized the recent hundreds of violations of Greek airspace since both US and Turkish military aircraft simultaneously participated in these violations.

As we have also declared in the past, the US military forces in our country constitute an occupation force, and as such we will strike against anyone who is a member of this force or an agent of its secret services. Our action today is the fourth anti-American anti-imperialist action in 1 year. The three previous actions are the bomb attack in Rendis suburb against the US military bus which was carrying military personnel who maintained US nuclear warheads in our country; the bomb attack in Kavouri against a US bus which was carrying the mercenary staff of a fighter bomber plane which is sent on missions to terrorize and bomb Middle East countries; and the bomb which failed to explode in Filothei against (Carros), the agent of the Army's secret service DIA.

These actions will continue and intensify until the last Turkish soldier leaves Cyprus and until the last American leaves our country.

FOR NATIONAL INDEPENDENCE.

FOR THE PEOPLE'S RULE WITH THE PEOPLE'S INSTITUTIONS OF DIRECT DEMOCRACY.

FOR SOCIALISM WITH DIRECT MANAGEMENT OF ECONOMIC UNITS BY ELECTED AND RECOGNISABLE COUNCILS OF WORKING PEOPLE.

THE STRUGGLE CONTINUES.

Athens, 14 June 1988
Revolutionary Organization 17 November

APPENDIX 5

RO-17N COMMUNIQUÉ ON THE
LOUISA RIANKOUR STREET INCIDENT
ON 27 MARCH 1992

17N text, dated 8 May 1992, sent to Eleftherotypia newspaper on 9 May

REVOLUTIONARY ORGANIZATION 17 NOVEMBER
PROCLAMATION

In the face of the new recital of lies, comical and at the same time contradictory scenarios the police devote themselves to via their journalists and in the face of confusion that they deliberately cultivate with regard to what happened on Friday morning, 27 March, on Riankour Street, and the laughable acts they committed on Monday, 30 March, through Friday, 3 April, in order to conceal their utter incapability and to justify the billions they squander, since they had discovered the revolver, we are now obliged to clear things up and to reveal what really happened.

The police were not informed by an informer of theirs inside or close to our organization, as they maintain and as anyone who reads the following will realize.

We did not go to the Riankour Street spot only on Friday, 27 March, but on Tuesday, 24 March and Thursday, 26 March. Some neighbour, a 60-year-old – perhaps a former cop – who was walking between the OTE [Greek Telecommunications Organization] building, the cafe, drugstore, and the opposite taverna, spotted us. He considered our movements suspicious and he saw us getting into the van, returning the next day, and he took us for robbers and notified the police. Thus, the police decided to send the Mavrouleas unit the next day to determine what happened since they did not know who was involved.

This is proved by the following impressive facts:

- The Mavrouleas unit was made up of three cops in a FIAT parked at the corner of Laskaridou and Riankour Streets together with another one who acted as a worker across the street. It is noteworthy that the cops were drinking coffee in plastic cups sitting in their vehicle! If is it possible that this is a stakeout! As soon as they saw our van being parked Mavrouleas got out, jotted down our tag number and went to the opposite kiosk to phone headquarters to learn if it were stolen, something that means that he did not know beforehand.
- As soon as they lost our van they notified headquarters again. Headquarters, in turn, communicated, via the radio transmitter on a joint frequency, with all police patrol cars and motorcycle police to tell them to find the vehicle saying that the tag number was of interest and that they should be careful because the three men inside, while actually we were five fully armed men. Something they would have not done if they had known who was involved because then they would have maintained radio silence and switched to other special and secret frequencies so that third parties might not listen in, as they moreover, did, beginning Monday, 30 March, when they finally set up the "stakeout".
- During our entire drive along Riankour and Lampsa Streets going up, there was absolutely no police car to cut us off as they should have if there was a stake out.
- The "stakeout", if this Punch-and-Judy show can be called a stakeout, was set up after the fact on Monday, 30 March, once, of course, they had discovered the revolver and had realized their monumental gaffe. The stakeout was not set up to catch us but for other reasons. In order to hide their inefficiency and in order to spread their fables, now playing with dates because of their panic since they did not know our target and also in order to put into action the new plot being prepared with alleged facts, videos and alleged photographs.

So that day, 27 March, the following occurred: As soon as we arrived and parked we saw them, we were at once spotted and decided to leave. Our cops, only three of them in the Fiat, followed at some distance not daring to approach us. It seems that Mavrouleas, in the short space of a few minutes, had begun to ask himself and to wonder what exactly was happening and he kept the Fiat away. He thus acted very correctly and coolly with the result that needless bloodshed that would have been fatal for them was avoided.

In fact, they did not have any chance in the Fiat. They would not have managed to fire even two shots since two of our commandos sitting in the back of the van were aiming at them with automatic weapons, ready to fire at them at their smallest move, while there were altogether five of us with a lot of weapons. It seems that the cops realized this and remained altogether motionless. So, here too, what we had said elsewhere has been confirmed. When cops won't fire on us, we won't fire on them. When cops pull out pistols we will fire on them with any hesitation.

The next two days, Saturday and Sunday, were days off for our supercops who are burdened with the task of guarding the state and thus they did absolutely nothing at the above-mentioned place.

In the meantime, they discovered the revolver. At this point let us be permitted not to say why it was left. We will merely observe that fact alone shows the size of our armaments inside the van. They, therefore, decided, for the reasons we have given, to set up their "stakeout" on 30 March, in other words three days after the event. Dozens of vehicles of all makes were mobilized, Audis, BMW's, Fiats, Toyotas, Renaults and Alfa Romeos, dozens of cops, motorcycles with cops were called up so that all the neighbours might see that the police did something. On the other hand, their panic and fear, from the fact that they did not know either the target or the exact spot where the act was to take place, was such that they reached the point where they were checking the Panormou-Kiffissia traffic light – as if the act were to occur there – in a black Suzuki Swift, among others, that they parked on the sidewalk at the corner of Panormou and Kiffisia Streets with two suspicious characters inside who took down the tag numbers of any cars that stopped there. They took their information to the headman, called Yiorgos, who drove around in an Alfa Romeo.

Needless to say, of course, that despite the fact that the operetta of catharsis had convinced the very last Greek that judges are all bought off and venal, and led police to believe that a judge was our target, unfortunately for them that was not so. As a consequence, all the confusion they are trying to create in our organization with stories about informers is done in vain.

The conclusion is clear and simple. Once they committed their monumental gaffe they thought they could pull off a new plot exploiting their failure as much as they could. Here, of course, our friends the Americans get involved. It is well-known that for some time now American experts of the FBI have been working on data that security authorities had from ancient stories having no connection with 17 November. Under the guidance and encouragement of the Americans they thought that anyone caught on the basis, really or not, of the ancient data, would have overwhelming proof currently against him. That they are recognized by cops on Riankour Street, that their fingerprints were found on the pick up truck and not in such and such an old hideout and above all that they were photographed. So, new provocative acts are being prepared. That perhaps is the primary reason why the alleged "stakeout" was set up on the Riankour Street following the holiday and why the police disclosed it today by way of their agent journalists it was not a leak from journalists as the minister mocked.

Needless to say that on that 27 March, just as they had not set up any stakeout they did not have any camera either. Because if they had, in fact photographed someone, if they had fingerprints of someone, the hawk-eyed fellows of the US secret services would have spotted him in 40 days and he would have been arrested especially now when they know that we are preparing an act. It is therefore crystal clear why they need so much time. The old data correspond somewhat to the description of those who were on Riankour Street.

Finally, let us add that the act of the low-down Greeks, [premier] Mitsotakis and [public order minister] Anagnostopoulos, of handing over data on all Greeks to the Americans of the FBI and CIA constitutes an act of extreme debasement of the Greek nation that is equivalent to high treason, an act about which no politician and no publication has said a word.

Athens, 8 May 92
Revolutionary Organization 17 November

APPENDIX 6

ELA COMMUNIQUÉ OFFERING TO HALT MILITARY ACTIVITY UNTIL SUMMER 1995

Excerpts of ELA text, dated 20 November 1993, published by Eleftherotypia newspaper on 22 November 1993

The state elections on 10 October 1993 brought PASOK back to government, that is, to the position of the central political manager of capitalism in our country.

Our political position regarding PASOK has been well-known and without retraction since October 1981, when PASOK became government for the first time. This party, together with New Democracy [ND] are the two main partners of the government-opposition. PASOK and ND take over successively, according to the development of social clashes and the class conjuncture, the management of the exploiting regime at the expense of the proletarians within the framework of world capitalism-imperialism. [passage omitted]

The only substantial difference between PASOK and ND concerns a big part of PASOK's social grassroots supporters, who inevitably vote for it. For historical reasons, many people are found and work within these grassroots who are socially conscientious, active, and are politically developing into prospective revolutionaries.

Given this state of affairs, the people who inevitably voted for PASOK have already realized that PASOK and ND share common denominators:

- The unimpeded advance of internationalised multinational capital.

- "Austerity" at the expense of the contemporary proletarians together with the social and physical infection.
- The sovereignty of the "European Union" and the IMF.
- The unlimited power of NATO and North American bases.
- Subjugation of the "new world order" to the United Nations and the European Union's TREVI.
- The unlimited exercise of police and judicial arbitrary procedures, suppression and terrorism. [passage omitted]

Given these facts, and in our attempt under the current circumstances to promote the goals off our political practice whose important elements are:

- The linking of all the various forms and ways of the anticapitalist, anti-imperialist struggle.
- The correction and combination of our actions with the antiregime resistance and aims of individuals, groups and movements.
- The liberation of the antiregime political detainees.

We have decided to take the following political initiative:

We will not carry out violent strikes until the summer of 1995 if, within a reasonable period of time, all those who are detained for their anticapitalist and anti-imperialist political stand and practice are released and if the unjust judicial pursuit of these people is stopped. The reasonable period of time cannot exceed 100 days from the time PASOK won the election.

We would also like to say to everyone, and particularly the proletarians of society wherever they may be, that: The only road to their liberation is revolutionary self-organization and illegal action and co-ordination outside and against the logic of accepting the regime's legal, judicial and ethical practices and the subjugation of the goals of the people's revolutionary struggle.

The struggle continues.

Epanastatikos Laikos Agonas – ELA

APPENDIX 7

ATTACKS BY RO-17N

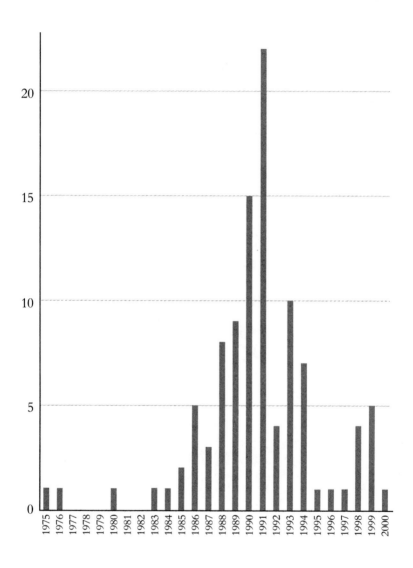

7.1 Number of attacks by RO-17N

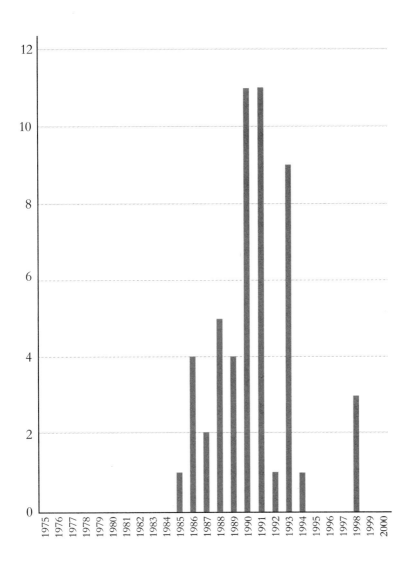

7.2 Number of bomb attacks by RO-17N

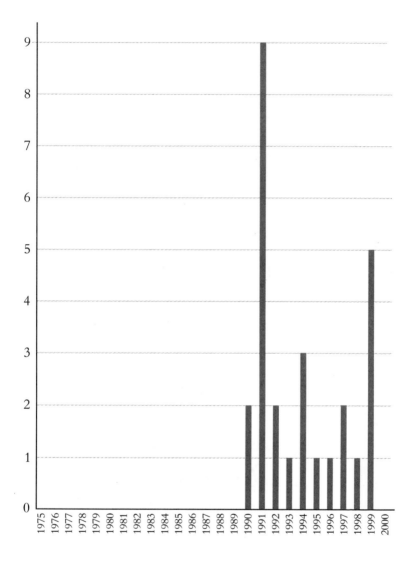

7.3 Number of rocket attacks by RO-17N

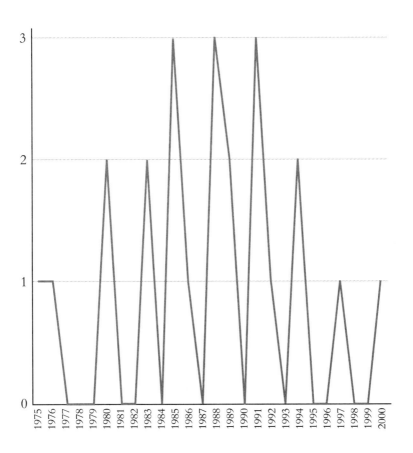

7.4 Number of murders by RO-17N

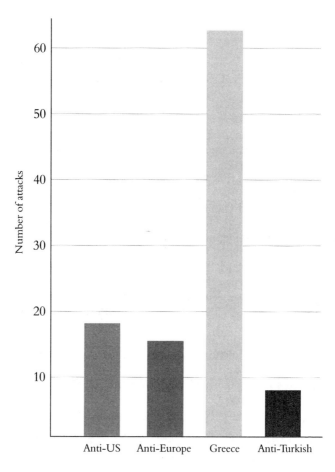

7.5 Targets of attacks by RO-17N

BIBLIOGRAPHY

I. STUDIES ON TERRORISM AND POLITICAL VIOLENCE

Alexander, Yonah and Richard Latter (eds), *Terrorism and the Media: Dilemmas for Governments, Journalists and the Public* (McLean, VA: Brassey's, 1990).

Alexander, Yonah and K.A. Meyers (eds), *Terrorism in Europe* (London: Croom Helm, 1982).

Alexander, Yonah and Dennis A. Pluchinsky (eds), *European Terrorism: Today & Tomorrow* (MacLean, VA: Brassey's, 1992).

Alexander, Yonah and Dennis A. Pluchinsky (eds), *Europe's Red Terrorists: The Fighting Communist Organizations* (London: Frank Cass, 1992).

Almagor-Cohen, Raphael, 'Foundations of Violence, Terror and War in the Writings of Marx, Engels and Lenin', in *Terrorism and Political Violence*, Vol. 3, No. 2 (Summer 1991), pp. 1–24.

Apter, David E. (ed.), *The Legitimization of Violence* (London: Macmillan, 1997).

Burton, Anthony, *Urban Terrorism* (London: Leo Cooper, 1975).

Carter, April F., 'Violence', in David Miller (ed.), *The Blackwell Encyclopaedia of Political Thought* (Oxford: Blackwell, 1987). pp. 540–41.

Catanzaro, Raimondo (ed.), *The Red Brigades and Left-wing Terrorism in Italy* (London: Pinter, 1991).

Chalk, Peter, *West European Terrorism and Counter-Terrorism* (London: Macmillan, 1996).

Crenshaw, Martha (ed.), *Terrorism, Legitimacy, and Power: The Consequences of Political Violence* (Middletown, CT: Wesleyan University Press, 1983).

Crenshaw, Martha (ed.), *Terrorism in Context* (Pennsylvania: Penn State Press, 1995).

Dartnell, Michael, 'France's *Action Directe*: Terrorists in Search of a Revolution', in *Terrorism and Political Violence*, Vol. 2, No. 4 (Winter 1990), pp. 457–83.

Dartnell, Michael Y., *Action Directe: Ultra-Left Terrorism in France, 1979–1987* (London: Frank Cass, 1995).

Della Porta, Donatella, *Il Terrorismo Di Sinistra* (Bologna: Il Mulino, 1990).

Drake, C. M., *Terrorists' Target Selection* (London: Macmillan, 1998).

Drake, Richard, *The Revolutionary Mystique and Terrorism in Contemporary Italy* (Bloomington, IN: Indiana University Press, 1989).

Drake, Richard, 'Ideology and Terrorism in Italy: Autobiography as Historical Source', in *Terrorism and Political Violence*, Vol. 4, No. 2 (Summer 1992), pp. 47–61.

Drake, Richard, *The Aldo Moro Case* (London: Harvard University Press, 1995).

Evans, Robert H., 'Terrorism and the Subversion of the State: Italian Legal Responses', in *Terrorism and Political Violence*, Vol. 1, No. 3 (July 1989), pp. 324–52.

Farnen, Russell F., 'Terrorism and the Mass Media: A Systemic Analysis of a Symbiotic Process, in *Terrorism: An International Journal*, Vol. 13, No. 2 (March-April 1990), pp. 99–143.

Fritzche, Peter, 'Terrorism in the Federal Republic of Germany and Italy: Legacy of the '68 Movement or "Burden of Fascism"?', in *Terrorism and Political Violence*, Vol. 1, No. 4 (Oct. 1989), pp. 466–81.

Fromkin, David, 'The Strategy of Terrorism', in *Foreign Affairs*, Vol. 53, No. 4 (July 1975), pp. 683–98.

Furet, François, Antoine Liniers and Philippe Reynaud, *Terrorisme et démocratie* (Paris: Librairie Antheme Fayard, 1983).

Gearty, Conor, *The Future of Terrorism* (London: Phoenix, 1997).

Guelke, Adrian, *The Age of Terrorism and the International Political System* (London: I.B. Tauris, 1995).

Hoffman, Bruce, *Inside Terrorism* (London: Victor Gollancz, 1998).

Horowitz, Irving Louis, *Taking Lives* (New Brunswick, NJ: Transaction Publishers, 1997).

Jamieson, Alison, *The Heart Attacked: Terrorism and Conflict in the Italian State* (New York: Marion Boyars, 1989).

Jamieson, Alison, 'Identity and Morality in the Italian Red Brigades', in *Terrorism and Political Violence*, Vol. 2, No. 4 (Winter 1990), pp. 508–20.

Kellen, Konrad, *The Impact of Terrorism on the Federal Republic of Germany: 1968–1982*, (St. Monica, CA: RAND Corporation, Oct. 1989).

Laqueur, Walter, *Terrorism* (London: Weidenfeld & Nicolson, 1977).

Laqueur, Walter, 'Reflections on Terrorism', in *Foreign Affairs*, Vol. 65, No. 1, (Fall 1986), pp. 86–100.

Lodge, Juliet (ed.), *Terrorism: A Challenge to the State* (Oxford: Martin Robertson, 1981).

Meade, Robert C. Jr., *Red Brigades: The Story of Italian Terrorism* (London: Macmillan, 1990).

Moss, David, *The Politics of Left-Wing Violence in Italy, 1969–1985* (London: Macmillan, 1989).

Ortner, Sherry B, 'On Key Symbols', in *American Anthropologist*, Vol. 75, No. 5 (Oct. 1973), pp. 1338–46.

O'Sullivan, Noel (ed.), *Terrorism, Ideology and Revolution* (Boulder, CO: Westview Press, 1986).

Pye, Lucian, 'Political Culture', in *International Encyclopedia of the Social Sciences*, Vol. 12, p. 218.

Rubenstein, Richard E., *Alchemists of Revolution: Terrorism in the Modern World* (New York: Basic Books Inc., 1987).

Schmid, A. P., 'Terrorism and the Media: The Ethics of Publicity', in *Terrorism and Political Violence*, Vol. 1, No. 4 (October 1989), pp. 539–65.

Schmid, Alex P. and Ronald D. Crelinsten (eds), *Western Responses to Terrorism* (London: Frank Cass, 1993).

Schmid, Alex P., Albert J. Jongman, et. al. *Political Terrorism: A New Guide to Actors, Authors, Concepts and Data Bases, Theories and Literature* (New Brunswik, NJ: Transaction Books, 1988).

Seliger, Martin, *Ideology and Politics* (London: George Allen & Unwin, 1976).

Smith, M. L. R., *Fighting for Ireland? The Military Strategy of the Irish Republican Movement* (London: Routledge, 1995).

Smith Davidson, G., *Combatting Terrorism* (London: Routledge, 1990).

Thornton, Thomas P., 'Terror as a Weapon of Political Agitation', in Harry Eckstein (ed.), *Internal War* (London: Free Press of Glencoe, 1964).

Toolis, Kevin, *Rebel Hearts: Journeys within the IRA's Soul* (London: Picador, 1995).

Tucker, H. H. (ed.), *Combating the Terrorists: Democratic Responses to Political Violence* (New York: Facts on File, 1988).

Wagner-Pacifici, Robin Erica, *The Moro Morality Play: Terrorism as a Social Drama* (Chicago: University of Chicago Press, 1986).

Wardlaw, Grant, *Political Terrorism* (2nd edition) (Cambridge: Cambridge University Press, 1990).

Weinberg, Leonard and William Lee Eubank (eds), *The Rise and Fall of Italian Terrorism* (Boulder, CO: Westview Press, 1987).

Wieviorka, Michel, *The Making of Terrorism* (Chicago: University of Chicago Press, 1993).

Wilkinson, Paul, *Terrorism and the Liberal State* (2nd edition) (London: Macmillan, 1986).

Wilkinson, Paul, 'The Media and Terror: A Reassessment', in *Terrorism and Political Violence*, Vol. 9, No. 2 (Summer, 1997), pp. 51–64.

II. GREEK POLITICAL CULTURE

Andreopoulos, George, *I Chrissi kai i Katachrissi tou Antiamerikanismou stin Ellada* [The Use and Abuse of Anti-Americanism in Greece] (Athens: Polytypo, 1994).

Bermeo, Nancy, 'Classification and Consolidation: Some Lessons from the Greek Dictatorship', in *Political Science Quarterly*, Vol. 110, No. 3 (1995), pp. 435–52.

Carabott, Phillip (ed.), *Greece and Europe in the Modern Period: Aspects of a Troubled Relationship* (London: King's College, 1995).

Carabott, Phillip (ed.), *Greek Society in the Making, 1863–1913* (Aldershot: Varorium, 1997).

Clogg, Richard, *A Short History of Modern Greece* (Cambridge: Cambridge University Press, 1979).

Clogg, Richard, *Parties and Election in Greece: The Search for Legitimacy* (London: Hurst & Company, 1987).

Clogg, Richard, *A Concise History of Greece* (Cambridge: Cambridge University Press, 1992).

Clogg, Richard (ed.), *Greece 1981–89: The Populist Decade* (London: Macmillan, 1993).

Clogg, Richard, 'Andreas Papandreou – A Profile', in *Mediterranean Politics*, Vol. 1, No. 3 (Winter, 1996), pp. 382–7.

Clogg, Richard and George Yannopoulos (eds), *Greece Under Military Rule* (London: Secker & Warburg, 1972).

Close, David H. (ed.), *The Greek Civil War, 1943–1950: Studies of Polarization* (London: Routledge, 1993).

Close, David H., *The Origins of the Greek Civil War* (London: Longman, 1995).

Cram, Laura, 'Women's Political Participation in Greece since the Fall of the Colonels: From Democratic Struggle to Incorporation by the Party-State?', in *Democratization*, Vol. 1, No. 2 (Summer 1994), pp. 229–50.

Davanellos, Antonis, *Noemvris 1973: I exegerssi* [November 1973: The Revolt] (Athens: Ekdosseis Ergatiki Dimokratia, 1995).

Demertzis, Nicolas, 'Greece', in Roger Eatwell (ed.), *European Political Cultures: Conflict or Convergence?* (London: Routledge, 1997), pp. 107–21.

Demertzis, Nikos (ed.), *I Elliniki Politiki Koultoura Simera* [The Greek Political Culture Today] (Athens: Odysseas, 1994).

Dertilis, George, *Koinonikos Metaschimatismos kai Stratiotiki Epemvassi, 1889–1909* [Social Change and Military Intervention, 1880–1909] (Athens, Exantas, 1977).

Diamandouros, Nikiforos P., 'Greek Political Culture in Transition: Historical Origins, Evolution, Current Trends', in Richard Clogg (ed.), *Greece in the 1980s* (London: Macmillan, 1983), pp. 43–69.

Diamandouros, Nikiforos P., 'Regime Change and the Prospects for Democracy in Greece: 1974–1983', in Guillermo O'Donnell, Philippe C. Schmitter, and Laurence Whitehead (eds), *Transitions from Authoritarian Rule: Prospects for Democracy* (Baltimore: Johns Hopkins University Press, 1986), pp. 138–64.

Elephantis, Angelos, *Ston Asterismo tou Laikismou* [In the Constellation of Populism] (Athens: O Politis, 1991).

Elephantis, Angelos, *Dia Gymnou Ofthalmou* [Through the Naked Eye] (Athens: Polis, 1998).

Featherstone, Kevin and Kostas Ifantis (eds), *Greece in a Changing Europe: Between European Inegration and Balkan disintegration?* (Manchester: Manchester University Press, 1996).

Featherstone, Kevin and Dimitrios K. Katsoudas (eds), *Political Change in Greece: Before and After the Colonels* (London: Croom Helm, 1987).

Fouskas, Vassilis, 'The Left and the crisis of the Third Hellenic Republic, 1989–97', in Donald Sassoon (ed.). *Looking Left: European socialism after the Cold War* (London: I.B. Tauris, 1997), pp. 64–87.

Gunther, Richard, P. Nikiforos Diamandouros and Hans-Jurgen Puhle (eds), *The Politics of Democratic Consolidation: Southern Europe in Comparative Perspective* (Baltimore: Johns Hopkins University Press, 1995).

Haralambis, Dimitris, *Stratos kai Politiki Exoussia: I domi tis exoussias stin metemfyliaki Ellada* [Political Power and the Military: The Power Structure in post-Civil War Greece] (Athens: Exandas, 1985).

Hatzivassiliou, Evanthis, 'Security and the European Option: Greek Foreign Policy, 1952–62', in *Journal of Contemporary History*, Vol. 30 (1995), pp. 187–202.

Higham, Robin and Thanos Veremis (eds), *The Metaxas Dictatorship: Aspects of Greece, 1936–40* (Athens: ELIAMEP -Vryonis Center, 1993).

Iatrides, J. O. and Linda Wringley (eds), *Greece at the Crossroads: The Civil War and its Legacy* (University Park, Penn: Pennsylvania University Press, 1995).

Ifantis, Konstantinos, 'From Factionalism to Autocracy: PASOK's De-radicalization during the Regime Transition of the 1970s', in *Democratization*, Vol. 2, No. 1 (Spring 1995), pp. 77–89.

Kalogeropoulou, Efthalia, 'Election promises and government performances in Greece: PASOK's fulfilment of its 1981 election pledges', in *European Journal of Political Research*, 17 (1989), pp. 289–311.

Kapetanyiannis, Vassilis, 'The Making of Greek Eurocommunism', in *Political Quarterly*, Vol. 50, No. 4 (Oct.–Dec. 1979), pp. 445–60.

Kapetanyiannis, Vassilis, *Socio-Political Conflicts and Military Intervention: The case of Greece, 1950–1967*, (Unpublished PhD dissertation, University of London, 1986).

Karambelias, George, *Kratos kai Koinonia stin Metapolitefsi: 1974–1988* [State and Society in Metapolitefsi, 1974–1988] (Athens: Exandas, 1989).

Kariotis, Theodore C. (ed.), *The Greek Socialist Experiment: Papandreou's Greece, 1981–1989* (New York: Pella, 1992).

Kitroeff, Alexander, 'Andreas Papandreou: A Brief Political Biography', in *Journal of the Hellenic Diaspora*, Vol. 23, No. 1 (Special Issue, 1997), pp. 7–32.

Kitromilides, Paschalis, 'The Vision of Freedom in Greek Society', in *Journal of the Hellenic Diaspora*, Vol. 19, No. 1 (1993), pp. 5–29.

Koutsoukis, Kl. S., 'Sleaze in Contemporary Greek Politics', in *Parliamentary Affairs*, Vol. 48, No. 4 (October 1995), pp. 688–96.

Legg, Keith R., *Politics in Modern Greece* (Stanford: Stanford University Press, 1969).

Legg, Keith R. and John Roberts, *Modern Greece: A Civilization on the Periphery* (Boulder, CO: Westview Press, 1997).

Livieratos, Dimitris, *Koinonikoi Agones stin Ellada, 1927–31* [Social Struggle in Greece, 1927–31] (Athens: Ennalaktikes Ekdosseis, 1987).

Loulis, John, 'Papandreou's Foreign Policy', in *Foreign Affairs*, (Winter 1984/85), pp. 375–91.

Lygeros, Stavros, *To Pechnithi tis Exoussias* [PowerGames] (Athens: Nea Synora, 1996).

Lyrintzis, Christos, 'Political Parties in Post-Junta Greece: A Case of "Bureucratic Clientelism"', in Geoffrey Pridham (ed.), *The New Mediterranean Democracies* (London: Frank Cass, 1984), pp. 99–118.

Lyrintzis, Christos, 'The power of populism: The Greek case', in *European Journal of Political Research*, 15 (1987), pp. 667–86.

Macridis, Roy C., *Greek Politics at a Crossroads: What kind of Socialism?* [Stanford: Hoover Institution Press, 1984).

Mangakis, George, 'Letter to Europeans', in *An Embarrassment of Tyrannies: Twenty-five Years of Index on Censorship*, (London: Gollancz, 1997), pp. 25–38.

Mardas, Alexis, *Pisso apo ton Illio: Andreas Papandreou, Oramata kai Efialtes* [Behind the Sun: Andreas Papandreou, Visions and Nightmares] (Athens: Gnossi, 1995).

Mavrogordatos, George Th., *Stillborn Republic: Social Coalitions and Party Strategies in Greece, 1922–1936* (Berkeley: University of California Press, 1983).

Mazower, Mark, *Greece and the Inter-War Economic Crisis* (Oxford: Clarendon Press, 1991).

Mazower, Mark, *Inside Hitler's Greece: The Experience of Occupation, 1941–44* (New Haven: Yale University Press, 1993).

Meynaud, Jean, *Les Forces Politiques en Grèce* (Paris: Etudes de Science Politique, 1965).

Mouzelis, Nicos P., *Modern Greece: Facets of Underdevelopment* (London: Macmillan, 1978).

Mouzelis, Nicos P., 'Greece in the Twenty-first Century: Institutions and Political Culture', in Dimitri Constas & Theofanis G. Stavrou (eds), *Greece Prepares for the Twenty-first Century* (Baltimore: Johns Hopkins University Press, 1995).

Murtagh, Peter, *The Rape of Greece: The King, The Colonels and the Resistance* (London: Simon & Schuster, 1994).

Nachmani, Amikam, 'Civil War and Foreign Intervention in Greece, 1946–9', in *Journal of Contemporary History*, Vol. 25 (1990), pp. 489–522.

Noutsos, Panayiotis, *I Sossialistiki Skepssi stin Ellada: 1875–1974* [The Socialist Thought in Greece: 1875–1974] (Athens: Gnossi, 1994).

Papachelas, Alexis, *O Viasmos tis Ellinikis Dimokratias: O Amerikanikos Paragon, 1947–1967* [The Rape of Greek Democracy: The American Factor, 1947–1967] (Athens: Estia, 1997).

Papadopoulos, Yannis, 'Parties, the State and Society in Greece: Continuity within Change', in *West European Politics*, Vol. 12, No. 2 (April 1989), pp. 55–71.

Papandreou, Andreas, *Democracy at Gunpoint: The Greek Front* (London: Andre Deutsch, 1971).

Pappas, Takis S., *Making Party Democracy in Greece* (London: Macmillan, 1999).

Penniman, Howard (ed.), *Greece at the Polls: The National Elections of 1974 and 1977* (Washington DC: American Enterprise Institute, 1981).

Petras, James, 'The Contradictions of Greek Socialism', in *New Left Review*, 163 (May–June, 1987), pp. 3–25.

Petropulos, John Anthony, *Politics and Statecraft in the Kingdom of Greece, 1833–43* (Princeton, NJ: Princeton University Press, 1968).

Pettifer, James, *The Greeks: The Land and People since the War* (London: Viking, 1993).

Pollis, Adamantia, 'Modernity, Civil Society and the Papandreou Legacy', in *Journal of the Hellenic Diaspora*, Vol. 23, No. 1 (Special Issue, 1997), pp. 59–82.

Pretenteris, I.K., *I Thefteri Metapolitefsi: prosopikes simeiosseis apo mia megali anatropi* [The Second Metapolitefsi: personal notes from a big upset] (Athens: Polis, 1996).

Pridham, Geoffrey and Paul G. Lewis (eds), *Stabilising Fragile Democracies: Comparing new party systems in Southern and Eastern Europe* (London: Routledge, 1996).

Psomiades, Harry J., 'Greece: From the Colonels' Rule to Democracy', in John H. Herz (ed.), *From Dictatorship to Democracy* (Westport, CO: Greenwood Press), pp. 251–73.

Psomiades, Harry J. and Stavros B. Thomadakis (eds), *Greece, the New Europe, and the Changing International Order* (New York: Pella, 1993).

Rigos, Alkis, *I B' Elliniki Dimokratia, 1924–1935: Koinonikes Diastasseis tis Politikis Skinis* [The Second Greek Republic, 1924–1935: Social Dimensions on the Political Scene] (Athens: Themelio, 1992).

St Martin, Katerina, *Lambrakides: I Istoria mia Yenias* [Lambrakides: The History of a Generation] (Athens: Polytypo, 1987).

Samatas, Minas, 'Greek McCarthyism: A Comparative Assessment of Greek Post-Civil War Repressive Anticommunism and the US Truman-McCarthy Era', in *Journal of Hellenic Diaspora*, Vol. 13, Nos. 3–4 (Fall-Winter 1986), pp. 5–75.

Samatas, Minas, 'The Populist Phase of an Underdeveloped Surveillance Society: Political Surveillance in Post-Dictatorial Greece', in *Journal of the Hellenic Diaspora*, Vol. 19, No. 1 (1993), pp. 31–70.

Smith, Michael Llewellyn, *Ionian Vision: Greece in Asia Minor 1919–1922* (London: Hurst & Company, 1998).

Sotiropoulos, Dimitrios A., 'Bureaucrats and Politicians: a case study of the determinants of perceptions of conflict and patronage in the Greek bureaucracy under PASOK rule, 1981–1989', in *British Journal of Sociology*, Vol. 45, No. 3 (September 1994), pp. 349–65.

Spanou, Calliope, 'Penelope's Suitors: Administrative Modernization and Party Competition in Greece', in *West European Politics*, Vol. 19, No. 1 (January 1996), pp. 97–124.

Spourdalakis, Michalis, *PASOK: Domi, Essokomatikes Krisseis kai Sygkentrossi tis Exoussias* [PASOK: Structure, Intraparty Crises and Power Concentration] (Athens: Exandas, 1988).

Spourdalakis, Michalis, *The Rise of the Greek Socialist Party* (London: Routledge, 1988).

Spourdalakis, Michalis, 'PASOK's Second Chance', in *Mediterranean Politics*, Vol. 1, No. 3 (Winter 1996), pp. 320–36.

Theodoraki-Loule, Nitsa, *Harilaos Florakis* (Athens: Ellinika Grammata, 1995).

'Thucydides', 'Greek Politics: Myth and Reality', in *Political Quarterly*, Vol. 41, No. 2 (1970), pp. 455–66.

Tsoucalas, Constantine, *The Greek Tragedy* (Harmondsworth: Penguin, 1969).

Tsoucalas, Constantine, 'Class Struggle and Dictatorship in Greece', in *New Left Review*, No. 65 (July-August 1969), pp. 3–16.

Tsoucalas, Konstantinos, *Taxidi sto Logo kai stin Istoria, Tomoi A&B* [Journeys to Logos and History, Vols. 1 & 2] (Athens: Plethro, 1996).

Tsoukalis, Loukas, 'Beyond the Greek Paradox', in Graham T. Allisson and Kalypso Nicolaidis (eds), *The Greek Paradox: Promise vs. Performance* (Cambridge, MA: MIT Press, 1997), pp. 163–74.

Vatikiotis, P. J., *Popular Autocracy in Greece, 1936–1941: A Political Biography of General Ioannis Metaxas* (London: Frank Cass, 1998).

Venizelos, Evangelos, *I Logiki tou Politevmatos kai i Domi tis Ektelestikis Exoussias sto Syndagma tou 1975* [The Logic of the Regime and the structure of the Executive in the 1975 Constitution] (Thessaloniki: Paratiritis, 1980).

Veremis, Thanos, *Greece's Balkan Entanglement*, (Athens: ELIAMEP, 1995).

Veremis, Thanos, *The Military in Greek Politics: From Independence to Democracy* (London: Hurst & Company, 1997).

Vernardakis, Christoforos and Yiannis Mavris, *Kommata kai Koinonikes Symachies stin prodiktatoriki Ellada* [Parties and Social Alliances in pre-dictatorial Greece] (Athens: Exandas, 1987).

Verney, Susannah, 'To be or not to be within the European Community: the party debate and democratic consolidation in Greece', in Geoffrey Pridham (ed.), *Securing Democracy: Political Parties and Democratic Consolidation in Southern Europe* (London: Routledge, 1990), pp. 203–23.

Vlavianos, Haris, 'The Greek Communist Party: In Search of a Revolution', in Tony Judt (ed.), *Resistance and Revolution in Mediterranean Europe, 1939–1948* (London: Routledge, 1989).

Votsis, Yiorgos, *Se Mavro Fondo* [Against the dark background] (Athens: Stochastis, 1984).

Woodhouse, C. M., *Karamanlis: The Restorer of Greek Democracy* (Oxford: Clarendon Press, 1982).

III. THE GREEK STUDENT MOVEMENT AND THE EXTRA-PARLIAMENTARY LEFT

Axelos, 'Publishing Activity and the Movement of Ideas in Greece', in *Journal of the Hellenic Diaspora*, Vol. 11, No. 2 (Summer 1984), pp. 5–46.

Dafermos, Olympios, *To antidiktatoriko foititiko kinima, 1972–1973* [The anti-dictatorial student movement, 1972–1973] (Athens: Themelio, 1992).

Dekapenthimeros Politis, 'To Polytechneio mesa apo ta keimena tou' [The Polytechnic through its texts], No. 2 (19 November 1983).

EKKE, *Vassika Politika Keimena, 1970–1974* [Essential Political Texts, 1970–1974] (Athens, 1974).

Eleftherotypia, 'The left of the Left', 15–25 June 1976.

Eleftherotypia, 'The November '73 events', Special Section, (15–16 November, 1976).

Eleftherotypia, 'Student Movement, 1975–1995', Special Section, (17 November, 1995).

Kapsalis, Dionyssis, 'Antidiktatoriko Kinima: istoria kai ideologia' [The anti-dictatorial student movement: history and ideology] *O Politis*, No. 30 (November 1979).

Kathimerini, 'Polytechnic: 25 years', (15 November, 1998).

Kazamias, Andreas M. (ed.), 'Symposium on Educational reform in Greece', in *Comparative Education Review*, Vol. 22, No. 1 (February 1978).

KKE/M-L, *Kokkini Simaia* [Red Flag], No. 1 (October 1974) and Nos. 2–3 (November-December 1974).

Lazos, Christos, *Elliniko Foititiko Kinima, 1821–1973* [The Greek Student Movement, 1821–1973] (Athens: Gnossi, 1987).

Lygeros, Stavros, *Foititiko Kinima kai Taxiki Pali stin Ellada, 2 Tomoi* [The Student Movement and Class Struggle in Greece, 2 Vols.] (Athens: Ekdotiki Omada Ergassia, 1977).

'Maoists: The Last of the Romantics', *To Vima*, Special Section on youth political movements in Greece, 23 July, 1995.

OMLE, *Thesseis tis K.E tis OMLE yia ta 56 chronia apo tin idryssi tou KKE* [Positions of the Central Committee of the OMLE for the 56 years since the formation of the KKE], 1975.

OMLE, *Laiki Foni* [Popular Voice] Nos. 35–36 (February– March 1974).

OPA-RIXI, *Enopli Pali kai Tromokratia* [Armed Struggle and Terrorism] (Athens: Kommouna, 1985).

OSE, *Sossialistiki Epanastassi* [Socialist Revolution] No. 1 (September 1974).

Organosseis kai Exokoinovouleftika kommata: Aporrito Enimerotiko Simeioma/Ypodiefthynssi Genikis Asfalleias Athinon: Ypiressia Pliroforion [Extra-parliamentary organizations and parties: Classified Report/Greek Intelligence Service] 29 March 1984.

Psacharopoulos, George and Andreas M. Kazamias, 'Student Activism in Greece: A Historical and Empirical Analysis', in *Higher Education*, No. 9 (1980), pp. 127–38.

Rigos, Alkis, 'Foititiko Kinima kai Diktatoria' [The Student Movement and the Military Dictatorship], in *Anti*, No. 344, (1987).

Wasser, Henry, 'A Survey of Recent Trends in Greek Higher Education', in *Journal of the Hellenic Diaspora*, Vol. 6, No. 1 (1979), pp. 85–95.

IV. ULTRA-LEFT TERRORISM IN GREECE: INTERPRETATIONS

Bakoyiannis, Dora, 'Allages sta Valkania: Messa Mazikis Enimerossis kai Tromokratia' [Changes in the Balkans: Terrorism and the Media], in Yiorgos Voukelatos (ed.), *Tromokratia kai Messa Mazikis Enimerossis* [Terrorism and the Media] (Athens: Elliniki Euroekdotiki, 1993), pp. 15–32.

Bakoyiannis, Dora, 'Terrorism in Greece', in *Mediterranean Quarterly*, Vol. 6, No. 2 (Spring 1995), pp. 17–28.

Bossis, Mary, *Ellada kai Tromokratia: Ethnikes kai Diethneis Diastasseis* [Greece and Terrorism: National and International Dimensions] (Athens: Sakkoulas, 1996).

Confidential Report: *I Ideologiki, Politiki kai Epicheirissiaki Physiognomia tis EO 17 Noemvri* [The Ideological, Political and Operational Physiognomy of RO-17 November] Criminal Intelligence Directorate, Anti-Terrorism Branch, Athens, May 1995.

Confidential Report: *Ekthessi schetika me tin Epanastatiki Organossi 17 November kai alla themata* [Report on the Revolutionary Organization 17 November and other issues] Criminal Intelligence Directorate, Anti-Terrorism Branch, Athens, March 1995.

Corsun, Andrew, 'Group Profile: The Revolutionary Organization 17 November in Greece', in Yonah Alexander & Dennis A. Pluchinsky (eds), *European Terrorism: Today & Tomorrow* (McClean, VA: Brassey's, 1992), pp. 93–125.

Greek Parliament, Parliamentary Discussion Papers: 'Bill to combat against terrorism and protect the democratic polity, 774/1978', (10–17 April 1978).

Greek Parliament, Parliamentary Discussion Papers: 'The Abolition of Law 774/1978', (16–23 May 1983).

Greek Parliament, Parliamentary Discussion Papers: 'Bill for the Protection of Society against Organized Crime, 1916/1990', (10–13 December 1990).

Karambelias, Yiorgos, *To Elliniko Andarktiko ton Poleon, 1974–1985* [Urban Guerrilla Warfare in Greece, 1974–1985] (Athens: Roptron, 1985).

Karambelias, Yiorgos, *Enopli Pali kai Enallaktiko Kinima* [Armed Struggle and the Alternative Movement] (Athens: Kommouna, 1986).

Kassimeris, George, 'The Greek State Response to Terrorism', in *Terrorism and Political Violence*, Vol. 5, No. 4 (Winter 1993), pp. 288–310.

Kassimeris, George, 'Greece: Twenty Years of Political Violence', in *Terrorism and Political Violence*, Vol. 7, No. 2 (Summer 1995), pp. 74–92.

Kassimeris, George, 'Two decades of terrorism in Greece', in *Jane's Intelligence Review*, Vol. 8, No. 3 (March 1996), pp. 117–19.

Konstandaras, Nikos, 'Dark Star: The Story of November 17', in *Odyssey*, (February-March, 1994), pp. 28–34.

Symeonides, A. T., 'Greek Internal Security Policy', delivered at a Europe 2000 conference on *Organized Crime and Terrorism in New Europe*, (Athens: 26–28 November 1991).

INDEX

Evénéments de Mai, 49
extra-parliamentary action, 58
extra-parliamentary left, 69–70

Fakelos, 18
FBI, 85, 101, 144, 197
Florakis, Harilaos, 17n, 167
Follini, Maurizio, 82
foreign intervention, 33
France, 52, 181–2
Fromkin, David, 199
Fyntanidis, Seraphim, 187–8

Gaulle, Charles de, 28
General Motors, 103
Germany, 137, 158, 170, 176, 178, 182
Gladio, 143
Gorgu, Cettin, 95, 141n
Greece: civil war, 16, 27, 46, 65; economic independence, 29; entry to EC, 29; political culture, 4, 8, 41; political discourse, 207; political structures, 41; society, 7; 'Two Continents and Five Seas', 12–13, 30;
Grenada, 130
Guevara, Ernesto 'Che', 52, 90, 149
Gulf War, 93, 140

hafiethismos, 165, 182, 184, 186
Halivourgiki Steel company, 79–80
Halyps, 94
Hamby, Alonzo, 17n
Haralambis, Dimitris, 51
Holbrooke, Richard, 102
Holy Alliance, 147
Hussein, Saddam, 141

Iatrides, J.O., 16n, 36n
IBM, 69, 98
Imia, islet of, 102
imperialism, US, 33, 66, 77, 107, 110, 131
International Federation of Journalists, 188
Interpol, 82
IRA, 88, 102, 122, 208

Iran, 68
Iraq, 93
Italy, 49, 52, 68, 115, 137, 158, 160, 169–70, 176, 178–9, 181–2, 186, 205

Jamieson, Alison, 190
Judd, Robert, 77, 123
June '78, 64
JUSMAGG, 76

Kaltezas, Michalis, 79, 126
Kanellopoulos, Thanassis, 175
Kapetanyiannis, Vassilis, 17n, 20n, 34n, 45n, 55n
Kapsalakis, Zacharias, 81, 128
Karamanlis, Konstantinos, 6, 20, 23n, 24–5, 26n, 27–30, 32, 55–6, 59, 61–2, 75, 78n, 109, 112–13, 116–17, 149, 155–6, 159, 167, 193, 204
Karambelias, George, 21n
Karapiperis 6 (boat), 94
katestimeno (present regime), 106, 121, 123
kathestos (present regime), 100
Katrantzos store, 118–19
Katsaounis, Aristeidis, 157
Kececi, Nilgun, 95, 141n
Keely, Robert, 82
Kinima 20is Oktovri, 53
Kinissi Ellinon Marxiston Leniniston (KEML), 57n
Kitromilides, Paschalis, 10n
KKE, 14, 16, 18, 28–9, 43–44, 47, 54, 57, 59, 61, 66, 113, 149, 159, 166, 168
KKE-es, 28, 30, 48, 54
KKE (m-l), 60
Kommounistiki Organossi Machitis (KO. MACHITIS), 56n
Kommounistiki Diethnistiki Enossi (KDE), 57n
Kommounistiko Epanastatiko Metopo (KEM), 57n, 61–4
Korahais, Vassilios, 177–9
Korydallos, prison, 188
Koskotas, George, 86, 132–3, 135
Kosovo, 104, 148